THE ECONOMICS OF INTEGRATION

THE ECONOMICS
OF INTEGRATION

A BOOK OF READINGS

Edited and Introduced by
MELVYN B. KRAUSS
Johns Hopkins University, Bologna Center
and
London School of Economics

London
GEORGE ALLEN & UNWIN LTD
Ruskin House   Museum Street

First published in 1973

© George Allen & Unwin Ltd 1973

ISBN 0 04 330221 1 hardback
0 04 330222 x paperback

Printed by offset in Great Britain
in 10 point Times Roman type
by Alden & Mowbray Ltd
at the Alden Press, Oxford

PREFACE

I would like to thank all of the contributors of articles to this symposium and the sources of original publication for their most generous assistance in permitting the idea of a book of readings on this most important topic to become a reality. Special thanks are due to my wife Irene Krauss, whose cooperation in preparing the book has been substantial and deeply appreciated. Financial assistance has been rendered by the 'Europa Instituut' of the University of Amsterdam.

M.B.K.
Bologna, Italy
September, 1972

CONTENTS

CONTENTS

1

INTRODUCTION

MELVYN B. KRAUSS

The formation of the European Economic Community, or the Common Market as it is more popularly known, represents what will certainly be recorded as one of the major events of the post-Second World War period. Indeed, well before the War had come to a close, interest already had developed in economic integration as a means for rebuilding and sustaining the health of the economies of the Western European Allies; while on both sides of the Atlantic there was hope in the hearts of more than a few that the economic integration of all of Western Europe would serve as a prelude to its political integration – a United States of Europe, so to speak – which would, on the one hand, serve as a buffer between the then two great superpowers the U.S.A. and U.S.S.R and, on the other, reduce the likelihood that European nationalistic aspirations and rivalries would again throw the world into global conflict. This concern was codified in the rules of the General Agreement on Trade and Tariffs in the form of the special exemption granted customs unions to the general principle of geographical non-discrimination (most favoured nation clause) adopted for the conduct of post-War commercial policy. Arrangements entailing 100% discrimination on an 'across the board' basis are allowed under the GATT rules, though less extreme forms of geographic discrimination are not.

The central position played by the European Economic Community in the development of the theory of economic integration constitutes the major reason for its central position in this collection of essays. Customs union theory as developed by Viner and those following him was essentially a response to the European experiment; and the same is true of those special branches of monetary and public finance theory respectively concerned with the problems of monetary union and fiscal harmonization. This is not to say, of course, that other influences have not been present. The interest in economic integration on the part of the world's developing countries as a means for accelerating their rate of economic progress un-

11

doubtedly has strongly influenced not only the included contributions of Cooper and Massell and of Johnson, but others which because their interest lies more in development economics than economic integration have been regretfully omitted [1]. Still the influence of the Common Market has been dominant, and this is reflected in the Readings selected for this collection.

The problem of the number of themes and the extent to which each is covered is normally a difficult one for an editor, often resulting in a choice between depth and breadth. In the present case, the choice as to the number of themes was more apparent than real due to the limited number of important policy aspects of the economic integration problem for which an adequate literature exists, the two criteria used for selection purposes. The result has been not only a division of the Readings into four topics; customs-union theory, monetary union, fiscal harmonization and agricultural policy; but a reminder that the subject is still in its formative years.

CUSTOMS UNION THEORY

In a consideration of the question of whether customs union represented a movement towards freer trade or greater protection, Jacob Viner developed the basic theoretical concepts of 'trade creation' and 'trade diversion' [2]. Using a Ricardian model of production which focused on the welfare effect of changes in the location of production, Viner demonstrated that there can be no general presumption as to the welfare orientation of a customs union; that is, inherently the union provokes two contrasting forces – a trade-creating force resulting from the elimination of protection of domestic producers from their counterparts in partner countries, and a trade-diverting force resulting from the increased protection granted to domestic producers *vis-à-vis* third country producers through the extension of their protected market to the partner country – whose net effect depends on the particular circumstances of each case. The economic welfare of the world increases to the extent that customs union creates trade by diverting demand from higher-cost domestic to lower-cost partner products, and decreases to the extent that it diverts trade from lower-cost foreign to higher-cost partner sources.

Viner's analysis of the production effects of customs union was later supplemented by the analyses of Meade, Lipsey, and Gehrels, all of whom independently analysed the question of the union's consumption effects [3]. Lipsey's 1960 survey of the customs union literature is included in this volume not for the usual purpose of bringing the student up to date with recent developments in the field, but for his analysis of consumption effects and his highlighting of the second-best aspects of the customs union problem, an insight that had been originally discovered by Viner in his production-oriented analysis. Lipsey shows that similar to production effects, consumption effects could serve either a welfare-increasing or welfare-decreasing function. In a later analysis that is highly recommended but not included, Johnson redefined the terms 'trade creation' and 'trade diversion' each to include a production and consumption component [4]. This is a superior procedure to that employed by Lipsey, who defines trade creation and trade diversion solely in terms of the location of production, and considers consumption effects as something additional [5].

Under Viner's influence, the early writers on customs unions were content to start their analysis with the existence of a problem rather than with the reasons for its existence. Accordingly, the question of the rationale or motivation for customs union was not raised in the formal literature until the Cooper–Massell analysis, here included, which argued that since it could be established that a non-preferential tariff policy is necessarily superior to customs union as a trade-liberalizing device, a more efficient allocation of resources could not be the reason why customs unions are formed, the popular view of the matter. By eliminating resource allocation as a possible economic rationale for customs union, the Cooper–Massell analysis has had the effect of focusing attention on three other potential sources of gain from customs union; the union's so-called 'dynamic effects', its terms-of-trade effects and the public good argument for protection. The dynamic effects consist of two separate and different arguments which have proved particularly resistant to rigorous analysis. The first is concerned with the effects of protection on the efficiency with which the firm operates, according to a given technology and market structure; what Leibenstein has labelled 'X-efficiency' [6]. The second is that larger markets would permit the exploitation of economies-of-scale and the adoption of more up-to-date technology. Theoretical objection can be raised with respect to both arguments. Leibenstein's analysis of 'X-efficiency' is based on a not-so-wide set of *ad hoc* experience for which he offers no theoretical rationale other than the

13

naive 'cold shower of competition' argument. The economies-of-scale argument suffers from a variety of weaknesses; first, its assumption that countries of different average income levels and culture can simply be lumped together to increase the effective demand for commodities; second, that if it were really true that the larger the total output of any given industry the lower the cost of production, by and large, we ought to observe small countries having lower standards of living than large ones – an expectation that is contradicted by actual experience as frequently as it is confirmed; and third, its assumption that there exists a single producer for each commodity, a situation not often observed in the real world. Furthermore, the theory of economies-of-scale implies an average cost theory of pricing for the firm which is inconsistent with traditional profit maximization theory. Finally, and most important, even if the validity of both arguments could be established in any particular case, they are in essence arguments for free trade not customs union.

A more convincing economic argument for customs union is that related to its terms-of-trade effects. If a country is assumed large enough to affect the prices it pays in international markets for its traded goods, non-preferential tariff reduction will provoke a terms-of-trade loss which in combination with the terms-of-trade gain resulting from customs union (should trade with third countries survive the formation of the customs union) can provide an economic argument for customs union, especially as the loss from the trade diversion effect will be less the greater the improvement in the terms-of-trade. Johnson has called this argument the only valid one for customs union along classical or orthodox lines. It should be noted, however, that this is not a general *a priori* argument for customs union but one which essentially depends on the empirical question of whether the sum of the terms-of-trade and trade creation gains less the trade diversion loss from customs union is greater or less than the welfare loss from unilateral tariff reduction.

Cooper–Massell contend that the essence of the problem of rationalizing customs union on economic grounds is that classical trade theory with its free trade orientation is, with few exceptions, unable to explain what motivates a tariff. What is needed is an 'economic' theory of protectionism, whose development would allow a comparison of non-preferential tariff policy with customs union as alternative protectionist rather than trade-liberalizing mechanisms. This is the task undertaken by Johnson in his paper, here included, and by

14

Cooper–Massell in independent analyses; and they achieve the required re-orientation of theoretical framework from free trade to protection by introducing the concept of 'public goods' into the community's social welfare function along with private goods [7]. In these models, the form of the public good is a collective preference for certain types of economic activity, namely industrial production, which is assumed to yield the community satisfaction over and above that obtained through the private consumption of industrial products; but, in fact, the public good can take any number of forms and thus is potentially applicable to a wide variety of different situations. The Common Agricultural Policy of the EEC, for example, can be rationalized by this model if it is assumed that a public preference exists for agricultural rather than industrial production, and the model has been used by others to defend a variety of other apparently 'irrational' policy decisions by governments.

The danger with the Johnson–Cooper–Massell type models, including those that view the 'preferred' activity simply as yielding externalities to the community, is that they lend themselves easily to abuse by governments as a justification for whatever they have chosen or might choose to do. As is well known from the famous infant-industry argument for protection, the problem is operational rather than conceptual. There is, in certain cases, a perfectly valid argument for protection on public good grounds; but the argument is not a general one. The problem, on the one hand, is identifying those activities that have legitimate public good characteristics and which do not, and, on the other, determining whether protection is indeed required for welfare-maximization in cases where a legitimate public good interest can be demonstrated. In the event that a valid argument for protection can be established, there is the further problem of an efficient protection mechanism.

The purpose of Johnson's 'An economic theory of protectionism . . .' is to explain, in economic terms, why governments behave as they do in their economic policies. However, the failure of economists to develop a *generally* valid *a priori* argument for customs union on economic grounds implies that a proper interpretation of governmental policy in this area may be to take the motivation for such policy as being non-economic in nature. The establishment of the Common Agricultural Policy in the EEC, for example, has been hailed by many in the Community as a great achievement not for economic reasons, but for the political one that it demonstrated the

15

capacity of the member states to co-operate with each other in a common pursuit, regardless of how irrational that pursuit might turn out to be from an economic viewpoint. It further explains why the customs union rather than the free trade area solution to the problem of trade deflection was adopted by the EEC. Trade deflection refers to third country trade that enters the market of one country through that of a second country when the latter two agree to abolish customs duties on each other's trade, but maintain their own separate rates of customs duty on trade with the outside world. In order to prevent the tariff of the low-tariff country from becoming the *de-facto* common external tariff for the members in this case, either 'rules of origin' at the common border must be adopted, in which case only commodities originating in the member states can cross the border duty free, or a common external tariff established in fact. Since the latter implies a much greater degree of political cooperation between the members in determining what the common rates of tariff against outsiders will be, the common external tariff solution to the trade deflection problem was favoured by those who sought to nurture this type of cooperative spirit in Community affairs.

What is the proper role for economic research when it is accepted that the objective of governmental policy is non-economic in nature? The question is a controversial one, which resolves itself into two essentially conflicting points of view. The first tacitly accepts the non-economic objective of governmental policy and tries to work within it by developing analyses whose purpose is to achieve the non-economic objective at a minimum cost in terms of foregone real income to the community. The second approach to non-economic government asks what are the economic costs or perhaps incidental economic benefits of government 'irrationality', and poses the question as to whether the non-economic benefits are worth the net economic costs. One important by-product of such research is the questioning of the value of the non-economic objective and the possibility of its rejection should its costs to the community be deemed greater than its benefits.

The conceptualization of customs union as an essentially non-economic arrangement underlines the importance of empirical investigation to ascertain their economic costs or benefits. This would seem to be particularly relevant for the European Economic Community where according to one's perspective the customs union, and indeed the entire range of harmonization proposals concerned with fiscal, monetary and agricultural union, can be envisioned

16

either as a necessary prelude to eventual full political union in Europe (the supra-nationalists), or a mechanism by which either the real income of a member state can be increased at the expense of other members or non-members (the Gaullists) or a mechanism for re-distributing world welfare to a particular group existing within the country or union rather than the country or union itself. In the latter view, the Common Market can be thought of as a device for en-riching French farmers and German industrialists for example at the expense of both their fellow countrymen and foreigners rather than one for just enriching Frenchmen or Germans considered as homogeneous structural entities. In either event, the relevant question for economic research in these cases is the efficiency of the Common Market as a redistributor of the world's real income.

The major consensus of empirical studies of the potential welfare gains or losses of customs unions has been their smallness when expressed as a percentage of national income or GNP. This is due, on the one hand, to the inherent nature of the trade creation and trade diversion concepts themselves and, on the other, to the fact that any relevant number when divided by such a large aggregate as GNP can be expected to constitute a rather small percentage thereof. The point is that though small when expressed as a fraction of GNP, in absolute terms the welfare gains or losses from customs union can be very substantial. Furthermore, the problem must be considered in the context of other policies for increasing national income, if that is one's view of customs union; and all of these also produce changes which are small in relation to national income. This question of the apparent smallness of orthodox resource allo-cation effects has been interpreted as a challenge to orthodoxy by some who for one reason or another want large numbers to come out of customs union calculations rather than small ones. This ex-plains the recent popularity of the so-called 'dynamic effects' argu-ment for customs unions with advocates of British entry into the Common Market, who would like to establish the economic profit-ability of such entry in the face of a considerable amount of orthodox evidence to the contrary [8].

MONETARY UNION

The readings concerned with the monetary aspects of economic integration can be divided into two inter-related groups; the theory of monetary union, and problems of monetary union in the context of the European Economic Community. The former, which is another name for that branch of international monetary theory known as the theory of optimum currency areas, is concerned with the issue of the appropriate domain of an area in which the exchange rates between the currencies of the units comprising the area are fixed, appropriateness being defined in terms of the ability of the area to achieve balance-of-payments equilibrium without creating either inflation or unemployment in any of the component units (an alternative but identical way of putting the issue is that of the appropriate domain of an area for which a policy of flexible exchange rates can be employed). Meade, in his seminal paper on the subject, utilizes the standard trade theory assumption of the international immobility of the factors of production but full factor mobility within the nation when arguing for a policy of freely floating exchange rates between nations. The point is that unobstructed trade and factor movement promotes homogeneous economic conditions throughout the nation as economic disturbance in any one region tends to spread to the others via the inter-regional balance of trade and factor movement. Accordingly, an adjustment mechanism such as the exchange rate, whose effect is proportional in all regions of the nation's economy, can adjust international monetary disturbances without creating either inflation or unemployment in the nation.

Building on Meade's analysis, Mundell notes that there is no *a priori* reason for identifying the nation-state, a political entity, with an optimum currency area, which in the Mundell analysis is an economic entity determined by the criteria of the free movement of the factors of production. According to Mundell, the optimal currency area may be a region which cuts across national boundaries, in which case internal and external equilibrium requires flexible exchange rates between regions (and thus implicitly regional currencies) not nations. This has an important implication for the European Economic Community. Can an optimum currency area be identified with the whole of the Common Market as it presently exists, or will it cut across national boundaries including for example the north of Western Europe but not the south? In the latter eventuality monetary union in the EEC, implying rigidly fixed rates of exchange between the currencies of the partner countries, and perhaps one day a common currency, but a more flexible rate between the EEC and the rest-of-the-world, may prove an unstable arrangement.

Mundell's argument that the optimum currency area may be a region rather than a nation-state can be extended to include the possibility of an optimal currency area defined along sectorial lines, namely industry and agriculture. Because of the oft-noted absence of factor movement between these two sectors, optimal currency area logic implies that separate currencies be used in the industrial and agricultural sectors each bearing a flexible relationship to the other. The problem is illustrated by reference to Josling's analysis of the present situation in Germany where productivity in the agricultural sector significantly lags behind that in the industrial sector, the two sectors being separated by factor immobility. Because of the relative efficiency of German industrialists both *vis-à-vis* German agriculture and foreign industry, Germany's balance of payments moves towards surplus, resulting in an appreciation of the deutschemark. Such appreciation, while potentially capable of restoring equilibrium to the German balance of payments, tends to reduce the income position of the German agriculture sector through an adverse movement in its terms of trade and in so doing imparts a deflationary bias to the balance of payments adjustment process. What is needed is an exchange rate change between agriculture and industry in this case not Germany and the rest-of-the-world; and the argument can be extended to apply to Community agriculture and industry and as such constitute an implicit criticism of EEC monetary union as envisioned by the Werner Report.

The essence of the Meade–Mundell analysis is that there must exist homogeneous economic conditions within an area for exchange-rate flexibility to promote internal and external equilibrium. Such conditions are assumed to be related to the free movement of the factors of production but, as Haberler recently has pointed out, the condition of homogeneity may exist even if all regions of the area are isolated from one another if there exists a harmony of views as to the proper demand-management policies to be followed by each region within the area [9]. Thus, if all the member-states of the Community were to have similar national policy objectives with respect to the trade-off between inflation and unemployment, a policy of fixed rates of monetary exchange between the currencies of these countries could be maintained without creating excessive strains on any one of the members; while differences between the common Community rate of inflation and that obtaining in the rest-of-the-world could be adjusted by a change in the value of the harmonized

Community exchange rate in terms of foreign currency. Haberler makes the criteria for an optimum currency the existence of similar attitudes toward the proper rate of inflation within the units of the area just as Mundell made it the extent to which the factors of production can freely circulate [10].

The identification of the optimum currency area with the nation-state implies that each nation has autonomy in its monetary policy and thus permits an alternative concept of an optimum currency area defined by Haberler's criteria of similar attitudes toward the inflation–unemployment trade-off; namely that of an area where internal and external equilibrium can be obtained without any of the members foregoing their independent monetary policies. Put another way, the commitment of each member-state to a fixed rate of exchange and the constraint imposed upon the group by internal and external equilibrium requires each nation to adjust its monetary policy to the average of the other nations unless all have the same notion as to the proper rate of inflation. The importance of national sovereignty in monetary matters is highlighted by Cooper's, here included, description of the 1971 appreciation of the German deutschemark resulting from Germany's attempt to run a more restrictive monetary policy than its Common Market partners. The German experience implies not only that, in 1971 at least, the conditions of an optimum currency area according to the Haberler definition were not present in the EEC, but that, when the chips are down, members will prefer to terminate their commitment to a fixed exchange rate rather than surrender national sovereignty over their monetary policies.

Haberler's definition of an optimum currency area also is relevant to the present controversy in the European Economic Community over economic and monetary union, between the so-called 'economists', on the one hand, and 'monetarists' on the other. The former advocate the postponement of monetary union until the conditions for an optimal currency area are firmly established in the EEC, in order to avoid the stresses and strains on individual members that premature monetary union necessarily entails. The latter, who should not be confused with the school of thought often identified with Milton Friedman of the University of Chicago, favour premature monetary union precisely because of these stresses and strains, which they believe will serve as a means of coercing the individual member-states to harmonize their demand management policies even though the members themselves may have different ideas as to the proper trade-off between inflation and unemployment. The evidence from the period of the mid-1960s onward reflects the failure of such past coercion in the form of the supposed requirement of the Common Agricultural Policy for fixed exchange rates and the misplaced hope that, in some sense, the outward symbol of harmonized demand management policies could substitute for the real thing; demand management policies have differed between EEC members and exchange rates have changed. These issues have been admirably surveyed by Johnson in Chapters 9 and 10, which should be considered as a single paper in two parts.

TAX HARMONIZATION

The tax harmonization programme of the EEC, as set out in the 1963 *Report of the Fiscal and Financial Committee*, more popularly known as the Neumark Report, consists of three parts; the adoption of the value-added tax, the abolition of tax frontiers between member-states with respect to their intra-union trade, and the equalization of value-added tax rates. Properly interpreted, the adoption of the value-added tax, which refers to a method of taxation and not to some specific new kind of tax on economic activity, is not essentially a matter of tax harmonization, a concept whose underlying principle is that tax systems in no way interfere with the benefits accruing to the members of an economic union from trade liberalization and/or factor mobility; but is more a matter of tax reform, in that in most of the Common Market countries, with the prime exception being France, the value-added tax has replaced the cumbersome, iniquitous, and inefficient gross turnover or cascade-type sales tax, a change warranted more by the desire to bring a greater degree of equity and efficiency into the tax structure than by participation in an economic integration project. Still, perhaps because of the success the Benelux countries and Germany are making of the transition to a system of value-added taxes, itself in no small part due to the fact that politicians have seized upon the introduction of the new tax as a convenient smokescreen behind which they could raise average sales tax rates and blame it on the new tax – a situation observed most recently in the Netherlands – the value-added tax has come to be regarded as the symbol if not the essence of the EEC tax harmonization programme.

The prime objective of the tax harmonization programme, however, is the abolition of tax frontiers between member-states in their intra-union trade, though retention of tax frontiers is envisaged with respect to trade between third countries and the Community. Tax frontiers refer to destination principle border tax adjustments, which are one of the two possible principles of border tax adjustment that a nation can apply to its international trade – the other being the origin principle. Under the destination principle, explicit export tax rebates and import compensatory duties are intended to guarantee that all goods consumed within the taxing jurisdiction are equally taxed regardless of where they are produced; while under the origin principle exports are taxed and imports exempted to insure that all goods produced within the taxing jurisdiction are equally burdened regardless of where they are consumed. Most sales taxes in the world today – not just those collected by the VAT methods – are on the destination basis. The introduction of value-added taxation and the adoption of a principle of border tax adjustment are, of course, logically quite separate questions.

It should be mentioned in connection with the issue of border tax adjustments that, as Johnson and Krauss demonstrate, there is an essential distinction to be drawn between a *border tax*, which properly understood is a tax on the crossing by trade of international frontiers (a tariff, for example) and hence restricts trade volumes below what would be indicated as desirable by the principle of comparative advantage; and a *border tax adjustment*, which is an adjustment of the taxes imposed on a producer when the goods he produces cross an international border. Such an adjustment may involve an addition to or a subtraction from the taxes he has already paid; and if the adjustment in question implies either equal rates of taxation of imports and subsidization of exports, the destination principle, or equal rates of subsidization of imports and taxation of exports, origin principle, the effect of the adjustment is to leave the relative competitive positions of exporting and import-competing industries in the domestic market unchanged. This merely is an application of the well-known principle that taxation of imports and subsidization of exports is equivalent to a devaluation of the currency, and that under long-run full employment and price-flexibility conditions a devaluation will be offset by an equal inflation of domestic prices.

The equivalency of border tax adjustments with changes in the currency exchange rate has been the principal contribution of economic science to the issue of border tax adjustments. Imposing destination principle border tax adjustments is equivalent in effect to currency depreciation, while currency appreciation has the same effect as that of imposing origin principle adjustments – at least with respect to the balance of trade. Taking this one step further, switching principles of border tax adjustment can also be expressed in terms of equivalent changes in currency values; substituting origin for destination principle border tax adjustments, for example, involves a change from taxing imports and subsidizing exports to subsidizing imports and taxing exports, and thus is equivalent to currency appreciation; while a change in the opposite direction is equivalent to currency depreciation. Finally, if two countries both switch to the origin principle, the currency of the country which has the higher average rate of tax – and thus the higher rate of border tax adjustment – depreciates relative to that of the currency of the low tax country. Thus switching to the origin principle can improve the balance-of-payments position of the country making the change, and thus be equivalent in effect to currency depreciation rather than currency appreciation if other countries also switch to the origin principle, but impose higher rates of origin principle border tax adjustments than it does. In any event, the issue of border tax adjustments is essentially a monetary one; so long as taxation is general, different rates of commodity taxation in different countries are compatible with efficient resource allocation regardless of whether destination or origin principle border tax adjustments apply to those countries' international trade. However, the principle of border tax adjustment will be a matter of importance when taxation is not general; a partial commodity tax will distort comparative costs unless destination principle border tax adjustments are applied, while a tax on the production of a single commodity will create consumption inefficiencies unless the origin principle is in force. To translate this rather abstract piece of analysis to the real world of policy, its implication is that participation by a country in an economic union requires neither large-scale structural changes between direct and indirect taxation, nor substantial changes in the level of tax rates, nor modification of existing systems of border tax adjustment for reasons of efficient resource allocation. The sole adjustment necessary is to make the effect of the tax system as general as possible [11].

The purpose of the abolition of tax frontiers in the Community, and the Neumark Report is very clear on this, is not related to an economic objective, however, by which I mean an objective defined in terms of the traditional private consumption oriented concepts of welfare economics, but the political one of establishing within the Community conditions analogous to those of an internal market. After all, it is argued, internal markets are seldom partitioned by tax frontiers, and since this is envisioned to be the goal to which the Common Market aspires, tax frontiers have been deemed incompatible with the Common Market concept. But the question arises as to whose Common Market concept the intra-Community tax frontiers are incompatible with? The European Economic Community means different things to different people, and it is imperative for the relevance of economic research to know what the objective of Community policy really is, rather than what economists assume it should be.

In the case of the Neumark Report, it is clear that the Common Market concept referred to above is that of the establishment of a supra-nationalistic United States of Europe. It is not only the Neumark Report's call for the abolition of tax frontiers with respect to intra-union trade that implies this interpretation of tax harmonization in the EEC; it is also its call for the adoption of value-added taxation and the equalization of value-added tax rates, which on economic grounds cannot be justified by participation in an economic union. Why else should such importance be placed on having all members of the Community use the same type of tax, imposed at the same *ad valorem* rate, on goods whose trade will not be subject to tax inspection at common frontiers but only at the border with third countries, if not to promote a federal Western European political structure? A major issue in the Common Market is that of supra-nationalism versus national sovereignty, and the lack of any genuine enthusiasm for the Neumark Report's recommendations in the EEC to present can be taken as an indication either that the United States of Europe concept is an idea whose time has not yet come or, as I suspect, one which died when the euphoria immediately following the successful termination of the Second World War had passed.

AGRICULTURAL POLICY

Farmers are protected in most of the major industrialized countries of the West, and it seems unfair to single out the agricultural policy of the Common Market on this account alone. However, criticism of the Common Agricultural Policy of the EEC (CAP) has not centred primarily on the fact that European farmers receive protection, but rather over the form such protection has taken. Josling's paper outlines and analyses three possible methods of protecting farmers: deficiency payment schemes, which are equivalent in effect to direct production subsidies; the variable levy system, which imposes a levy on imports equal to the difference between the level of world prices and that fixed in the Community; and direct lump-sum payments to farmers. The latter is shown to be the most efficient in terms of economic cost per unit of income transferred to farmers and the variable levy system the least efficient. The adoption by the Common Market of the variable levy system for protecting Community agriculture thus has been the focal point of criticism against the CAP.

Josling's demonstration of the relative inefficiency of the variable levy system is based on standard welfare analysis which abstracts from distributional considerations by assuming that all other things being equal an additional unit of income in the hands of the consumer increases the welfare of the community by the exact amount that welfare would increase had the producer or the government received the extra unit of income under *ceteris paribus* conditions. However, the question of the motivation of the income transfers to producers (farmers) is left unexplained in this analytical framework, for if the producers of agricultural products count the same to the community as do consumers of such products, why are producers treated in a special way? Possible rationales for such support are that the production of agricultural products yields external economies to the rest of the community, so that under free trade conditions the output of agricultural products will be below the optimal amount; or the agricultural activity yields collective or public utility to the entire community over and above that derived from the private consumption of agricultural products. Some have argued that the widespread support of agricultural production is itself proof of the existence of externalities in agricultural production, but this essentially circular line of reasoning assumes that governments are all-wise and all-knowing, an assumption for which there is a considerable amount of contrary evidence. A more acceptable approach would appear to be to take motivation of the policy as political rather than try to justify it on economic grounds, and consider the question of the efficiency of government in achieving this objective. This, of course, could have the further benefit of leading to a discussion of whether or not the political benefits from the subsidization of farmers are worth their economic costs.

The free trade in agricultural products within the Community that was permitted by the setting of common agricultural prices well above their world price level was hailed by many Europeans as one of the Community's finest achievements until the consequences of this policy began to take full impact. Specifically, by artificially restricting consumption and stimulating domestic production, the high common price level has generated a surplus of agricultural products which has proved costly both to the Community and the outside world. The Community has suffered from the costs of storing the surpluses, or should the surpluses be sold on world markets, the loss that buying at a high price and selling at a low one necessarily entails; while producers of agricultural products in third countries have witnessed a deterioration in their terms-of-trade as a result of the Community's disposal of surplus production on world markets. The result has been a constant barrage of criticism from both inside and outside the Community, eventually leading to the reform of the CAP known as 'Agriculture 1980'. This programme, which is largely the work of the influential Dutchman Sicco Mansholt, author of the original CAP, ignores the critical influence of the high common price level in producing the costly surpluses, and instead blames the problems of European agriculture on the supposed low level of agricultural efficiency in the EEC. 'Agriculture 1980' calls for a rationalization of European farming along modern technological lines and a massive re-deployment of workers from the agricultural to the industrial sector of the Community; but its refusal to come to grips with what in my view is the essence of the problem implies rough going for this particular reform. Large-scale subsidization of a profession never has been the quickest nor the most efficient way of inducing persons to leave it. Indeed so flagrant is the contradiction within 'Agriculture 1980' on this point that one cynically surmises that the issue of costly surpluses may have been raised merely as a diversion for some other more fundamental purpose. What this purpose is can only be a matter of conjecture, but given the demonstrated reformist zeal of its author together with his rural fundamentalist background, it may be nothing less than the establishment of a new way of agricultural life in Europe, whose basic structural unit would be the middle-income, socially responsible and respectable European farmer.

26

OTHER POLICIES

This particular collection of Readings, which focuses on a relatively narrow range of important subjects that are topical in the EEC at the present time and promise to remain so, unfortunately suffers from the necessary exclusion of other aspects of the economic integration problem that are both interesting and potentially important. Primary amongst these is the Commission's Competition policy which at present seems more interested in replacing American industrial giants with European giants, than with coming to terms with the more important problem of the protection of the consumer from the abuse of monopoly power regardless of who the monopolist is and where he comes from. Indeed one fears that anti-Americanism in this aspect of European affairs has been and is being used more as a cover for the development of European-based monopolies than for 'liberating' Europeans from alleged American domination, an unfortunate development since it would seem to be a matter of little difference to European consumers if 'exploitation' by American producers simply was replaced by 'exploitation' by European ones.

Notwithstanding the above, the pressure for competition with the Americans in the EEC has been supported by both the left and right ends of the European political spectrum. The motivation of European business is obvious, though it is a real question whether the interests of European consumers would be better served by European-owned and managed firms than American ones; while right-wing nationalism in Western Europe is as economically 'irrational' as it is anywhere else. The Socialists, on the other hand, seem to prefer a European takeover for the reason that European business would be more susceptible to control by European governments than American business; and a similar motive may be ascribed to the environmentalists, though the right of the host country to tax foreign offenders to the ecological balance would seem to be sufficient protection in this respect.

Besides Competition Policy, other policies that warrant attention are the common transport policy, the common energy policy the social policy and the regional policy of the EEC. The last in particular promises to be a subject of importance in the near future with British entry and the generalized fear that Britain will become the Quebec or West Virginia of the Common Market. Optimal currency area theory has an important implication for this question.

27

If Britain's average productivity is lower than that of its partners and the Community goes ahead with monetary union according to the Werner Report's recommendations, balance-of-payments equilibrium for the Community as a whole entails a deflationary bias in the low productivity countries. As the experience of Canada and the United States clearly implies, regional problems are particularly difficult to solve and create considerable political tensions since residents of the depressed area often are unwilling to move to the high productivity areas, yet demand a decent standard of living, while residents in the high productivity areas come to resent the high cost of bringing industry to depressed areas when it cannot be justified on economic grounds. This should prove a sobering thought for those who see British entry into Europe as the mechanism by which Britain regains a lost empire. In the modern world, political power follows economic power not the opposite.

NOTES AND REFERENCES

[1] F. and S. Andic and D. Dosser, *A Theory of Economic Integration for Developing Countries*, London: Allen and Unwin, 1971; S. B. Linder, Customs union and economic development, in M. S. Wionczek (ed.), *Latin American Economic Integration*, New York: Praeger, 1966; and R. F. Mikesell, The theory of common markets as applied to regional arrangements among developing countries, in R. F. Harrod and D. C. Hague (eds.), *International Trade Theory In A Developing World*, London: Macmillan, 1963, pp. 205–29.

[2] J. Viner, *The Customs Union Issue*, New York: Carnegie Endowment For International Peace, 1950.

[3] J. E. Meade, *The Theory of Customs Unions*, Amsterdam: North-Holland, 1955; and F. Gehrels, 'Customs unions from a single country viewpoint,' *Review of Economic Studies*, 1956–7, 24 (1), pp. 61–4.

[4] H. G. Johnson, The economic theory of customs unions, *Pakistan Economic Journal*, vol. 10, pp. 14–32, 1960. Reprinted in *Money, Trade and Economic Growth*, London: George Allen and Unwin, 1962, pp. 46–73.

[5] M. B. Krauss, Recent developments in customs union theory: an interpretive survey, *Journal of Economic Literature*, June 1972, pp. 413–36.

[6] H. Leibenstein, Allocative efficiency versus X-efficiency, *American Economic Review*, June 1966, pp. 392–415.

[7] C. A. Cooper and B. F. Massell, Towards a general theory of customs unions for developing countries, *Journal of Political Economy*, Oct. 1965, pp. 461–76.

[8] The reader is advised to see, in this respect, J. Williamson, Trade and economic growth, in J. Pinder (ed.), *The Economics of Europe*, London: Charles Knight and Co. Ltd., 1971, pp. 19–45.

[9] G. Haberler, The international monetary system: some recent developments and discussions, in G. N. Hahn (ed.), *Approaches To Greater Flexibility of Exchange Rates: The Bürgenstock Papers*, Princeton: Princeton University Press, 1970, pp. 115–23.

[10] Other noteworthy contributions to the discussion of optimum currency areas are R. I. McKinnon, Optimum currency areas, *American Economic Review*, 1963, **53**, pp. 717–24; and P. B. Kenen, The theory of optimum currency areas: an eclectic view, in R. A. Mundell and A. K. Swoboda (eds.), *Monetary Problems of the International Economy*, Chicago: Chicago University Press, 1970.

[11] The seminal paper on the tax harmonization problem is: C. S. Shoup, Taxation aspects of international economic integration, in *Travaux de l'Institut International de Finances Publiques*, Neuvième Session, W. P. van Stockum et Fils, 1953, pp. 89–107. An up-to-date survey of tax harmonization issues can be found in, Mel Krauss, The tax harmonization problem in free trade areas and common markets, *The Manchester School*, June 1971, vol. XXXIX/no. 2, pp. 71–82. Several interesting studies can be found in C. S. Shoup (ed.), *Fiscal Harmonization in Common Markets*, 2 vols, New York, Columbia University Press, 1967.

PART ONE

CUSTOMS UNION

2

THE THEORY OF CUSTOMS UNIONS:
A GENERAL SURVEY [1]*

Queen's University

This paper is devoted mainly to a survey of the development of
customs-union theory from Viner to date; since, however, the theory
must be meant at least as an aid in interpreting real-world data, some
space is devoted to a summary of empirical evidence relating to the
gains from European Economic Union. It is necessary first to define
customs-union theory. In general, the tariff system of any country
may discriminate between commodities and/or between countries.
Commodity discrimination occurs when different rates of duty are
levied on different commodities, while country discrimination occurs
when the same commodity is subject to different rates of duty, the rate
varying according to the country of origin. The theory of customs
unions may be defined as that branch of tariff theory which deals with
the effects of geographically discriminatory changes in trade barriers.

Next we must turn our attention to the scope of the existing theory.
The theory has been confined mainly to a study of the effects of
customs unions on welfare rather than, for example, on the level of
economic activity, the balance of payments or the rate of inflation.
These welfare gains and losses, which are the subject of the theory
may arise from a number of different sources: (1) the specialization
of production according to comparative advantage which is the basis
of the classical case for the gains from trade; (2) economies of
scale [2]; (3) changes in the terms of trade; (4) forced changes in
efficiency due to increased foreign competition; and (5) a change in
the rate of economic growth. The theory of customs unions has been
almost completely confined to an investigation of (1) above, with
some slight attention to (2) and (3), (5) not being dealt with at all,
while (4) is ruled out of traditional theory by the assumption (often
contradicted by the facts) that production is carried out by processes
which are technically efficient.

* *Economic Journal*, September 1960, 70, pp 496–513.

Throughout the development of the theory of customs unions we will find an oscillation between the belief that it is possible to produce a general conclusion of the sort: 'Customs unions will always, or nearly always, raise welfare', and the belief that, depending on the particular circumstances present, a customs union may have any imaginable effect on welfare. The earliest customs-theory was largely embodied in the oral tradition, for it hardly seemed worthwhile to state it explicitly, and was an example of an attempt to produce the former sort of conclusion. It may be summarized quite briefly. Free trade maximizes world welfare; a customs union reduces tariffs and is therefore a movement towards free trade; a customs union will, therefore, *increase* world welfare even if it does not lead to a world-welfare *maximum*.

Viner showed this argument to be incorrect. He introduced the now familiar concepts of trade creation and trade diversion [3] which are probably best recalled in terms of an example. Consider the figures in Table 2·1.

TABLE 2·1. *Money prices (at existing exchange rates) of a single commodity (X) in three countries*

Country	A	B	C
Price	35s	26s	20s

A tariff of 100% levied by country A [4] will be sufficient to protect A's domestic industry producing commodity X. If A forms a customs union with either country B or country C she will be better off; if the union is with B she will get a unit of commodity X at an opportunity cost of 26 shillingsworth of exports instead of at the cost of 35 shillingsworth of other goods entailed by domestic production [5]. This is an example of trade creation. If A had been levying a somewhat lower tariff, a 50% tariff, for example, she would already have been buying X from abroad before the formation of any customs union. If A is buying a commodity from abroad, and if her tariff is non-discriminatory, then she will be buying it from the lowest-cost source – in this case country C. Now consider a customs union with country B. B's X, now exempt from the tariff, sells for 26s, while C's X, which must still pay the 50% tariff, must be sold for 30s. A will now buy X from B at a price, in terms of the value of exports, of 26s, whereas she was formerly buying it from C at a price of only 20s. This is a case of Viner's trade diversion, and since it entails a movement from lower to higher real cost sources of supply, it represents a movement from a more to a less efficient allocation of resources.

This analysis is an example of what Mr Lancaster and I have called 'The General Theory of Second Best': [6] if it is impossible to satisfy *all* the optimum conditions (in this case to make all relative prices equal to all rates of transformation in production), then a change which brings about the satisfaction of *some* of the optimum conditions (in this case making some relative prices equal to some rates of transformation in production) may make things better or worse [7].

Viner's analysis leads to the following classification of the possibilities that arise from a customs union between two countries, A and B:

1. Neither A nor B may be producing a given commodity. In this case they will both be importing this commodity from some third country, and the removal of tariffs on trade between A and B can cause no change in the pattern of trade in this commodity; both countries will continue to import it from the cheapest possible source outside of the union.

2. One of the two countries may be producing the commodity inefficiently under tariff protection while the second country is a non-producer. If country A is producing commodity X under tariff protection this means that her tariff is sufficient to eliminate competition from the cheapest possible source. Thus if A's tariff on X is adopted by the union the tariff will be high enough to secure B's market for A's inefficient industry.

3. Both countries may be producing the commodity inefficiently under tariff protection. In this case the customs union removes tariffs between country A and B and ensures that the least inefficient of the two will capture the union market [8].

In case 2 above any change must be a trade-diverting one, while in case 3 any change must be a trade-creating one. If one wishes to predict the welfare effects of a customs union it is necessary to predict the relative strengths of the forces causing trade creation and trade diversion.

This analysis leads to the conclusion that customs unions are likely to cause losses when the countries involved are complementary *in the range of commodities that are protected by tariffs*. Consider the class of commodities produced under tariff protection in each of the two countries. If these classes overlap to a large extent, then the most efficient of the two countries will capture the union market and there will be a re-allocation of resources in a more efficient direction. If these two classes do not overlap to any great extent, then the protected industry in one country is likely to capture the whole of the union market when the union is formed, and there is likely to be a re-allocation of resources in a less-efficient direction. This point of Viner's has often been misunderstood and read to say that, in some general sense, the economies of the two countries should be competitive and not complementary. A precise way of making the point is to say that the customs union is more likely to bring gain, the greater is the degree of overlapping between the class of commodities produced under tariff protection in the two countries.

A subsequent analysis of the conditions affecting the gains from union through trade creation and trade diversion was made by Drs Makower and Morton [9]. They pointed out that, *given that trade creation was going to occur*, the gains would be larger the more dissimilar were the cost ratios in the two countries. (Clearly if two countries have almost identical cost ratios the gains from trade will be small.) They then defined competitive economies to be ones with similar cost ratios and complementary economies to be ones with dissimilar ratios, and were able to conclude that unions between complementary economies would, if they brought gain at all, bring large gains. The conclusions of Viner and Makower and Morton are in no sense contradictory. Stated in the simplest possible language, Viner showed that gains will arise from unions if both countries are producing the same commodity; Makower and Morton showed that these gains will be larger the larger is the difference between the costs at which the same commodity is produced in the two countries [10].

We now come to the second major development in customs-union theory – the analysis of the welfare effects of *the substitution between commodities* resulting from the changes in relative prices which necessarily accompany a customs union. Viner's analysis implicitly assumed that commodities are consumed in some fixed proportion which is independent of the structure of relative prices. Having ruled out substitution between commodities, he was left to analyse only bodily shifts of trade from one country to another. The way in which Viner's conclusion that trade diversion necessarily lowers welfare depends on his implicit demand assumption is illustrated in Fig. 2·1. Consider the case of a small country, A, specialized in the

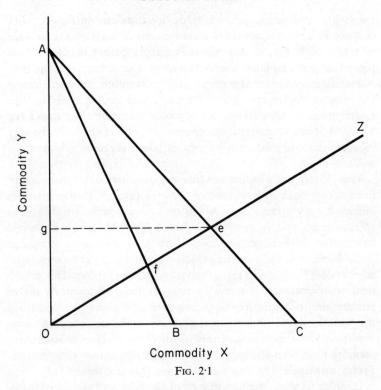

FIG. 2·1

production of a single commodity, Y, and importing one commodity, X, at terms of trade independent of any taxes or tariffs levied in A. The fixed proportion in which commodities are consumed is shown by the slope of the line OZ, which is the income- and price-consumption line for all (finite) prices and incomes. OA indicates country A's total production of commodity Y, and the slope of the line AC shows the terms of trade offered by country C, the lowest cost producer of X. Under conditions of free trade, country A's equilibrium will be at e, the point of intersection between OZ and AC. A will consume Og of Y, exporting Ag in return for ge of X. Now a tariff which does not affect A's terms of trade and is not high enough to protect a domestic industry producing Y will leave her equilibrium position unchanged at e [11]. The tariff changes relative prices, but consumers' purchases are completely insensitive to this change and, if foreign trade continues at terms indicated by the slope of the line AC, the community must remain in equilibrium at e. Now consider a

37

case where country A forms a trade-diverting customs union with country B. This means that A must buy her imports of X at a price in terms of Y higher than she was paying before the union was formed. An example of this is shown in Fig. 2·1 by the line AB. A's equilibrium is now at f, the point of intersection between AB and OZ; less of both commodities are consumed, and A's welfare has unambiguously diminished. We conclude therefore that, under the assumed demand conditions, trade diversion (which necessarily entails a deterioration in A's terms of trade) *necessarily* lowers A's welfare [12].

Viner's implicit assumption that commodities are consumed in fixed proportions independent of the structure of relative prices is indeed a very special one. A customs union necessarily changes relative prices and, in general, we should expect this to lead to some substitution between commodities, there being a tendency to change the volume of already existing trade with more of the now cheaper goods being bought and less of the now more expensive. This would tend to increase the volume of imports from a country's union partner and to diminish both the volume of imports obtained from the outside world and the consumption of home-produced commodities. The importance of this substitution effect in consumption seems to have been discovered independently by at least three people, Professor Meade [13], Professor Gehrels [14] and myself [15].

In order to show the importance of the effects of substitutions in consumption we merely drop the assumption that commodities are consumed in fixed proportions. I shall take Mr Gehrels' presentation of this analysis because it illustrates a number of important factors. In Fig. 2·2 OA is again country A's total production of Y, and the slope of the line AC indicates the terms of trade between X and Y when A is trading with country C. The free-trade equilibrium position is again at e, where an indifference curve is tangent to AC. In this case, however, the imposition of a tariff on imports of X, even if it does not shift the source of country A's imports, will cause a reduction in the quantity of these imports and an increase in the consumption of the domestic commodity Y. A tariff which changes the relative price in A's domestic market to, say, that indicated by the slope of the line $A'C'$ will move A's equilibrium position to point h. At this point an indifference curve cuts AC with a slope equal to the line $A'C'$; consumers are thus adjusting their purchases to the market rate of transformation and the tariff has had the effect of

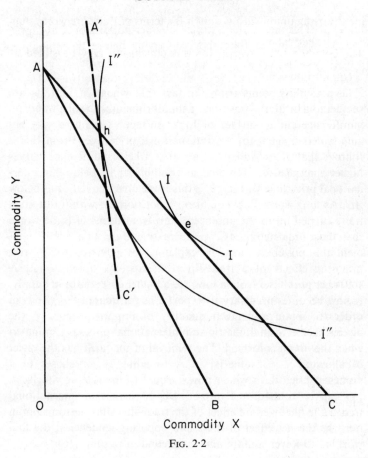

FIG. 2·2

reducing imports of X and increasing consumption of the home good Y. In these circumstances it is clearly possible for country A to form a trade-diverting customs union and yet gain an increase in its welfare. To show this, construct a line through *A* tangent to the indifference curve *I″* to cut the X axis at some point *B*. If A forms a trade-diverting customs union with country B and buys her imports of X from B at terms of trade indicated by the slope of the line *AB*, her welfare will be unchanged. If, therefore, the terms of trade with B are worse than those given by C but better than those indicated by the slope of the line *AB*, A's welfare will be increased by the trade-diverting customs union. A's welfare will be diminished by this trade-diverting union with B only if B's terms of trade are worse than those indicated by the slope of AB.

The common-sense reason for this conclusion may be stated as follows:

'The possibility stems from the fact that whenever imports are subject to a tariff, the position of equilibrium must be one where an indifference curve [surface or hyper-surface as the case may be] cuts (*not* is tangent to) the international price line. From this it follows that there will exist an area where indifference curves higher than the one achieved at equilibrium lie below the international price line. In Fig. [2·2] this is the area above I'' but below AC. As long as the final equilibrium position lies within this area, trade carried on in the absence of tariffs, at terms of trade worse than those indicated by AC, will increase welfare. In a verbal statement this possibility may be explained by referring to the two opposing effects of a trade-diverting customs union. First, A shifts her purchases from a lower to a higher cost source of supply. It now becomes necessary to export a larger quantity of goods in order to obtain any given quantity of imports. Secondly, the divergence between domestic and international prices is eliminated when the union is formed. The removal of the tariff has the effect of allowing . . . consumer[s] in A to adjust . . . purchases to a domestic price ratio which now is equal to the rate at which . . . [Y] can be transformed into . . . [X] by means of international trade. The final welfare effect of the trade-diverting customs union must be the net effect of these two opposing tendencies; the first working to lower welfare and the second to raise it' [16].

On this much there is general agreement. Professor Gehrels, however, concluded that his analysis established a general presumption in favour of gains from union rather than losses. He argued that 'to examine customs unions in the light only of *production* effects, as Viner does, will give a biased judgement of their effect on countries joining them' [17], and he went on to say that the analysis given above established a general presumption in favour of gains from union. Now we seemed to be back in the pre-Viner world, where economic analysis established a general case in favour of customs unions. In my article 'Mr. Gehrels on customs union' [18], I attempted to point out the mistake involved. The key is that Gehrels' model contains only two commodities: one domestic good and one import. There is thus only one optimum condition for consumption: that the relative price between X and Y equals the real rate of transformation (in domestic production or international trade, whichever is relevant) between these two commodities. The general problems raised by customs unions must, however, be analysed in a model containing a minimum of three types of commodities: domestic commodities (A), imports from the union partner (B) and imports from the outside world (C). When this change is made Gehrel's general presumption for gain from union disappears. Table 2·2

TABLE 2·2

Free trade	Uniform *ad valorem* tariff on all imports	Customs union with country B
$\dfrac{P_{Ad}}{P_{Bd}} = \dfrac{P_{Ai}}{P_{Bi}}$	$\dfrac{P_{Ad}}{P_{Bd}} < \dfrac{P_{Ai}}{P_{Bi}}$	$\dfrac{P_{Ad}}{P_{Bd}} = \dfrac{P_{Ai}}{P_{Bi}}$
$\dfrac{P_{Ad}}{P_{Cd}} = \dfrac{P_{Ai}}{P_{Ci}}$	$\dfrac{P_{Ad}}{P_{Cd}} < \dfrac{P_{Ai}}{P_{Ci}}$	$\dfrac{P_{Ad}}{P_{Cd}} < \dfrac{P_{Ai}}{P_{Ci}}$
$\dfrac{P_{Bd}}{P_{Cd}} = \dfrac{P_{Bi}}{P_{Ci}}$	$\dfrac{P_{Bd}}{P_{Cd}} = \dfrac{P_{Bi}}{P_{Ci}}$	$\dfrac{P_{Bd}}{P_{Cd}} < \dfrac{P_{Bi}}{P_{Ci}}$

Subscripts A, B and C refer to countries of origin, d to prices in A's domestic market, and i to prices in the international market.

shows the three optimum conditions that domestic prices and international prices should bear the same relationship to each other for the three groups of commodities, A, B and C [19]. In free trade all three optimum conditions will be fulfilled. If a uniform tariff is placed on both imports, then the relations shown in column 2 will obtain, for the price of goods from both B and C will be higher in A's domestic market than in the international market. When a customs union is formed, however, the prices of imports from the union partner, B, are reduced so that the first optimum condition is fulfilled, but the tariff remains on imports from abroad (C) so that the third optimum condition is no longer satisfied. The customs union thus moves country A from one non-optimal position to another, and in general it is impossible to say whether welfare will increase or diminish as a result. We are thus back to a position where the theory tells us that welfare may rise or fall, and a much more detailed study is necessary in order to establish the conditions under which one or the other result might obtain.

The above analysis has lead both Mr Gehrels and myself [20] to distinguish between *production effects* and *consumption effects* of customs unions. The reason for attempting this is not hard to find. Viner's analysis rules out substitution in consumption and looks to shifts in the location of production as the cause of welfare changes in customs unions. The analysis just completed emphasizes the effects of substitution in consumption. The distinction on this basis, however, is not fully satisfactory, for consumption effects will themselves cause changes in production. A more satisfactory distinction would seem to be one between *inter-country substitution* and *inter-commodity substitution*. Inter-country substitution would be Viner's trade creation and trade diversion, when one country is substituted for another as the source of supply for some commodity. Inter-commodity substitution occurs when one commodity is substituted, at least at the margin, for some other commodity as a result of a relative price shift. This is the type of substitution we have just been analysing. In general, either of these changes will cause shifts in both consumption and production.

Now we come to Professor Meade's analysis. His approach is taxonomic in that he attempts to classify a large number of possible cases, showing the factors which would tend to cause welfare to increase when a union is formed and to isolate these from the factors which would tend to cause welfare to diminish [22]. Fig. 2·3 (a) shows a demand and a supply curve for any imported commodity. Meade observes that a tariff, like any tax, shifts the supply curve to the left (to $S'S'$ in Fig. 2·3) and raises the price of the imported commodity. At the new equilibrium the demand price differs from the supply price by the amount of the tariff. If the supply price indicates the utility of the commodity to the suppliers and the demand price its utility to the purchasers, it follows that the utility of the taxed import is higher to purchasers than to suppliers, and the money value of this difference in utility is the value of the tariff. Now assume that the marginal utility of money is the same for buyers and for sellers. It follows that, if one more *unit of expenditure* were devoted to the purchase of this commodity, there would be a net gain to society equal to the proportion of the selling price of the commodity composed of the tariff. In Fig. 2·3 the rate of tariff is $cb/ab\%$, the supply price is ab and the demand price is ac, so that the money value of the 'gain' ('loss') to society resulting from a marginal increase (decrease) in expenditure on this commodity is bc.

Now assume that the same *ad valorem* rate of tariff is imposed on

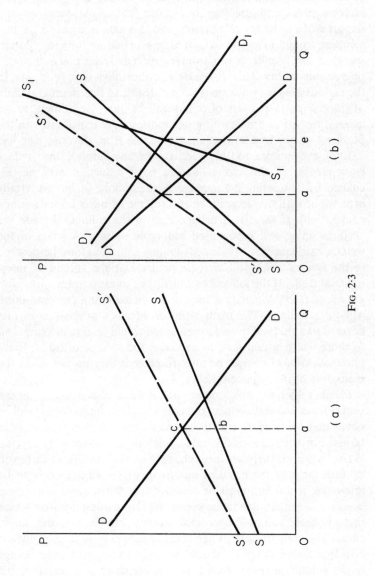

FIG. 2·3

all imports so that the tariff will be the same proportion of the market price of each import. Then the gain to society from a marginal increase in expenditure (say one more 'dollar' is spent) on any import is the same for all imports, and this gain is equal to the loss resulting from a marginal reduction in expenditure (one less 'dollar' spent) on any import. Now consider *a marginal reduction* in the tariff on one commodity. This will cause a readjustment of expenditure, in the various possible ways analysed by Meade, so that in general more of some imports and less of others will be purchased. Since, *at the margin*, the gain from devoting one more unit of expenditure to the purchase of any import is equal to the loss from devoting one less unit of expenditure to the purchase of any import, the welfare consequences of this discriminatory tariff reduction may be calculated by comparing the increase in the volume of imports (trade expansion) with the decrease in the volume of other imports (trade contraction). If there is a net increase in the volume of trade the customs union will have raised economic welfare. A study of the welfare consequences of customs unions can, therefore, be devoted to the factors which will increase or decrease the volume of international trade. If the influences which tend to cause trade expansion are found to predominate it may be predicted that a customs union will raise welfare. The main body of Meade's analysis is in fact devoted to a study of those factors which would tend to increase, and to those which would tend to decrease, the volume of trade. Complications can, of course, be introduced, but they do not affect the main drift of the argument [23].

Meade's analysis, which makes use of demand and supply curves, suffers from one very serious, possibly crippling, limitation. It will be noted that we were careful to consider only *marginal reductions* in tariffs. For such changes Meade's analysis is undoubtedly correct. When, however, there are *large* changes in many tariffs, as there will be with most of the customs unions in which we are likely to be interested, it can no longer be assumed that the demand and supply curves will remain fixed; the *ceteris paribus* assumptions on which they are based will no longer hold, so that both demand and supply curves are likely to shift. When this happens it is no longer obvious how much welfare weight should be given to any particular change in the volume of trade (even if we are prepared to make all of the other assumptions necessary for the use of this type of classical welfare analysis). In Fig. 2·3 (b), for example, if the demand curve

44

shifts to $D_1 D_1$ and the supply curve to $S_1 S_1$, what are we to say about the welfare gains or losses when trade changes from Oa to Oe?

There is not time to go through a great deal of Professor Meade's or my own analysis which attempts to discover the particular circumstances in which it is likely that a geographically discriminatory reduction in tariffs will raise welfare. I shall, therefore, take two of the general conclusions that emerge from various analyses and present these in order to illustrate the type of generalization that it is possible to make in customs-union theory.

The first generalization is one that emerges from Professor Meade's analysis and from my own. I choose it, first, because there seems to be general agreement on it and, second, although Professor Meade does not make this point, because it is an absolutely general proposition in the theory of second best; it applies to all sub-optimal positions, and customs-union theory only provides a particular example of its application. Stated in terms of customs unions, this generalization runs as follows: when only some tariffs are to be changed, welfare is more likely to be raised if these tariffs are merely *reduced* than if they are completely *removed*. Proofs of this theorem can be found in both Meade [23] and Lipsey and Lancaster [24] and we shall content ourselves here with an intuitive argument for the theorem in its most general context. Assume that there exist many taxes, subsidies, monopolies, etc., which prevent the satisfaction of optimum conditions. Further assume that all but one of these, say one tax, are fixed, and inquire into the second-best level for the tax that is allowed to vary. Finally, assume that there exists a unique second-best level for this tax [25]. Now a change in this one tax will either move the economy towards or away from a second-best optimum position. If it moves the economy away from a second-best position, then, no matter how large is the change in the tax, welfare will be lowered. If it moves the economy in the direction of the second-best optimum it may move it part of the way, all of the way or past it. If the economy is moved sufficienty far past the second-best optimum welfare will be lowered by the change. From this it follows that, if there is a unique second-best level for the tax being varied, a small variation is more likely to raise welfare than is a large variation [26].

The next generalization concerns the size of expenditure on the three classes of goods – those purchased domestically, from the union partner, and from the outside world – and is related to the gains from inter-commodity substitution. This generalization follows from the analysis in my own thesis [27] and does not seem to have been stated in any of the existing customs-union literature. Consider what happens to the optimum conditions, which we discussed earlier, when the customs union is formed (see Table 2·2). On the one hand, the tariff is taken off imports from the country's union partner, and the relative price between these imports and domestic goods is brought into conformity with the real rates of transformation. This, by itself, tends to increase welfare. On the other hand, the relative price between imports from the union partner and imports from the outside world are moved away from equality with real rates of transformation. This by itself tends to reduce welfare. Now consider both of these changes. As far as the prices of the goods from a country's union partner are concerned, they are brought into equality with rates of transformation *vis-à-vis* domestic goods, but they are moved away from equality with rates of transformation *vis-à-vis* imports from the outside world. These imports from the union partner are thus involved in both a gain and a loss and their size is *per se* unimportant; what matters is the relation between imports from the outside world and expenditure on domestic commodities: the larger are purchases of domestic commodities and the smaller are purchases from the outside world, the more likely is it that the union will bring gain. Consider a simple example in which a country purchases from its union partner only eggs while it purchases from the outside world only shoes, all other commodities being produced and consumed at home. Now when the union is formed the 'correct' price ratio (i.e. the one which conforms with the real rate of transformation) between eggs and shoes will be disturbed, but, on the other hand, eggs will be brought into the 'correct' price relationship with all other commodities – bacon, butter, cheese, meat, etc., and in these circumstances a customs union is very likely to bring gain, for the loss in distorting the price ratio between eggs and shoes will be small relative to the gain in establishing the correct price ratio between eggs and all other commodities. Now, however, let us reverse the position of domestic trade and imports from the outside world, making shoes the only commodity produced and consumed at home, eggs still being imported from the union partner, while everything else is now bought from the outside world. In these circumstances the customs union is most likely to bring a loss; the gains in establishing the correct price ratio between eggs and shoes are indeed likely to be very small compared with the losses of distorting the price ratio between eggs and all other commodities. If, to take a third example, eggs are produced at home, shoes imported from the outside world, while everything else is obtained from the union partner, the union may bring neither gain nor loss; for the union disturbs the 'correct' ratio between shoes and everything else except eggs, and establishes the 'correct' one between eggs and everything else except shoes. This example serves to show that the size of trade with a union partner is not the important variable; it is the relation between imports from the outside world and purchases of domestic goods that matters.

This argument gives rise to two general conclusions, one of them appealing immediately to common sense, one of them slightly surprising. The first is that, *given a country's volume of international trade*, a customs union is more likely to raise welfare the higher is the proportion of trade with the country's union partner and the lower the proportion with the outside world. The second is that a customs union is more likely to raise welfare the lower is the total volume of foreign trade, for the lower is foreign trade, the lower must be purchases from the outside world relative to purchases of domestic commodities. This means that the sort of countries who ought to form customs unions are those doing a high proportion of their foreign trade with their union partner, and making a high proportion of the total expenditure on domestic trade. Countries which are likely to lose from a customs union, on the other hand, are those countries in which a low proportion of total trade is domestic, especially if the customs union does not include a high proportion of their foreign trade.

We may now pass to a very brief consideration of some of the empirical work. Undoubtedly a serious attempt to predict and measure the possible effects of a customs union is a very difficult task. Making all allowances for this, however, a surprisingly large proportion of the voluminous literature on the subject is devoted to guess and suspicion, and a very small proportion to serious attempts to measure. Let us consider what empirical work has been done on the European Common Market and the Free Trade Area, looking first at attempts to measure possible gains from specialization. The theoretical analysis underlying these measurements is of the sort developed by Professor Meade and outlined previously.

The first study which we will mention is that made by the Dutch economist Verdoorn, subsequently quoted and used by Scitovsky [28]. The analysis assumes an elasticity of substitution between domestic goods and imports of minus one-half, and an elasticity of sub-stitution between different imports of minus two. These estimates are based on some empirical measurements of an aggregate sort and the extremely radical assumption is made that the same elasticities apply to all commodities. The general assumption, then, is that one import is fairly easily substituted for another, while imports and domestic commodities are not particularly good substitutes for each other [29].

Using this assumption, an estimate was made of the changes in trade when tariffs are reduced between the six Common Market countries, the United Kingdom and Scandinavia. The estimate is that intra-European trade will increase by approximately 17%, and, when this increase is weighted by the proportion of the purchase price of each commodity that is made up of tariff and estimates for the reduction in trade in other directions are also made, the final figure for the gains from trade to the European countries is equal to about one-twentieth of one per cent of their annual incomes. In considering this figure, the crude estimate of elasticities of substitution must cause some concern. The estimate of an increase in European trade of 17% is possibly rather small in the face of the known fact that Benelux trade increased by approximately 50% after the formation of that customs union. A possible check on the accuracy of the Verdoorn method would have been to apply it to the pre-customs union situation in the Benelux countries, to use the method to predict what would happen to Benelux trade and then to compare the prediction with what we actually know to have happened. Whatever allowances are made, however, Scitovsky's conclusion is not likely to be seriously challenged:

'The most surprising feature of these estimates is their smallness. ... As estimates of the total increase in intra-European trade contingent upon economic union, Verdoorn's figures are probably under estimates; but if, by way of correction, we should raise them five- or even twenty-five-fold, that would still leave unchanged our basic conclusion that the gain from increased intra-European specialisation is likely to be insignificant' [30].

A second empirical investigation into the possible gains from trade, this time relating only to the United Kingdom, has been made by Professor Johnson [31]. Johnson bases his study on the estimates made by *The Economist* Intelligence Unit of the increases in the value of British trade which would result by 1970, first, if there were only the Common Market and, second, if there were the Common Market and the Free Trade Area. Professor Johnson then asks what will be the size of the possible gain to Britain of participation in the Free Trade Area? His theory is slightly different from that of Professor Meade, but since it arrives at the same answer, namely that the gain is equal to the increased quantity of trade times the proportion of the purchase price made up of tariff, we do not need to consider the details. From these estimates Johnson arrives at the answer that the possible gain to Britain from joining the Free Trade Area would be, *as an absolute maximum*, 1% of the national income of the United Kingdom.

Most people seem to be surprised at the size of these estimates, finding them smaller than expected. This leads us to ask: might there not be some inherent bias in this sort of estimate? and, might not a totally different approach yield quite different answers? One possible approach is to consider the proportion of British factors of production engaged in foreign trade. This can be taken to be roughly the percentage contribution made by trade to the value of the national product, which can be estimated to be roughly the value of total trade as a proportion of GNP, first subtracting the import content from the GNP. This produces a rough estimate of 18% of Britain's total resources engaged in foreign trade. The next step would be to ask how much increase in efficiency of utilization for these resources could we expect: (1) as a result of their re-allocation in the direction of their comparative advantage, and (2) as a result of a re-allocation among possible consumers of the commodities produced by these resources. Here is an outline for a possible study, but, in the absence of such a study, what would we guess? Would a 10% increase in efficiency not be a rather conservative estimate? Such a gain in efficiency would give a net increase in the national income of 1·8%. If the resources had a 20% increase in efficiency, then an increase in the national income of 3·6% would be possible. At this stage these figures can give nothing more than a common-sense check on the more detailed estimates of economists such as Verdoorn and Johnson. Until further detailed work has been done, it must be accepted that the best present estimates gives figures of the net gain from trade amounting to something less than 1% of the national income (although we may not, of course, have a very high degree of confidence in these estimates) [32].

When we move on from the possible gains from new trade to the question of the economic benefits arising from other causes, such as economies of scale or enforced efficiency, we leave behind even such halting attempts at measurement as we have just considered. Some economists see considerable economies of scale emerging from European union. Others are sceptical. In what follows, I will confine my attention mainly to the arguments advanced by Professor H. G. Johnson [33]. His first argument runs as follows:

'It is extremely difficult to believe that British industry offers substantial potential savings in cost which cannot be exploited in a densely-populated market of 51 million people with a GNP of £18 billion, especially when account is taken of the much larger markets abroad in which British industry, in spite of restrictions of various kinds, has been able to sell its products' [34].

Let us make only two points about Professor Johnson's observation. First, many markets will be very much less than the total population. What, for example, can we say about a product sold mainly to upper middle-class males living more than 20 miles away from an urban centre? Might there not be economies of scale remaining in the production of a commodity for such a market? Secondly, in the absence of some theory that tells us the statement is true for 51 and, say, 31, but not 21, million people, the argument must remain nothing more than an unsupported personal opinion. As another argument, Professor Johnson asks, 'Why are these economies of scale, if they do exist, not already being exploited?' [35] It is, of course, well known that unexhausted economies of scale are incompatible with the existence of perfect competition, but it is equally well known that unexhausted economies of scale are compatible with the existence of imperfect competition as long as long-run marginal cost is declining faster than marginal revenue. Here it is worth while making a distinction, mentioned by Scitovsky [36], between the long-run marginal cost of producing more goods, to which the economist is usually referring when he speaks of scale effects, and the marginal cost of making and selling more goods (which must include selling costs). This leads to a distinction between increasing sales when the whole market is expanding and increasing sales when the market is static, and thus increasing them at the expense of one's competitors. The former is undoubtedly very much easier than the latter. It is quite possible for the marginal costs of *production* to be declining while the marginal costs of *selling* in a static market are rising steeply.

This would mean that production economies would not be exploited by the firms competing in the market, but that if the market were to expand so that *all* firms in a given industry could grow, then these economies would be realized.

Let us also consider an argument put forward in favour of economies of scale. Writing in 1955, Gehrels and Johnson argue that very large gains from economies of scale can be expected [37]. In evidence of this they quote the following facts: American productivity (i.e. output per man) is higher than United Kingdom productivity for most commodities; the differential is, however, greatest in those industries which use mass-production methods. From this they conclude that there are unexploited economies of mass production in the United Kingdom. Now this may well be so, but, before accepting the conclusion, we should be careful in interpreting this meagre piece of evidence. What else might it mean? Might it not mean, for example, that the ratios of capital to labour differed in the two countries so that, if we calculate the productivity of a factor by dividing total production by the quantity of one factor employed, we will necessarily find these differences? Secondly, would we not be very surprised if we did not find such differences in comparative costs between the two countries? Are we surprised when we find America's comparative advantage centred in the mass-producing industries, and, if this is the case, must we conclude that vast economies of mass production exist for Europe?

Finally, we come to the possible gains through forced efficiency. Business firms may not be adopting methods known to be technically more efficient than those now in use due to inertia, a dislike of risk-taking, a willingness to be content with moderate profits, or a whole host of other reasons. If these firms are thrown into competition with a number of firms in other countries who are not adopting this conservative policy, then the efficiency of the use of resources may increase because technically more efficient production methods are forced on the businessman now facing fierce foreign competition. Here no evidence has as yet been gathered, and, rather than report the opinions of others, I will close by recording the personal guess that this is a very large potential source of gain, that an increase in competition with foreign countries who are prepared to adopt new methods might have a most salutary effect on the efficiency of a very large number of British and European manufacturing concerns [38, 39].

NOTES AND REFERENCES

[1] An earlier version of this paper was read before the Conference of the Association of University Teachers of Economics at Southampton, January 1959. I am indebted for comments and suggestions to G. C. Archibald, K. Klappholz and Professor L. Robbins.

[2] Points (1) and (2) are clearly related, for the existence of (1) is a *necessary* condition for (2), but they are more conveniently treated as separate points, since (1) is not a *sufficient* condition for the existence of (2).

[3] Jacob Viner, *The Customs Union Issue*, New York: Carnegie Endowment for International Peace, 1950. See the whole of Chapter 4, especially pp. 43–4.

[4] In everything that follows the 'home country' will be labelled A, the 'union partner' B and the rest of the world C.

[5] This argument presumes that relative prices in each country reflect real rates of transformation. It follows that the resources used to produce a unit of X in country A could produce any other good to the value of 35s and, since a unit of X can be had from B by exporting goods to the value of only 26s, there will be a surplus of goods valued at 9s accruing to A from the transfer of resources out of X when trade is opened with country B.

[6] R. G. Lipsey and K. J. Lancaster, The general theory of second best, *Review of Economic Studies*, vol. XXIV (1), no. 63, 1956–7.

[7] The point may be made slightly more formally as follows: the conditions necessary for the maximizing of *any* function do not, in general, provide conditions sufficient for an increase in the value of the function when the maximum value is not to be obtained by the change.

[8] One of the two countries might be an efficient producer of this commodity needing no tariff protection, in which case, *a fortiori*, there is gain.

[9] H. Makower and G. Morton, A contribution towards a theory of customs unions, *Economic Journal*, vol. LXII, no. 249, March 1953, pp. 33–49.

[10] Care must be taken to distinguish between complementarity and competitiveness in costs and in tastes, both being possible. In the Makower–Morton model these relations exist only on the cost side. An example of the confusion which may arise when this distinction is not made can be seen in F. V. Meyer's article, Complementarity and the lowering of tariffs, *The American Economic Review*, vol. XLVI, no. 3, June 1956. Meyer's definitions, if they are to mean anything, must refer to the demand side. Hence he is not entitled to contrast his results with those of Makower and Morton, or of Viner, all of whom were concerned with cost complementarity and competitiveness.

[11] It is assumed throughout all the subsequent analysis that the tariff revenue collected by the government is either returned to individuals by means of lump-sum subsidies or spent by the government on the same bundle of goods that consumers would have purchased.

[12] It is also necessary to assume that country A is the only country in the world that levies tariffs! This was pointed out in my thesis referred to subsequently but omitted from the original text of this article.

[13] J. E. Meade, *The Theory of Customs Unions*, Amsterdam: North-Holland, 1956.

[14] F. Gehrels, Customs unions from a single country viewpoint, *Review of Economic Studies*, vol. XXIV (1), no. 63, 1956–7.

[15] R. G. Lipsey, The theory of customs unions: trade diversion and welfare, *Economica*, vol. XXIV, no. 93, February 1957. My own paper was first written in 1954 as a criticism of the assumption of fixed ratios in consumption made by

Dr Ozga in his thesis (S. A. Ozga, The Theory of Tariff Systems', University of London Ph.D. thesis, unpublished).

[16] R. G. Lipsey, Trade diversion and welfare, pp. 43–4. The changes made in the quotation are minor ones necessary to make the notation in the example comparable to the one used in the present text.

[17] F. Gehrels, Customs unions, p. 61.

[18] R. G. Lipsey, Mr Gehrels on customs unions, *Review of Economic Studies*, Vol. XXIV (3), no. 65, 1956–7, pp. 211–14.

[19] If we assume that consumers adjust their purchases to the relative prices ruling in their domestic markets, then the optimum conditions that rates of substitution in consumption should equal rates of transformation in trade can be stated in terms of equality between relative prices ruling in the domestic markets and those ruling in the international market.

[20] Gehrels, Customs unions, p. 61, and Lipsey, Trade diversion and welfare, pp. 40–1.

[22] The point of his taxonomy or of any taxonomy of this sort, it seems to me, must be merely to illustrate how the model works. Once one has mastered the analysis it is possible to work through any particular case that may arise, and there would seem to be no need to work out all possible cases beforehand.

[22] For example, the same rate of tariff might not be charged on all imports. In this case it is only necessary to weight each dollar's increase or decrease in trade by the proportion of this value that is made up by tariff – the greater is the rate of tariff the greater is the gain or loss. It is also possible, if one wishes to make inter-country comparisons, to weight a dollar's trade in one direction by a different amount than a dollar's trade in some other direction. These complications, however, do not affect the essence of Meade's analysis, which is to make a *small change* in some tariffs and then to observe that the welfare consequences depend on the net change in the volume of trade and to continue the study in order to discover in what circumstances an increase or a decrease in the net volume of trade is likely.

[23] *Theory of Customs Unions*, pp. 50–1.

[24] The general theory of second best, section V.

[25] A unique second-best level (i.e. the level which maximizes welfare subject to the existence and invariability of all the other taxes, tariffs, etc.) for any one variable factor can be shown to exist in a large number of cases (see, for example, Lipsey and Lancaster, sections V and VI), but cannot be proved to exist in general (section VIII).

[26] This may be given a more formal statement. Consider the direction of the change – towards or away from the second-best optimum position – caused by the change in the tax. Moving away from the second-best optimum is a *sufficient*, but not a necessary, condition for a reduction in welfare. Moving towards the second-best optimum is a *necessary*, but not a sufficient, condition for an increase in welfare.

[27] R. G. Lipsey, 'The Theory of Customs Unions: A General Equilibrium Analysis', University of London Ph.D. thesis, unpublished, pp. 97–9, and Mathematical Appendix to Chapter VI. The thesis has since been published under the above title by Weidenfeld & Nicolson, London, 1970. The reference to the printed version is pp. 50–6.

[28] T. de Scitovsky, *Economic Theory and Western European Integration*, London, Allen and Unwin, 1958, pp. 64–78.

[29] Note also that everything is assumed to be a substitute for everything else; there are no relations of complementarity.

[30] Scitovsky, *Economic Theory*, p. 67.

[31] H. G. Johnson, The gains from free trade with Europe: an estimate, *Manchester School*, vol. XXVI, September 1958.

[32] Perhaps a more intuitively appealing argument as to why these estimates probably do not over-estimate the order of magnitude of the gain is as follows: Typical European tariffs on manufactured goods were in the order of 20%. This means that industries from 1 to 20% less efficient than foreign competitors will be protected by these tariffs. If the costs of different industries are spread out evenly, then some tariff-protected industries would be 20% less efficient than foreign competitors, but others would be only 1% less efficient, and their average inefficiency would be in the order of half the tariff rate, which is 10% less efficient than foreign competitors. Typically, the margin of production is unlikely to be moved further forward or backward on average across all products by more than 10%. In other words, it seems unlikely that more than 10% of a country's resources are, as a result of a tariff policy, producing goods other than what they would have produced under free trade. Thus 10% of a country's resources might be producing 10% less efficiently than if there were no tariffs. This has the overall effect of reducing national income by approximately 1%.

[34] In singling out Professor Johnson, I do not wish to imply that he is alone in practising the sort of economics which I am criticizing. On the contrary, he is typical of a very large number of economists who have attempted to obtain quantitative conclusions from qualitative arguments.

[34] H. G. Johnson, The criteria of economic advantage, *Bulletin of the Oxford University Institute of Statistics*, vol. 19, February 1957, p. 35. See also The economic gains from free trade with Europe, *Three Banks Review*, September 1958, for a similar argument.

[35] Johnson, Economic gains, p. 10, and Economic advantage, p. 35.

[36] Scitovsky, *Economic Theory*, pp. 42 ff.

[37] Gehrels and Johnson, The economic gains from European integration, *Journal of Political Economy*, August 1955.

[38] Milton Friedman's argument that survival of the fittest proves profit maximization notwithstanding (see *Essays in Positive Economics*, Chicago: University of Chicago Press, 1953). What seems to me to be a conclusive refutation of the Friedman argument is to be found in G. C. Archibald, The state of economic science, *British Journal of the Philosophy of Science*, June 1959.

[39] I have since changed my mind in respect to this belief. See the more detailed arguments in Lipsey (1967, The balance of payments and the Common Market, *Economics: The Journal of the Economics Association*, Autumn, p. 12). The following quotation should indicate the nature of my present disagreement with the argument in the text. 'Before you accept this argument which is usually thrown about quite uncritically ask yourself what the text books all say about the argument that a poor, low productivity country cannot trade profitably with a rich, high productivity one. "Nonsense," says the books, "it is comparative not absolute advantage that determines the flow of trade and the gains from it." Assume, for example, that everybody in Britain is absolutely 20% less efficient than everybody on the Continent. If we go into the common market on an exchange rate which will yield an external balance, then there will be *no* effect on overall efficiency: some industries will have a comparative advantage, some will not, and payments will be balanced at the present levels of efficiency. The only way in which increased efficiency could be forced on Britain would be if we went in at an over-valued exchange rate. This means that very few industries would be able to export and that imports would flood in from the continent. We would then be hoping that the domestic level of efficiency would react so that the overall level of costs and prices would fall in Britain, *vis-à-vis* Europe, and that a

balance of payments would be achieved at the formerly over-valued rate once the increase in efficiency had occurred. But there is no reason to think that a rise in efficiency with a constant price level which is the equivalent to a temporary increase in the rate of economic growth would improve the balance of payments. Certainly there is little in our recent history to suggest that it would cause a deflation. Probably the best we could hope for would be a parallel rise in wages and no change in the price level. Thus, even if the gain were realized, we would have to contemplate a subsequent devaluation of the pound. This in itself would be no disaster but it is not easy to devalue a single currency within the rules of the Common Market nor is there any evidence that the Six would contemplate allowing us to enter on an over-valued rate. We would also be taking the chance – in my opinion a very outside one in light of evidence of the 1920s – that an over-valued exchange rate would produce a rise in efficiency rather than a decline in employment and in national income.'

3

A NEW LOOK AT CUSTOMS UNION THEORY [1]*

C. A. COOPER

The Rand Corporation, Santa Monica, California

B. F. MASSELL

*Food Research Institute,
Stanford University*

Customs union theory can be said to date from the publication in 1950 of Viner's pioneering work [2]. Viner showed that a customs union can result in either trade creation or trade diversion: the former involves a shift from high-cost domestic production to lower-cost production in a partner country; the latter a shift from the lowest-cost external producer to a higher-cost partner. Viner pointed out that trade creation raises the home country's welfare, and trade division lowers it. This distinction has formed the basis of most subsequent analysis of the welfare implications of customs unions.

Viner's analysis has been extended and modified by Lipsey, Meade, Gehrels and others [3] to take account of intercommodity substitution, or 'consumption effects'. Lipsey, for example, argues that 'when consumption effects are allowed for, the simple conclusions that trade creation is "good" and trade diversion "bad" are no longer valid' [4]. Although he does not try to establish that trade creation can lower welfare, he does show that trade diversion can raise welfare [5]. When a tariff is imposed it introduces a divergence between relative prices facing consumers and real opportunity costs of goods to the economy. It is, in this respect, identical to an excise tax, and constrains consumers to a non-optimal consumption equilibrium. When a customs union is formed, some dutiable goods formerly imported from outside sources will be replaced by the same goods imported from a partner country, duty-free but at a higher real

* *Economic Journal*, December 1965, 75, pp. 742–747.

cost. The shift to a higher-cost source of supply tends to lower the country's real income, and consequently consumer welfare; but the removal of the constraint on consumption may raise welfare. If the second effect is favourable, and outweighs the first effect, there is a net rise in welfare.

This paper is concerned with the 'pure theory' of customs unions – as surveyed in Lipsey's classic articles [5] – and rules out gains from changes in the terms of trade, economies of scale and other considerations not forming part of the pure theory.

We shall argue the following:

1. Analytically the welfare effect of a customs union – whether trade creating, trade diverting or both – can be split into two components: (*a*) a tariff reduction component, and (*b*) a pure trade diversion component.

2. Using the standards of traditional customs union analysis, the tariff reduction component is the sole source of any gain in consumers' welfare that might result from a customs union. It accounts for both trade creation and the consumption effect.

3. Using as a point of reference an *appropriate* policy of non-preferential protection, a customs union necessarily results in pure trade-diversion, and is consequently 'bad' in the traditional welfare sense.

4. The 'free trade point of view' underlying the Vinerian analysis fails to explain why a customs union would ever be preferred to a non-preferential tariff policy.

5. Recognition of the purposes served by tariffs permits an explanation of the existence of customs unions, and the extension of customs-union analysis to a greater variety of issues than has hitherto been the case.

CUSTOMS UNIONS AND CONSUMER WELFARE

Fig. 3·1 shows the home market for any individual product affected by the customs union [6]. In the figure D is the home demand curve; S_h is the supply curve of domestic producers; S_{h+p}, the supply curve of the home-plus-partner countries, assuming that the partner's goods are admitted duty free; and S_w, the world supply curve [7]. For greater generality, we have assumed rising costs in the home

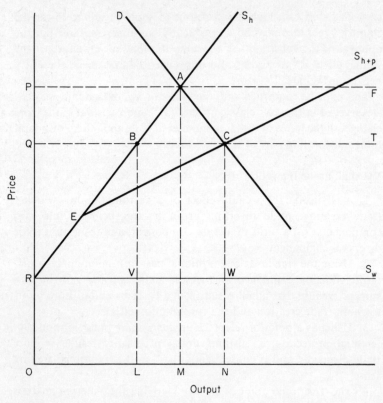

FIG. 3·1.—The welfare effects of a customs union

and partner countries [8]. But to rule out terms-of-trade effects, the home country is assumed not to account for a substantial proportion of total world imports of the item; consequently the world supply curve, S_w will appear horizontal in this market, even if there are rising costs [9].

First, consider that the country initially has a non-preferential tariff equal to RQ, so that the relevant supply curve is RBT. Then quantity ON will be consumed at price OQ. Of this amount, OL will be produced domestically and the remainder, LN, imported from the lowest-cost (world) supplier.

Second, consider an initial non-preferential tariff below RQ. The price is then below OQ, consumption in excess of ON and local production less than *OL*, with imports supplying that part of consumption that is not locally supplied.

In either of these two cases forming a customs union leaves the price, quantity consumed and level of local production unchanged [10]. However, the higher-cost partner country displaces the lowest-cost world supplier [11], raising the real cost of the item to the economy, and reducing the customs revenue [12]. We shall term this *pure* trade diversion.

Third, consider a tariff in excess of *RP*. The effective world supply curve (including the tariff) then lies above *PF*, and the entire local demand is supplied out of local production. Quantity *OM* is sold at price *OP*. In this case forming a customs union results in trade creation; the partner displaces (in part) local production. The price falls to *OQ*, consumption increases to *ON*, local production declines to *OL* and the partner supplies *LN*.

Fourth, if the tariff is between *RQ* and *RP* the price is between *OQ* and *OP*. Local demand is then supplied jointly by local production and imports. The quantity consumed is between *OM* and *ON*; local production between *OL* and *OM*; and imports make up the difference. A customs union then results in both trade creation and trade diversion. The price is again reduced to *OQ*, consumption increases to *ON* and local production is reduced to *OL*, with the partner supplying *LN*.

Present theory argues that trade creation is beneficial, that trade diversion is harmful and that the consumption effect may be either [13]. Whether a customs union on balance raises or lowers consumer welfare depends on whether or not trade creation plus (or minus, as the case may be) the consumption effect outweigh trade diversion.

According to present theory, then, our first two examples (pure trade diversion) are bad. The third and fourth examples cannot be evaluated without reference to what is happening elsewhere in the economy. The type of analysis regarded as appropriate is the theory of second-best.

We establish our first two points by noting that in examples 3 and 4 the country has the option of selecting a tariff equal to *RQ*, making *RBT* the effective supply curve. Consumption will be equal to *ON*; the price *OQ*; domestic production *OL*; and imports *LN*. Thus, this lower tariff will provide the same price, level of consumption and domestic production obtained in the customs union. But with the lower non-preferential tariff (as compared with the customs union), imports from the outside world (the lowest-cost supplier) entirely displace imports from the partner, providing a net gain to the country equal to the difference in the total cost of supply from the two alternative sources: the area of rectangle $BCWV$. Moreover, customs revenue will be greater by the same amount.

It is then convenient to split the effect of a customs union into two components: (1) a non-preferential tariff reduction to RQ, and (2) a move from this position to a customs union with the initial tariff [14]. This analytical distinction shows clearly that any rise in consumer welfare as a consequence of forming a customs union, whether as a result of trade creation or a favourable consumption effect, is due entirely to the tariff reduction component of the move. Moving to a customs union from the position obtainable as a result of the non-preferential tariff reduction is simply pure trade diversion – a substitution of the high-cost partner's goods for goods from the lowest-cost world supplier – which lowers welfare. Whether a customs union is on balance beneficial (compared with the initial non-preferential tariff) will depend on whether the tariff-reduction effect outweighs the pure trade diversion effect.

But this result implies that a customs union is necessarily inferior to an *appropriate* policy of non-preferential protection. Even without the option of forming a customs union, the home country already has the option of lowering its initial tariff and thereby reaping the beneficial effects that a customs union would provide without the offsetting costs. Moreover, because a customs union is always purely trade-diverting compared with the best non-preferential tariff, then the theory of second-best is not helpful in evaluating the welfare effects of the customs union *per se*; second-best theory is relevant only for evaluating the welfare effect of the tariff reduction component.

The difficulty posed for customs union analysis by the intermingling of tariff reduction and pure trade diversion effects shows up clearly in Lipsey's classic article [15]. In order to analyse the consumption effect of a customs union, Lipsey must first neutralize the impact of the implicit tariff reduction. He does this by assuming 'that the tariff revenue collected by the government is either returned to individuals by means of lump-sum subsidies or spent by the government on the same bundle of goods that consumers would have purchased' [16]. Without this assumption, which eliminates the revenue effect of tariffs, it would be necessary to consider the economic consequences of replacing the revenue lost in forming a customs union. Since forming a customs union does not, *per se*, generate new sources of revenue, the Government must employ an alternative that existed before. As this source of revenue was previously by-passed, there is a presumption that the Government regarded it as inferior to the tariff actually chosen. If not, the Government could shift to this alternative source of revenue even without forming a customs union. But this means that a customs union cannot be judged 'good' or 'bad' without taking into account the harmful effects of raising the revenue previously generated by the pre-union tariff. Moreover, this difficulty is not confined to the issues of replacing revenue. Whatever the purpose of pre-union tariffs – whether as revenue-raising, protective or balance-of-payments devices – the cost of replacing them in a customs union must be considered.

Viner was explicit that trade creation is good and trade diversion bad *from a free trade point of view*. As he also regarded tariffs as an inefficient means of raising revenue, it followed that any pre-union tariff has to be ill-advised. It is then certainly possible for a customs union to bring about a gain – even though an even larger gain could be achieved through a simple reduction in the non-preferential tariff.

We certainly do not question the logic of Viner's analysis. What we do question is the usefulness of this type of analysis as a basis for the evaluation of customs unions. It fails to show why a customs union may be acceptable when a tariff reduction is not, and it fails to analyse how a customs union may more efficiently serve the ends previously served by non-preferential protection. We would argue that the answer to the latter is the key to the former. It may be that policy-makers are sufficiently obtuse not to notice that a 'good' customs union has moved them towards free trade and away from protection, but this assumption of political myopia does not appear to be well founded. And without this assumption, by failing to explain why countries have tariffs, customs-union theory fails to explain also why customs unions are formed.

By making explicit the economic ends served by tariffs, the stage is set for an extension of customs-union analysis. Much of the recent controversy surrounding customs unions has, in fact, been carried on from this point of view. The possible gains from a customs union resulting from improvements in the terms of trade, economies of scale and reductions in disguised unemployment have received considerable attention. These gains, of course, do not show up as the simple trade-creation gains considered in the Vinerian model.

Little, if any, attention has been given, however, to the comparison of the relative efficiency of preferential and non-preferential tariff systems as protective devices. By permitting customs-union participants to draw on one another's markets, a customs union may make it possible for its members to maintain a protected domestic market at less sacrifice in income than is possible through non-preferential protection. To analyse the prospective gains from such 'market-swapping' requires a different analytical framework from that provided by traditional customs-union theory [17]. By departing from the traditional framework, economists will have more to say about issues hitherto left for the policy-makers to grapple with.

NOTES AND REFERENCES

[1] Any views expressed in this paper are those of the authors. They should not be interpreted as reflecting the view of the Rand Corporation or of the Centre for Economic Research. The authors are indebted to Professors Richard N. Cooper and Harry G. Johnson for helpful comments.

[2] Jacob Viner, *The Customs Union Issue*, New York: Carnegie Endowment for International Peace, 1950.

[3] See, for example, R. G. Lipsey, Trade diversion and welfare, *Economica*, vol. XXIV, February 1957, pp. 40–6; R. G. Lipsey, The theory of customs unions: a general survey, *Economic Journal*, September 1960, pp. 496–513; J. E. Meade, *The Theory of Customs Unions*, Amsterdam: North-Holland, 1956; F. Gehrels, Customs unions from a single country viewpoint, *Review of Economic Studies*, vol. XXIV (1), no. 63, 1956–7.

[4] Lipsey, Trade diversion and welfare, p. 41.

[5] Lipsey, Theory of customs unions, pp. 506–9.

[6] The diagram is similar to that used by Harry G. Johnson in *Money, Trade, and Economic Growth*, Cambridge: Harvard University Press, 1962, p. 65.

[7] For clarity of exposition, it is assumed that the partner country cannot sell in the home-country market in the absence of a tariff preference. This assumption is not essential to the analysis.

[8] Constant costs in either country can be treated as a limiting case of the following analysis without materially affecting the results.

[9] In other words, with respect to imports, the country is a price-taker rather than a price-maker.

[10] We are making the traditional assumption that the pre-union tariff remains effective with respect to imports from countries other than the partner.

[11] The partner will displace at least some imports if the tariff is high enough for the customs union to be effective, i.e., if the tariff shifts S_w enough to intersect S_h above point E. The partner will *entirely* displace imports if the tariff is equal to RQ.

[12] From the home country's point of view the increase in real cost will equal the loss in customs revenue. If the tariff equals RQ this will be shown by the area of the rectangle $BCWV$; if the tariff is less than RQ the increase in cost will be less.

[13] In the diagram the consumption effect is necessarily beneficial; but it

may be more than offset by harmful effects possibly arising from a reduction in the consumption of other items.

[14] If the initial tariff is no greater than RQ, then there is no tariff reduction.

[15] Theory of customs unions.

[16] *Ibid.*, p. 500.

[17] For our own attempt to provide an analytical discussion of market-swapping, see C. A. Cooper and B. F. Massell, Toward a general theory of customs unions for developing countries, *The Journal of Political Economy*, Oct. 1965, pp. 461–76.

4

AN ECONOMIC THEORY OF PROTECTIONISM, TARIFF BARGAINING, AND THE FORMATION OF CUSTOMS UNIONS*

HARRY G. JOHNSON

London School of Economics and Political Science and the University of Chicago

I. INTRODUCTION

The traditional approach to the theory of tariffs, which is embodied in the recently elaborated analysis of the effects of customs unions pioneered by Viner, Meade, Lipsey, and others, is concerned with such matters as the possibility of increasing real income by using the tariff to exploit monopoly or monopsony power in world markets, the 'welfare costs' of the tariff in terms of foregone real income, and the effects on real income of changes in particular tariffs or in tariff structures, such as are entailed by the formation of customs unions and free-trade areas. Implicit in this approach is the assumption that 'real income' is identifiable, on social welfare function lines, with the utility derived by individuals from their personal consumption of goods and services; and, except in the optimum tariff analysis, the further assumption that tariffs are arbitrary interferences with the freedom of international exchange, which may be changed equally arbitrarily by governments.

In two previous papers, written within the traditional approach, I have called attention to the special and restrictive nature of these assumptions and the implications of abandoning them. In my 'The cost of protection and the scientific tariff' [1] I assumed that the authorities of a country were attempting to achieve certain non-economic objectives by the use of the tariff, and worked out the implications for the structure of tariff rates of a 'scientific' effort to achieve these objectives at minimum cost in terms of foregone real

* *Journal of Political Economy*, June 1965, 73, pp. 256–283.

income. In my 'Optimal trade intervention in the presence of domestic distortions' [2], I remarked that the relevance of the traditional theory to the problems of economic policy depends on a particular assumption about the nature of government, namely, that government seeks to maximize real income but is ill-informed about how to do this. I also pointed out that under different assumptions about the nature of government the analysis would have to be interpreted differently: if government were assumed to be all wise, the traditional measures of marginal welfare loss would have to be reinterpreted as measures of the divergence of social from private costs or benefits of protection; if, on the other hand, government is regarded as an extra-market system for modifying the distribution of income and wealth, interest would focus on the tariff structure as measuring the political power of various claimants to the national income, and the traditional welfare costs would measure the in-efficiency of the political process as a redistributor of income.

The traditional approach explicitly adopts the orthodox econo-mist's judgement of what economic welfare consists in, which runs in terms of individual consumption of goods and services. This defini-tion of welfare leads virtually automatically to the recommendation of what Meade has called the 'modified free-trade position' [3], a position exemplified by my paper on 'Distortions' previously men-tioned. This policy recommendation, in turn, puts the economist in opposition to dominant strands in the actual formulation of inter-national economic policy, which have to be treated by definition as 'irrational' or 'non-economic', or as arbitrarily constraining analysis to the realm of 'second-best theory'. At the same time, the economist is left without a theory capable of explaining a variety of important and observable phenomena, such as the nature of tariff bargaining, the commercial policies adopted by various countries, the conditions under which countries are willing to embark on customs unions, and the arguments and considerations that have weight in persuading countries to change their commercial policies.

This paper attempts a sketch of such a theory [4]. The theory derives from the underlying analysis of my two previous papers, in that it accepts the relevance of 'non-economic' objectives and utilizes the suggested hypothesis that government action represents a rational attempt to offset divergences between private and social costs or benefits. But it departs from that analysis in abandoning the distinction between economic and non-economic objectives, which is ethically biased in favour of private consumption as the exclusive measure of welfare, in favour of a distinction between private and public consumption goods, and between 'real income' in the sense of utility enjoyed from both private and public consumption and 'real product' defined as total production of privately appropriable goods and services. The theory employs building blocks provided by a variety of recent contributions, notably Downs' economic theory of democracy, Becker's theory of discrimination, and Breton's economic theory of nationalism [5]. The theory presented does not claim to account for all aspects of commercial policy formation, only to provide a tool for dealing with some practically important aspects; in particular, it concentrates on industrial protection, to the exclusion of agricultural protection, though the latter may be dealt with by obvious extensions of the theory [6].

II. THE THEORY OF PROTECTIONISM AND TARIFF BARGAINING: INDUSTRIAL PRODUCTION AS AN AGGREGATE

The theory assumes, following Downs, that political parties in democratic countries (and, to a sufficient extent, in dictatorial systems) seek to gain and hold power by promising and implementing policies desired by the electorate; and that competition for office will result in the adoption of policies that tend to maximize the satisfaction enjoyed by the electorate. That satisfaction flows from two sources; private consumption of privately provided goods and services, and collective consumption of goods and services provided through the government at the cost of sacrifices of private consumption. (Consumption is used here as shorthand for both investment and consumption proper.) Competition among parties will tend to carry the allocation of the economy's productive resources between private and collective consumption to the point where the marginal return of satisfaction per unit of resources expended is the same in the two uses.

It is further assumed that there exists a collective preference for industrial production, in the sense that the electorate is willing to spend real resources through government action in order to make the volume of industrial production and employment larger than it would be under free international competition. Industrial production, in other words, appears as a collective consumption good yielding a flow of satisfaction to the electorate independent of the satisfaction they derive directly from the consumption of industrial products. The origins of the preference for industrial production may lie in any one of a number of sources – nationalist aspirations and rivalry with other countries, the power of owners of and workers in industrial facilities to achieve a redistribution of income toward themselves by political means [7], or the belief that industrial activity involves beneficial 'externalities' of various kinds. The precise source of the preference for industrial production will influence the form of expenditure of resources through government action, and especially the distribution of resources so spent among particular industries. In a detailed analysis of a particular nation's tariff policy, the nature of the preference for industrial production would be an important question, and could be inferred from the relative magnitudes of the premiums the public is willing to pay for different kinds of industrial production; for the present purpose, however, it is sufficient to work with a generalized preference for industrial production.

Resources for the support of industrial activity as a collective consumption good have to be provided by government action, since it is in no one's individual interest to provide them voluntarily. Such resources could be supplied in various ways: fundamentally, the choice lies between direct subsidy from tax revenue, indirect subsidy through tax concessions involving loss of tax revenue, and indirect subsidy through a tariff. The tariff involves the equivalent of an excise tax on the consumer the proceeds of which are paid to the producer to the extent that he produces the good and to the government to the extent that the producer is unable to compete with imports. Subsidy through tax concessions depends on the existence of sufficiently heavy taxes on productive activity, and hence has only become an important technique since the Second World War. Direct subsidy can be shown to be more efficient than the tariff as a means of promoting production, since it avoids the consumption cost of the tariff. But the tariff is invariably favoured, generally on the grounds that the revenue to finance a subsidy is difficult to collect. Other explanations are that the politicians and businessmen who exploit the preference for industrial production do not wish its alternative opportunity costs to be readily ascertainable, and that the preference for industrial production includes the specification that the country's industry must appear to be able to compete with imports without explicit governmental support. In other words, the collective utility derived from industrial production is conditional on the maintenance of the appearance of competitiveness.

On the assumption of the rationality of governmental processes, the government will tend to carry protection to the point where the value of the marginal collective utility derived from collective consumption of domestic industrial activity is just equal to the marginal excess private cost of protected industrial production. In so doing, the government will be maximizing the country's real income, properly defined. But it will not be maximizing the country's real product, since maximization of real income requires sacrificing real product in order to gratify the preference for collective consumption of industrial production.

The marginal private excess cost of protected industrial production consists of two components, the marginal production cost and the marginal private consumption cost. The marginal production cost, expressed as the proportion by which domestic cost exceeds world market cost, would be measured by the tariff rate, in the usual simple model of trade in which goods are assumed to be produced by production processes employing only original factors of production. In a more complex input–output model of production, the marginal production cost, similarly expressed as a proportional excess above world cost, would be measured by the tariff rate minus the proportion of world cost by which other tariffs on goods used as inputs raised domestic costs above world costs, all divided by the proportion of the value of the final product considered to constitute collective consumption. (If, for example, the country derives collective satisfaction from the sales value of automobiles assembled in the country, the divisor is unity; if it derives satisfaction from the value added in assembly, the divisor will be substantially less than one, for the automobile assembly industry.)

The marginal private consumption cost of protected industrial production comprises the loss of consumers' surplus due to the restriction of consumption by the increase in the tariff rate necessary to induce the marginal unit of domestic production. The magnitude of this marginal cost depends on the tariff rate and on the price sensitivity of demand relative to supply, increasing with the relative price sensitivity of demand [8].

If account were taken of the variety of industrial products available for protection, and the possibility that their contributions to satisfaction of the collective preference for industrial production might well vary were recognized, the foregoing principle that the government would equate marginal social utility of collective consumption of domestic industry to marginal excess private cost of protected production would have to be elaborated into the principle that the government would equate the values of the marginal utilities derived from the various lines of industrial production to their marginal excess private costs. This principle would not imply equalization of tariff rates, both because the marginal collective utility of a dollar's worth of industrial production might depend on what was produced, and because the relation of the proportional excess cost of marginal protected production to the tariff rate associated with it would vary, for two reasons. First, the relation of the tariff rate to the marginal excess production cost would vary due to the input–output complications just mentioned [9]; second, the relation of the consumption to the production cost component of the marginal excess private cost of protected production would, as already mentioned, vary with the price sensitivity of demand relative to supply. For all these reasons, the real-income-maximizing tariff structure would not entail equal tariff rates on all protected products. Thus variations in the tariff rates levied under existing national tariff structures cannot be adduced as evidence of 'irrationality' in tariff-making, contradicting the theory presented here. In what follows, these complications will be ignored, and industrial production treated as a single aggregate, produced entirely with domestic inputs.

In equilibrium, the proportional marginal excess private cost of protected production measures the marginal 'degree of preference' for industrial production. Its magnitude reflects the interaction of the demand for collective consumption of industrial production and the cost of supplying it. This interaction is depicted in Fig. 4·1.

In Fig. 4·1,1S_f is the supply curve of industrial products (measured in unit values at world market prices) from the world market, assumed to be perfectly elastic (probably a reasonably realistic assumption for most countries), and DD is a compensated (constant-utility) demand curve for such products (at the free-trade private utility level). $S_h S_h$ is the domestic supply curve, and PS_{h+u} is the marginal private cost curve of protected production, including excess private consumption cost, the vertical distance between PS_{h+u} and S_f representing the marginal excess private cost, of protected production, geometrically, PS_{h+u} must be so constructed in relation to $S_h S_h$ that, for any tariff t, the area PSR is equal to the area ABC. The

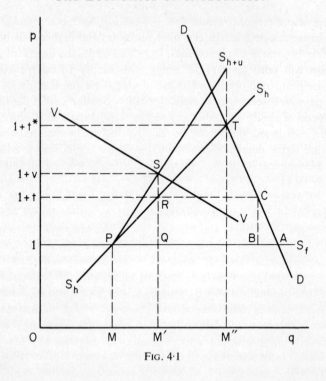

FIG. 4·1

height of the curve VV above S_f represents the marginal value of industrial production in collective consumption, measured in units of world purchasing power. The maximization of real national income is achieved at the intersection S of VV with PS_{h+u}, requiring the use of the tariff rate t to induce an increase in industrial production from OM to OM', and involving the marginal degree of preference for industrial production v.

The marginal 'degree of preference' for industrial production v will be higher, the higher is VV and the more elastic it is at the free-trade output, and the farther left and less elastic is PS_{h+u}. Given the slope of DD relative to that of S_hS_h, which determines the ratio of SR to RQ and hence of v to t, the higher also will be t, the tariff rate. It follows that, if the demand conditions and the preference for industrial production tend to be the same in all countries, the lower is a country's ability to compete in industrial production (as represented by the location of P relative to A, the free-trade production and consumption points, respectively), the higher will be its marginal

70

degree of preference for industrial production, and (except in certain circumstances detailed in the next footnote) the higher will be its tariff level (degree of protection). In other words, the degree of protection will tend to vary inversely with ability to compete with foreign industrial producers. This is a testable implication of the theory, which seems confirmed by reality. Similarly, if a country's competitive ability should change adversely (that is, S_hS_h shift leftward), continued maximization of real income would require an increase in the degree of protection; and vice versa. This is another testable implication of the theory, which again seems confirmed by reality [10].

As Fig. 4·1 is drawn, the preference for industrial production is satisfied with the country producing less industrial goods than it consumes. The limit to the gratification of the preference for industrial production that can be achieved by protection is the level of industrial production OM'' achievable by the self-sufficiency tariff rate t^*. Beyond that point, the country can gratify the preference for industrial production only by resorting to export subsidies. Since the domestic price is unsubsidized, and must rise with increased output if domestic sales are to be profitable to producers, the tariff must be increased along with the export subsidy to prevent imports (and reimports) from undercutting sales in the domestic market; thus this policy will continue to involve both excess production costs and excess consumption costs. The marginal private cost of such a policy would be represented in Fig. 4·1 by an extension of PS_{h+u} beyond S_{h+u}.

Fig. 4·1 assumes that the country depicted would be a net importer of industrial products under free trade. Countries that are net exporters of industrial products may also have a preference for industrial production. The preference of exporting countries for industrial production may be satiated by the level of industrial production their exports permit them (that is, VV may joint S_hS_h at a point below the world market price of industrial goods). If the preference is not satiated, the only policy open to the country is export subsidization coupled with a tariff at the same rate as the subsidy to prevent reimportation. This case is shown in Fig. 4·2, which is the same as Fig. 4·1 except that the locations of P and A are reversed, the world demand curve $1D_f$ replaces the world supply curve, and s, the subsidy and tariff rate, replaces t.

These last two implications of the theory – subsidization of industrial exports by both high-cost protectionist countries and countries competitive in the world market – are again testable and confirmed to some extent by practical experience. Examples are the practice of subsidizing exports of the products of 'new industries' in the less developed countries such as India, and the various arrangements for subsidizing exports through tax incentives, easy export credit, and so forth maintained by countries that have no balance-of-payments reason to transfer real product to foreigners by these means. Another implication, again in conformity with experience, is

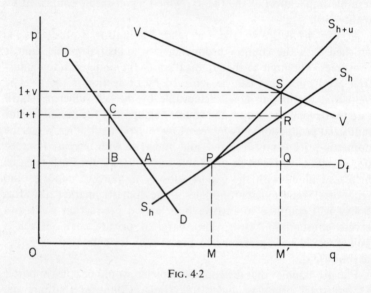

FIG. 4·2

that industrial exporting countries faced with adverse changes in their international competitive position will introduce export subsidies or raise existing export subsidies. (For possible exceptions to this proposition, refer back to the discussion of the effects of the same change on the industrial importing countries, and especially note 10.)

The subsidization of exports just discussed is, however, not a widespread practice and is usually disguised in some subtle fashion. The reason is that there is an international convention against explicit export subsidization, incorporated in the principles of GATT and backed up by national antidumping legislation. This convention and the associated national legislation are themselves explainable by reference to the preference for industrial production and the free enterprise philosophy that underlies the preference for tariffs over production subsidies. Export subsidization by a foreign country appears as an attempt by the foreigner to increase his collective utility from industrial production at the expense of one's own by unfair means. What is more important, direct export subsidization is visible and can be counteracted by use of one's own tariff. Enforcement of a prohibition on export subsidization implies that only industrial importing countries are free to maximize their real incomes by gratifying the preference for industrial production: industrial exporting countries are (or may be) confined to a suboptimal level of real income by the inability to subsidize exports. This constraint has important consequences for tariff policy and bargaining, which will be developed subsequently.

The analysis thus far has implicitly assumed a typical country small enough for changes in the volume of its imports or exports of industrial products to make no difference in the price it pays for its imports (if it is a net industrial importer) or receives for its exports of the other products (if it is a net industrial exporter) [11]. If this is not true, and the terms of trade are affected by the country's tariff policy, the conditions of optimum tariff theory exist; and by the initial assumption of governmental rationality they will be exploited. It is clear, however, that importers of industrial products will adopt a higher tariff level (against industrial products) than the optimum tariff of conventional analysis, and conversely that countries that are net exporters of industrial products will adopt a lower tariff level (against non-industrial products) than the conventional optimum tariff – always provided that the preference for industrial production does not become satiated [12]. In both cases real incomes is maximized, and thus is higher than it would be under the conventionally determined optimum tariff. But in the net industrial importing country real product must be lower than it would have been under the conventional optimum tariff, and may be lower than it would have been under free trade; whereas in the net industrial exporting country, real product, though less than it would have been under the conventional optimum tariff, must be higher than it would have been under free trade – provided that the preference for industrial production is not strong enough to lead to free trade (or to export subsidization, if that is possible) rather than a tax on imports.

The introduction of monopoly-monopsony power in the world

market into a model in which industrial production is treated as a single aggregate provided a motive for industrial exporting countries as well as industrial importing countries to have tariffs, and therefore introduces the possibility of negotiation for the reciprocal reduction of tariffs. To investigate this possibility, I assume a world of two countries only, an industrial exporting ('advanced') country and an industrially importing ('less developed') country, each with a tariff on imports [13]. To allow scope for tariff bargaining, these tariffs must be assumed to have been arrived at by some process of independent tariff formation in the two countries, though this process may or may not be assumed to have involved recognition of the dependence of the welfare-maximizing tariff policy of each on the tariff policy of the other, without affecting the conclusions [14].

Under what conditions will a reciprocal reduction of tariffs by the two countries be mutually beneficial, in the sense that some combination of tariff reductions can be found that will raise the real income of both countries? In the traditional analysis, where the initial existence of tariffs is derived from the exercise of monopoly–monopsony power on the part of each country, reciprocal tariff reduction is always beneficial, and it can be shown that tariff bargaining would proceed to reduce tariffs until at least one country had eliminated its tariff entirely [15]. In the presence of a preference for industrial production, however, this proposition no longer holds, since this preference gives the less developed country a motive for imposing a tariff independent of the exploitation of monopoly–monopsony power, so that the existence of its tariff does not necessarily imply the presence of such power. In this case, mutually beneficial tariff reduction is possible only to the extent that the less-developed country's tariff involves the exploitation of monopoly–monopsony power, and would never lead to that country's abandoning protection in favour of free trade.

The point may be illustrated, without loss of generality, by considering the attractiveness to the two countries of a proposed slight reciprocal reduction of tariffs, so designed as to expand trade without changing the terms of trade. In the traditional model, the presence of tariffs means that in each country the marginal private value of an increment of imports exceeds its price (the tariff having been imposed because the marginal social cost of imports exceeds price), so that each country will gain by the reciprocal reduction of tariffs, and tariff reduction will proceed until one country reaches the free-trade point. In the present model, the marginal private value of an increment in imports also exceeds its price, owing to the tariff. But in the advanced country the marginal social value of an increment of imports is above the marginal private value, because an increment of imports carries with it an increment of exports and therefore of industrial production and the utility of collective consumption associated with industry. In the less developed country, on the other hand, the marginal social value of an increment of imports is below the marginal private value, because an expansion of trade entails a contraction of industrial production and a loss of utility from the collective consumption of industry. Given rational maximization of real income, the country will have fixed its tariff so that the marginal social value of an increment of imports is initially just equal to its marginal social cost, and unless the presence of monopoly–monopsony power makes marginal social cost exceed price, the country will derive no gain in real income (as distinct from real product) from an expansion of trade at constant terms of trade. In fact, a non-infinitesimal expansion of trade would impose a loss on it. Thus while the advanced country will have an incentive to accept the proposed reciprocal tariff reduction, the less developed country will have no incentive to do so unless it possesses monopoly–monopsony power that its tariff has exploited. If it possesses no monopoly–monopsony power, it would only accept a reciprocal tariff reduction proposal that promised an improvement in its terms of trade; but the advanced country would have no incentive to offer such a proposal since to do so would entail an unrequited sacrifice of the exploitation of its own monopoly–monopsony power [16]. If it does possess monopoly–monopsony power, it would be willing to accept reciprocal tariff reduction of the type described, but only to the point at which its tariff rate equalized the marginal excess private cost of protected production with the marginal degree of preference for industrial production. Thus reciprocal tariff reduction could only lead to one country's following a free-trade policy if that country were the advanced country; and this would require that that country's monopoly–monopsony power be relatively less, in some sense difficult to define except by its results, than that of the less developed country.

The case in which the less developed country has no monopoly–monopsony power is of special interest, since for the analysis of tariff bargaining (though not of the actual results of bargains) it can be

75

taken to represent the more realistic situation in which there are a large number of less developed countries, each too small to exercise any independent monopoly–monopsony power, even though the aggregate of less developed countries may possess such power. To be acceptable, a tariff-reducing bargain in this case must promise to improve the terms of trade of the less developed country and turn them against the advanced country; in monetary terms, it must threaten to worsen the advanced country's balance of payments at the existing exchange and money wage rates. If, as a matter of rational exploitation of monopoly–monopsony power (as in the preceding analysis), or more generally of bargaining tactics, balance of payments considerations or other reasons, the advanced country's negotiators insist that equity of bargains necessitates reciprocal tariff reductions that would produce a balanced expansion of trade at unchanged terms of trade (that is, equal increases in export and import values at current prices) the less developed country will refuse any bargain proposed, as involving a loss of real income to it. This point explains one aspect of the dissatisfaction that the less developed countries have recently been manifesting with respect to the GATT mechanism of bargaining for tariff reductions. Given the preference for industrial production, bargaining on GATT rules appears to offer no attractions to countries that do not export industrial products and lack monopoly–monopsony power in world markets; instead, it appears to such countries as a mechanism designed to enable the advanced countries to win benefits at their expense [17].

The aggregated two-good model of this section does not lend itself readily to extension to tariff-bargaining among a number of countries, which introduces the possibility of preferential arrangements. The analysis does, however, indicate the reasons why preferential arrangements between advanced and less developed countries may be attractive to both sides. The convention against export subsidies may prevent the advanced country from achieving a level of industrial production high enough to maximize its real income, and this may make it willing to pay a price, in terms of a preference-created increase in the cost of its imports of non-industrial goods, for a preference-created increase in its exports. To the less developed country, on the other hand, a preference toward a particular advanced country has the advantage that its price is an increase in the social cost of existing imports, rather than a decrease in the country's industrial production, which loss may be more than offset by the increased prices the country may obtain for its exports of non-industrial products.

III. THE THEORY OF PROTECTIONISM AND TARIFF BARGAINING: VARIETY OF INDUSTRIAL PRODUCTION

In this section I abandon the assumption that industrial production is a single aggregate, with countries having varying comparative advantage in industry as opposed to non-industrial production. Instead, I assume that industrial production comprises a variety of products, in which countries have varying degrees of comparative advantage. Such differences in comparative advantage among industries may be assumed to result from differences in the local availability of natural resources, in the general level of labour or management skill, in the availability of capital, in technological level, or in the size of the domestic market combined with the existence of economies of scale in certain industries. I continue to assume that countries differ in their over-all comparative advantage in industry as compared with non-industrial production.

The variety of industrial production allows countries to be both importers and exporters of industrial products, and in combination with the preference for industrial production will motivate each country to practise some degree of protection. It is therefore not necessary to appeal to monopoly–monopsony power in world markets to provide an environment of universal protection within which reciprocal tariff reduction is possible; and for analytical simplicity it will be assumed that no country has such power. It will also be assumed that the convention against export subsidization is fully effective; this is an important assumption, in that it creates an opportunity for mutually profitable tariff reduction, and in certain circumstances a motive for protection itself.

In the circumstances posited, a country can gratify its preference for industrial production only by protecting the domestic producers of commodities it imports. Acting rationally, it will carry protection to the point where the marginal social value of collective consumption of industrial production is equal to the marginal excess cost of industrial production. The latter, however, will be constituted somewhat differently in this model than in the previous one. Protection of import-competing industries will tend to some extent to reduce industrial exports, as well as non-industrial production; hence, in order to increase total industrial production by one unit, it will be necessary to increase protected industrial production by more than one unit to compensate for the induced loss of industrial exports, so that the marginal excess private production cost and consumption cost must be reckoned accordingly [18].

Protection of import-competing industries reduces industrial exports by raising their cost of production, either by raising the prices of factors of production common to the two sectors of industry or by raising the cost of outputs of the protected sector used as inputs in the export sector. The stronger are these effects of protection, other things equal, the higher will be the marginal excess cost of industrial production. These effects are likely to be larger, the larger the size of the total industrial sector relative to the non-industrial sector and the larger the size of the protected industrial sector relative to the exporting industrial sector.

These relationships would imply that the same marginal degree of preference for industrial production would entail (a) lower tariff rates in a country with a relatively small non-industrial sector than in one with a relatively large non-industrial sector, and (b) higher tariff rates in countries a relatively small proportion of whose industrial production is protected than in countries a relatively large proportion of whose industrial production is protected. These would appear to be testable implications of the theory: and the former seems in conformity with reality, while the latter does not. The tests, however, are not valid ones, because the marginal degree of preference for industrial production is not independent of the characteristics of the economy to which the implications refer. A country with a small non-industrial sector is virtually certain to be a net industrial exporter, and vice versa, so that with identical preferences for industrial production among nations a country with a small non-industrial sector would necessarily have a more fully gratified preference and hence a lower marginal degree of preference for industrial production: hence its tariff rates would tend to be lower anyway. Similarly, a country that protects relatively much of its industrial production presumably does so because it has a comparative disadvantage in industrial production, so that its marginal degree of preference for industrial production and hence its tariff rates would tend to be higher than those of a country which protects relatively little of its industrial production. Higher tariff rates in the former than in the latter are therefore not inconsistent with the theory.

As in the previous model, the theory implies that the degree of protection practised by the various countries will vary inversely with their net industrial export position; and that an improvement in a country's comparative advantage in industrial production as against non-industrial production will lead it to reduce its degree of protection, and vice versa. As already mentioned, these implications are consistent with experience – countries whose competitiveness in world markets is improving tend to move in the free-trade direction, while countries whose competitiveness is deteriorating tend to move toward increased protectionism [19].

The analysis just presented assumes that domestic and international trade is organized competitively, so that protection tends to divert resources away from production for export. If production is assumed to be carried on by monopolistic enterprises, so that discrimination by the producer between markets is possible, and these enterprises are assumed to be multiproduct firms operating under joint cost conditions, so that discrimination between the domestic and the foreign markets can be affected by loading different products with different proportions of overhead cost rather than by charging different prices for the same product in the two markets (thus circumventing the convention against dumping), the foregoing conclusions will be altered. A tariff will permit the protected producer to charge his overheads against the home-market consumer and, indirectly, to subsidize exports. By so doing, monopolistic market organization may permit the country, through its tariff policy, to achieve a given level of industrial production at a lower marginal excess cost than would rule under competition. Under these conditions, the tariff might increase rather than decrease industrial exports, thus yielding a double gain from protection. The implications of monopolistic market organization for the theory of tariff bargaining are obviously both complex and interesting; the former characteristic prevents them from being pursued further in this paper.

The analysis thus far has provided a rationale for the existence of universal tariff protection of industrial production and examined some of the implications of differences or changes in countries' circumstances for their protectionist policies. I now introduce the possibility of bargaining for reciprocal tariff reduction. To begin with, I assume a world of only two countries, though this does some violence to the assumption that no country has monopoly–monopsony power in the world market. One of these countries must be a net exporter, and the other a net importer, of industrial products; but it is no longer true (as in the previous model) that the expansion of industrial production in one must entail a contraction of industrial production in the other, since industrial production in both can expand at the expense of production of non-industrial products.

At the outset, it should be emphasized that for each country the prospective gain from reciprocal tariff reduction must lie in the expansion of exports of industrial products. By assumption, each country has been willing to reduce its real product by protection of domestic industrial producers against foreign competition in order to maximize its real income (including utility from collective consumption of industrial production), and any reduction in industrial production due to an expansion of imports adds less to real product that it subtracts from collective utility. Thus reduction of one's own tariffs is a source of loss, which can only be compensated for by a reduction of the other country's tariff. On the other hand, a reduction of the other country's tariff is a source of gain, since it expands one's own industrial production and yields an increased flow of utility from collective consumption of industrial production. The theory therefore accounts for the form and logic of bargaining for reciprocal tariff reductions, phenomena which are incomprehensible to the classical approach to tariff theory, according to which the source of gain is the replacement of domestic production by lower-cost imports, whereas increased exports yield no gain (improved terms of trade apart) to the exporting country, but a gain to the foreigner through the same replacement of domestic production by lower-cost imports. Since these gains are attainable by unilateral action, the classical approach provides no explanation of the necessity and nature of the bargaining process.

The gains from reciprocal tariff reduction are nevertheless of the same basic nature in this model as in the classical analysis, though their outward character is different: they result from the substitution of lower-cost for higher-cost sources of want satisfaction. The difference is that in the classical analysis it is lower-cost satisfaction of private consumer wants that is involved, and this could be achieved without the cooperation of the other country through unilateral tariff reduction; whereas in the preference for industrial production model it is lower-cost satisfaction of the demand for collective consumption of industrial production that is involved, and this can only be achieved through the cooperation (via bargaining) of the other country. Because of the convention preventing export subsidization, a country enters the bargaining situation in a 'second-best' equilibrium position, in which the marginal excess cost of industrial production achieved by additional exports is zero, whereas the marginal excess cost of additional industrial production achieved by protection is positive. Each country therefore stands to gain, in terms of real income, by exchanging a reduction of its industrial production through its own tariff reduction for an equal expansion of its industrial production through the other country's tariff reduction. Actually, however, reciprocal tariff reductions can be arranged that will increase each country's industrial production while lowering its marginal excess cost, since reciprocal tariff reduction will increase each country's aggregate consumption of industrial goods at the expense of its consumption of non-industrial goods [20]. And an individual country could gain from negotiated reciprocal tariff reductions that reduced its aggregate industrial production, providing that the resulting increase in real product outweighed the loss of utility from collective consumption of industrial production; at the initiation of bargaining, it could gain from any reciprocal tariff reduction that offered it any slight increase in exports [21]. It follows that reciprocal tariff-cutting would proceed so long as each country could offer the other a tariff reduction that would increase the other's exports. Consequently, just as in the classical model in which tariffs exist due to monopoly–monopsony power in world markets, bargaining for mutually beneficial tariff reductions would eliminate tariffs in one of the countries, and possibly in both.

This result depends, of course, on the assumptions of the model, and especially on the assumption that the preference for industrial production does not discriminate between industries. If countries attached separate collective consumption utility to different industries, a position could be reached in which a country could not be compensated for further reductions in the tariff on one of its (more highly valued) industries by a reduction in the other country's tariff or one of its (less highly valued) industries. Also, if a country's production is concentrated in the hands of monopolistic enterprises capable of effective price discrimination between the domestic and foreign market, reciprocal tariff reduction might involve a loss rather than a gain for that country.

The assumption of a two-country world and a general preference for industrial production leads to the conclusion that bargaining will result in the elimination of the tariffs of at least one of the countries. This result is due to the fact that in a two-country world it is always possible to arrange reciprocal tariff reductions that will increase industrial production in both countries while reducing the excess cost of industrial production. I now abandon the two-country assumption and assume the existence of many countries. In this case, as will be shown, there are limits to the extent of the reciprocal reduction of tariffs that can be negotiated on a most-favoured-nation basis; furthermore, these limits introduce the possibility that reciprocal preferential tariff reduction, that is, tariff reductions discriminating among foreign countries, will be more attractive than non-discriminatory tariff reduction, a possibility that would not exist apart from the preference for industrial production.

Assume that all reciprocal tariff reductions must be arrived at on a most-favoured-nation basis; that is, that each partner in the negotiation must extend the tariff reduction to all other nations, not merely to the negotiating partner. Reduction of a country's tariff on a particular item will then increase its total imports of that item by more than it increases imports from the partner country; it may or may not decrease the country's industrial production by more than it increases industrial production in the partner country, depending on the magnitudes of the parameters involved [22]. The same holds for a reduction of the partner country's tariff.

It follows, first, that countries negotiating for reciprocal tariff reductions will offer concessions on those items for which a reduction in their own tariff will yield the maximum increase in partner industrial production per unit reduction in domestic industrial production, and demand concessions on those items for which a reduction in the partner's tariff will yield the maximum increase in their own industrial production per unit reduction in the partner's industrial production. By so doing, they maximize their joint gains from the combination of substitution of lower-cost (exported) for higher-cost (protected import-competing) industrial production and expansion of aggregate industrial production. In other words, each country has an incentive to choose items for negotiation in a fashion that discriminates against expansion of trade with third parties in favour of expansion of trade with the partner country. In this way the most-favoured-nation principle, which proscribes tariff discrimination among countries, leads to indirect discrimination among countries through the choice of commodities for reciprocal tariff reduction.

Second, it follows that the process of reciprocal tariff reduction is likely to come to a halt well before either country approaches anything like complete elimination of tariffs. This is so because sooner or later the only reciprocal tariff reductions possible will be ones that will reduce the aggregate industrial production of one or both countries. And while reciprocal reductions of this kind will be mutually advantageous over a certain range, in the sense that the loss of utility from collective consumption of industrial production in a country whose industrial production fell would initially be out-weighed by the gain in real product resulting from tariff elimination, this must cease to be the case before the country's tariffs have been completely eliminated, because the loss of utility is constant or rising per unit of industrial production sacrificed while the gain of real product must fall as the tariff is reduced [23].

The foregoing propositions relate to the nature and effects of bilateral negotiation for reciprocal tariff reduction, subject to the rule of non-discrimination, in a multicountry world; and they bear a reasonably close relationship to the nature and results of tariff negotiations under the GATT system. In a rational world, however, negotiations for reciprocal tariff reduction would not be confined to bilateral negotiations between pairs of nations; and this is not entirely the case under GATT. What would be the results of multi-lateral negotiations for reciprocal tariff reductions?

It seems likely, on the analogy of Marcus Fleming's treatment of the problem of making the best of balance-of-payments restrictions on imports [24], that the outcome would be a situation in which countries could be arranged in an order of decreasing industrial strength (comparative advantage in industrial production) and increasing protectionism – though it is difficult to construct a rigorous formal argument leading to this conclusion, owing to the difficulty of defining 'industrial strength'. The basic logic behind the conclusion stems from the preceding analyses of two-country models, where it was shown (in the aggregate industrial production model) that a country with no industrial exports and no monopoly–monopsony power would have no incentive to negotiate tariff reductions; and (in the disaggregated industrial production model) that both countries would gain from negotiating reciprocal tariff reductions until at least one of them practised free trade. Multilateral negotiation, it may be presumed, will permit one country to deal with the rest as if they constituted a single country.

In a multicountry world it should always be possible to find at least one country ('the strongest industrial country') so situated with respect to its initial trade position in industrial products and the elasticities of demand and supply governing them that universal adoption of free trade would increase its industrial exports more than its industrial imports. Such a country could always gain by offering to pursue a free-trade policy in exchange for tariff concessions by the others, providing that it received sufficient concessions for its aggregate industrial production to remain unchanged or increase; and the other countries – except for the non-exporters of industrial products, who would have no incentive to participate – should always be able to find some set of individual non-discriminatory tariff concessions that, in combination with the effects of free trade in the strongest industrial country, would leave unchanged or increase their individual aggregates of industrial production [25]. Thus one country at least would end up with a commercial policy of free trade. After this negotiation, the next strongest industrial country would have an incentive to negotiate reciprocal tariff reductions with the rest; but the free-trade country would now appear as the third party in the preceding analysis of bilateral negotiation, since it would gain automatically from the non-discriminatory reciprocal tariff reductions of the rest without being able to offer them export-increasing tariff concessions in return. Thus this negotiation might or might not bring the second-strongest industrial country to free trade. At the opposite extreme, countries with no comparative advantage in industrial production – countries all of whose industrial production has to be protected – would have nothing to gain from reciprocal tariff negotiation, but industrial production to lose, and would retain their original tariffs. Thus some arrangement of countries in order of increasing protectionism and decreasing industrial strength would emerge from multilateral negotiation of reciprocal tariff reduction. But this arrangement would be subject to some inter-tariff reduction. But this arrangement would be subject to some indeterminacy, since the outcome would depend in part on the order in which negotiations took place and the way in which the gains from negotiated tariff reductions were divided among the participating countries.

Now introduce, in place of the most-favoured-nation principle, the possibility of preferential (discriminatory) reciprocal tariff reduction, that is, of reciprocal reduction of tariffs on imports from the partner country, tariffs on imports of the same commodity from third countries remaining unchanged. Starting from an initial position of non-discrimination, discriminatory tariff reduction has the advantage over non-discriminatory tariff reduction that it permits a country to offer its partner an increase in exports and industrial production without suffering any loss of its own industrial production, through diverting imports from third countries to the partner. After all such possible trade diversion has occurred, further discriminatory tariff reduction has the advantage over non-discriminatory tariff reduction of yielding the partner the whole of any increase in the tariff-cutting country's imports (which now occur partly at the expense of its domestic industrial production), whereas under non-discriminatory tariff reduction the partner's exports would expand less than the tariff-reducing country's imports, so that the partner's industrial production expands more under the former than under the latter type of tariff-cutting. Thus discriminatory reciprocal tariff reduction costs each partner country less, in terms of the reduction in domestic industrial production (if any) incurred per unit increase in partner industrial production, than does non-discriminatory reciprocal tariff reduction. On the other hand, preferential tariff reduction imposes an additional cost on the tariff-reducing country, the excess of the cost of imports from the partner country over their cost in the world market.

For the initial slight preferential tariff reduction, this cost will be smaller, the smaller the amount of the partner country's exports to the world market. (Under the assumed conditions of perfect competition, the partner's exports may be sold anywhere under non-discrimination, but any slight preference will divert them to the market of the preference-granting country. It is obvious that the preference-receiving country will only benefit from the preference if its initial export sales are less than the import quantity that would be demanded by the preference-granting country under free trade, since only in this case can the preference increase its sales; this sets limits on the conditions under which preferential arrangements can be mutually beneficial.) For subsequent preferential tariff reductions, the marginal cost per unit of increased imports will rise, both because the excess cost of the marginal unit of imports increases and because this excess price is paid on a larger volume of intramarginal trade with the partner. Once the partner country's exports have replaced imports from other countries, further preferential tariff reductions entail an additional element of cost through replacement of domestic by partner industrial production and a consequent loss of collective utility.

That part of the cost of the preference that corresponds to the higher price paid for intramarginal imports, however, is an income transfer to the partner, whose gains from the preference comprise this transfer and the collective utility derived from whatever expansion of its industrial exports results. Since the excess marginal cost of the increment of partner industrial exports resulting from an initial slight preferential tariff reduction is negligible, while there must be some increase in the partner's industrial production if the preference is to benefit it, it follows that an exchange of slight preferential tariff reductions between the partners must always be mutually beneficial. For further reciprocal tariff reductions, however, the increasing marginal cost of preferential tariff reductions to the two partners is likely to mean that preferential tariff reduction will not proceed to

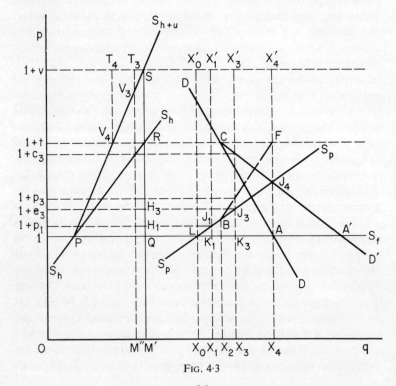

FIG. 4·3

the point of 100% preferences (reciprocal free trade in the commodities under negotiation). This conclusion parallels a proposition in standard customs union theory, to the effect that a partial preferential arrangement is more likely to raise the real income (real product, in the present terminology) of the preference-granting countries than a 100% preferential arrangement.

The cost of giving a preference is illustrated in Fig. 4·3, which reproduces the relevant parts of Fig. 4·1. For simplicity, it is assumed that the quantity of resources used in domestic production of the imported commodity has no influence on the quantity of resources used in the country's production of other industrial products, and that the marginal degree of preference for industrial production v is constant. The partner country's supply curve is represented by S_pS_p, quantity supplied being measured from the vertical SM'; the partner is assumed to be capable of supplying less than the total quantity of imports demanded when the country imposes a non-discriminatory tariff and the partner receives the world price, but more than that quantity of imports if it receives the domestic price. For simplicity, it is arbitrarily assumed that all of the exports of the partner in the initial non-discriminatory situation are directed to the preference-granting country.

So long as the preference is insufficient to enable the partner to supply the whole of the quantity of imports initially demanded, the granting of the preference simply enables the partner suppliers to charge a higher price than the world market price, and induces substitution of partner for foreign supplies (trade diversion). This case is represented in the figure by the preference p_1, which increases partner exports to the country from $M'X_0$ to $M'X_1$ (by X_0X_1); the cost of this preference to the country is $QH_1J_1K_1$, of which QH_1J_1L is an income transfer to the partner and J_1K_1L is the excess of the real production cost of the additional partner exports above the world market price.

Once the preference has become large enough for the partner country to supply the initial level of imports, the situation changes. For partner exports to increase, the domestic price must fall, to induce increased consumption and decreased domestic production (trade creation). In the figure, the effect on the quantity of imports demanded of the contraction of domestic production as the domestic price falls is represented by shifting the demand curve DD to the right below the point C by the amount of the corresponding contraction of domestic output, to give the demand curve for imports CA' continued (in the figure, $PQ = AA'$). The necessity for the domestic price to fall to induce increased imports means that part of any additional preference is absorbed in price reduction to domestic consumers, so that only a part of it accrues as an increase in the price received by partner suppliers. To represent this in the figure, the vertical distance between the horizontal line at $1 + t$ and CA' is added to S_pS_p to give the line BF, which represents the locus of the preferences necessary to induce various quantities of partner exports. With the preference p_3, for example, imports from the partner would be $M'X_3$; the excess of the price received by the partner over the world market price would be e_3; the domestic price would be above the world market price by c_3 and below the price in the absence of the preference by $t - c_3$; and domestic production would be below its level under non-discriminatory protection by the amount $M''M'$. The cost of the preference p_3 would consist of two parts: $QH_3J_3K_3$, the excess of the cost of imports from the partner country above world market prices, of which QH_3J_3L is an income transfer to the partner and J_3K_3L is the excess of the real production cost of the additional partner exports above the world market price; and ST_3V_3, the excess of the loss of utility from domestic industrial production over the saving of excess private cost of protected production.

Fig. 4·3 can also be used to depict the gains from preferential tariff reduction to the partner country, if it is assumed that the increase in partner exports represents the net increase in its industrial production resulting from the preference and that the partner country's marginal preference for industrial production is also v. Under the preference p_1, the partner gains an increment of producer's surplus (income transfer) equal to QH_1J_1L, and an increment of collective utility from industrial production $LX_0'X_1'K_1$; under the preference p_3, the corresponding gains are QH_3J_3L and $LX_0'X_3'K_3$.

Taking the two countries together, and cancelling out the income transfer, there is for preference p_1 a net benefit for the two together of $LX_0'X_1'J_1$: for preference p_2, there is a net benefit of $LX_0X_3'J_3 - ST_3V_3$. From the assumptions on which the figure is constructed it is obvious that the latter measure must be positive and must increase as the preference increases up to a 100% preference (a change from a preference p_3 to a preference t involves an addition to net benefit of $J_3X_3'X_4'J_4 - T_3V_3V_4T_4$, and since T_4T_3 is less than $X_3'X_4'$, and T_3V_3

and T_4V_4 are less than $X_3'J_3$ and $X_4'J_4$, this must be positive). If these assumptions held in both countries, the partners would therefore negotiate 100% preferences (reciprocal free trade) in the commodities concerned. The assumptions of the figure are highly restrictive, however: if the industrial production of the preference-receiving country increases by less than its exports, the gain of collective utility to the partner country will be less (say) than the area $LX_0'X_3'K_3$ and may fall short of the sum of the areas LJ_3K_3 (the excess real production cost of the increased exports) and ST_3V_3 (the net loss of real income to the home country from the reduction of its domestic production).

The potential benefit from discriminatory reciprocal tariff reduction, it should be noted, derives from two assumptions of the model: the preference for industrial production, and the convention against export subsidization. The first involves a willingness to sacrifice real product for the sake of greater industrial production, the second prevents countries from implementing the preference for industrial production by direct subsidization of exports. Reciprocal preferential tariff reduction is in fact an arrangement by which each partner indirectly subsidizes its own industrial exports by subsidizing its industrial imports from the other, the subsidy being given in the disguised form of preferential relief from tariffs otherwise payable.

It should also be noted that the foregoing analysis involves both of the effects considered in the standard analysis of preferential tariff reduction – trade diversion and trade creation – and that contrary to the standard analysis trade diversion as well as trade creation yields again to the partners; in fact, trade diversion is preferable to trade creation, for the preference-granting country, because it entails no sacrifice of domestic industrial production. This reversal of the usual conclusions is due to the presence of the preference for industrial production, and its frustration by the convention against export subsidization. In these circumstances, the gain of real product from trade creation to the importing country is insufficient to compensate for the loss of real income due to the resulting sacrifice of utility from collective consumption of domestic industrial production; and trade diversion is preferable because, though it involves a real product loss, it does not involve a sacrifice of domestic industrial production [26]. In both cases, however, the gain in a country's real income comes, not from a preponderance of the real product gains from trade creation over the real product losses from trade diversion resulting from the effects of the country's own preferential tariff reduction on its imports, but from the increase in the country's exports of industrial products resulting from the trade-diverting and trade-creating effects of the partner country's preferential tariff reduction in its favour. Consequently, preferential reciprocal tariff reductions may be negotiated even if they lead to a loss of real product for one or both parties [27].

The foregoing analysis also indicates the conditions under which reciprocal preferential tariff reduction will be beneficial to the countries concerned, and will therefore be resorted to. Implicit in the analysis are the assumptions that the parties concerned have a strong preference for industrial production, and a weak comparative advantage in industrial production, so that they each export relatively small quantities of industrial products, and gratify their preference for industrial production largely through protection of domestic industry against imports. A country with a strong comparative advantage in industrial production would both be able to seek expansion of its industrial production through multilateral tariff bargaining, and might be unable to benefit (in the competitive conditions of the model) from preferential entry to the other country's market, because such preferential entry might merely divert its exports from other countries' markets without significantly affecting their prices. The analysis also requires that the partners have differing comparative advantages (disadvantages) in the various lines of industrial production, so that each can benefit from preferences given by the other. In the preceding analysis, this was implicit in the assumption that each could export some quantity of a product that the other imported in spite of its protection of its domestic industry; that assumption is unnecessarily strong, all that is required being that tariff rates vary so that domestic costs of production of the various commodities exceed their world prices by different proportions in the two countries, the lower costs being found sometimes in one country and sometimes in the other.

Since in the model of protectionism presented above the marginal degree of preference for industrial production is equal in all industries, differences in tariff rates among industries must be due to differences in the behaviour of the consumption cost of protection among industries, or to differences in the extent to which resources employed in one branch of industry reduce production in others; and differences in tariff rate structures among countries must be due to differences in these factors among countries. For tariff rates to be sometimes higher and sometimes lower in one protectionist country than in the other, the latter differences must outweigh any differences in the marginal degree of preference for industrial production among countries. This last requirement implies that only countries with comparable degrees of preference for industrial production are likely to be in a position to benefit extensively from preferential reciprocal tariff-cutting schemes, a point relevant to the prediction of what countries or groups of countries are likely to engage in such schemes [28].

Under these conditions, countries can obtain increases in their individual aggregates of industrial production through preferential reciprocal tariff reduction that they could not obtain otherwise, while at the same time increasing their real incomes, and possibly but not necessarily their real products. The benefits accrue primarily through balanced exchanges of lower-cost industrial production in one country for higher-cost industrial production in the other (trade creation) and through balanced substitutions for foreign production of domestic industrial production whose collective consumption value exceeds its excess cost (trade diversion). There is, however, a further possible source of gain, not comprehended in the preceding analysis: if the reason for the excess cost of domestic industrial production is inefficiency promoted by the small scale of the domestic market and the monopolistic tendencies fostered by the tariff in each country, the trade-creating and especially the trade-diverting effects of reciprocal preferential tariff reduction may permit the harvesting of economies of scale. The preference for industrial production on which the analysis is posited will require that industries subject to the economies of scale be fairly divided up among the participants in the preferential arrangements. This consideration, however, is more relevant to the theory of customs union formation, the subject of the next section [29].

IV. THE THEORY OF CUSTOMS UNION FORMATION

Preferential tariff arrangements of the type discussed at the end of the previous section are inconsistent with the most-favoured-nation principle, and are frowned on for the quite valid reason that they are likely to be used mainly for protectionist rather than trade-liberalizing purposes. The most-favoured-nation principle can in fact be interpreted as a convention designed to protect the third parties at the expense of whose industrial production the mutual benefits of preferential reciprocal tariff reduction are in part obtained. Under the rules of GATT, however, an exception to the most-favoured-nation principle is made for customs unions and free-trade areas, on the quite questionable assumption that, since these arrangements demand 100% preferences across the board, they are likely to constitute movements in the free-trade rather than the protectionist direction. The standard theory of customs unions has shown that this is not necessarily so, if by 'the free-trade direction' is meant the direction of maximization of real product, while the emergence of the European Common Market has provided a practical demonstration of the protective potentialities of customs unions.

That customs unions will be formed with a protective intent is one of the implications of the analysis of protectionism in the preceding sections, and especially of the assumption of a preference for industrial production. The analysis of preferential tariff reduction is especially relevant, the customs union differing from preferential tariff reduction only in that preferences granted to participants in the arrangement have to be at the rate of 100%, and to apply across the board, and that the tariff rates of members against imports from the rest of the world have to be unified. The purpose of the present section is to apply the theory developed in the preceding sections to various aspects of the formation of customs unions (free-trade areas can be analysed by obvious extensions of the analysis).

The first problem to be considered is the nature of the gains that are generally alleged to follow from the formation of customs unions. The standard economic analysis of customs unions stresses the gains from trade creation, against which must be weighed the losses from trade diversion; and some weight is put on economies of scale and the promotion of efficiency through competition in a larger market area. These arguments, however, are equally arguments for unilateral tariff elimination, which would have the advantage of entailing no losses from trade diversion; and, apart from the economies of scale argument, which begs the question of why such economies are not exploitable through the world market but can be obtained by customs union, the only economic argument on classical lines for pursuing these gains through customs union rather than unilateral tariff elimination must rest on the possible terms-of-trade loss from unilateral tariff reduction and on the possible terms-of-gain for the union as a whole from discrimination against the outside world. The arguments usually advanced for customs unions in political discussion, however, generally ignore any possible gain from trade creation, in the sense of replacement of domestic production by cheaper imports, and instead regard this as a price to be paid for the benefits of expanded export markets, those benefits to result from both trade creation and trade diversion in favour of domestically produced products; and stress is laid on the gains to domestic industry from economies of scale and increased competition in a large market, as well as the 'growth potential' of a larger market area. In these arguments, trade diversion is valued for its effects in increasing production within the union, not for its effects in improving the terms of trade with the outside world; this is significant, because the conditions under which a customs union will divert the most trade are those under which its terms-of-trade effects will be least.

The difference between the two sets of arguments is clearly explainable by the hypothesis that standard economic analysis is concerned with maximization of real product, whereas political discussion derives from a preference for industrial production and is concerned with the maximization of real income conceived to include utility from the collective consumption of industrial production. The latter concern is bound to concentrate on the potentialities of a customs union for increasing the industrial output of the country and the efficiency of its industrial production, rather than on its potentialities for satisfying private consumption demand at lower cost by increased imports; and to regard such imports as a necessary cost of rather than a benefit from joining a customs union.

A second problem is the characteristics of countries likely to be successful in forming a customs union. As the preceding analysis of preferential reciprocal tariff reduction has shown, an arrangement of this kind will be attractive to countries with a strong preference for industrial production that are (or feel themselves to be) at a comparative disadvantage in industrial production in relation to the world market. A customs union enables them to gratify the preference for industrial production through trade creation and trade diversion, to an extent that would not be possible through negotiation of non-discriminatory tariff reduction.

In contrast to preferential tariff reduction, however, a customs union involves 100% preferential treatment of partners on an across-the-board basis. Instead of being able to pick and choose among commodities on which to give and demand preferences, a country must choose whether or not to participate in the customs union, and it will only choose to participate if there is a reasonable probability of a net gain, by comparison with *either* the situation in the absence of a customs union, *or* the situation in the presence of a union to which it does not belong. In either case, broadly speaking, a country will be motivated to join the union only if it judges that its industrial competitiveness or comparative advantage in industrial production is strong enough for its industrial production to increase within the union (or for any loss in aggregate industrial production to be compensated by increased efficiency). Conversely, the other members will be willing to have it join only if its membership does not threaten to increase its industrial production unduly at the expense of their own. Consequently, customs unions are most likely to be negotiable among countries with a similar degree of preference for industrial production, and with a similar degree of comparative advantage in industrial production [30], or, as it is sometimes put, countries at a similar stage of economic development. This implication of the theory of protectionism advanced here is confirmed by the formation of the European Common Market, and by the actual and prospective formation of customs unions among groups of less developed countries, in both of which connections much has been made of the 'similar stage of economic development' argument.

A third and final problem concerns the internal arrangements of the customs union. Standard trade theory would suggest that these arrangements would seek to maximize efficiency of production within the union, regardless of where production was located. The preference for industrial production hypothesis, however, would imply that any customs union agreement would include provisions to insure that each member obtains a 'fair share' of industrial production, and particularly that the growth of production in the union does not concentrate in one or a few countries at the expense of the rest. Such provisions are written into the Treaty of Rome, in the arrangements for a Development Fund, and incorporated more generally in the Common Market through the recognition of an obligation to contribute to the development of southern Italy. They are even more explicit in the provisions of the Latin American Free Trade Area Treaty, which envisage the Treaty as applying mostly to the establishment of new industries, and are concerned with a fair allocation of the new industries among the participating countries.

V. CONCLUDING COMMENTS

This paper has departed from the conventional assumptions of international trade theory and welfare economics, that welfare depends on private consumption of goods and services, in an attempt to construct a theory of protectionism, tariff bargaining, and customs union formation. In order to do so, it has posited a 'preference for industrial production', involving the treatment of industrial production as a collective consumption good the quality of which is governed by commercial policy. The intention has been to provide a logically coherent explanation of why commercial policy is conducted the way it is.

Any such attempt runs the risk of being misinterpreted as a justification of whatever countries have chosen or choose to do, and a demonstration that economics has nothing to say about what public policy should be. These are misinterpretations, because they fail to distinguish between two separate levels of analysis. At one level an economic decision unit is treated, as in this paper, as an objective actor in the economic process, with certain preferences whose satisfaction it seeks to maximize, the assumption being that the actor rationally connects means with ends. At a different level of analysis, the analytical problem is precisely what the actor should do to maximize its satisfaction, the assumption being that the actor does not, or does not fully, understand the connections between means and ends. Thus one branch of economics is concerned with the consequences of the assumption that firms act rationally to maximize profits, while another branch is concerned with devising decision rules and operations on data that will yield the profit-maximizing decisions. In the present paper, problems at the second level of analysis have been deliberately concealed in the concept of 'a preference for industrial production', in order to explore and rationalize the behaviour of governments. That preference, it will be recalled, was so defined as to comprise the effects of electoral ignorance and the influence of power groups on government policy. There is nothing in the analysis of this paper to prevent an economist from asking whether industrial production yields the economic benefits believed to flow from it, from calculating the real product cost of protection and asking whether the benefits repay this cost, or from insisting that the consumer's interest in low-cost consumption, as contrasted with the producer's interest in high-priced production, deserves more representation in government policy-making than it usually receives.

This appendix develops a simple and somewhat artificial model to demonstrate the proposition stated in the text, that bilaterally negotiated reciprocal tariff reduction on a non-discriminatory basis may cease to be profitable before free trade is reached.

Assume that each country produces exports at constant cost, and import substitutes at increasing cost. Let each country's import demand function (imports being measured in dollar's worth at world market prices) be $M_i(1 - m_i t_i)$, where M_i is the free-trade level of imports, m_i is the slope of the demand curve for imports, and t_i is the tariff rate (expressed as a proportion). The slope of the import demand curve is the absolute sum of the slopes of the consumption demand and domestic supply curves; let x_i be the proportion of $m_i(0 < x_i \leqslant 1)$ composed of the domestic supply slope. Assume further that each country j receives a fixed share s_{ij} in country i's imports

$$0 < s_{ij} \leqslant 1, \qquad \sum_{j \neq i} s_{ij} = 1,$$

this share being determined by some economic mechanism not investigated here. (In fact, these shares can be defined less restrictively, as applying only to the imports excluded by country i's tariff.) Finally, assume that each country attaches a constant social value v_i to a unit increase in industrial production achieved through an increase in exports or in production for the domestic market (by protection). The cost of protection is, of course, appropriately equal to $\frac{1}{2} m_i t_i^2 M_i$.

The difference between the real income of the country under general protection and under general free trade is

$$R_i = -v_i \sum_{j \neq i} s_{ij} M_j m_j t_j + v_i x_i m_i t_i M_i - \frac{1}{2} m_i t_i^2 M_i. \tag{1}$$

If each country takes the tariffs of the others as given, it will maximize its real income by setting its tariff rate at the level required by

$$\frac{\partial R_i}{\partial t_i} = m_i M_i (v_i x_i - t_i) = 0, \tag{2}$$

96

that is, it will establish the tariff rate $t_i = v_i x_i$. This is the tariff rate from which bilaterally negotiated tariff reductions are assumed to commerce.

Now consider reciprocal tariff reduction by countries i and j. Assume that the negotiation comprises a series of exchanges of small tariff reductions, symbolized by $T_i = -dt_i$ and $T_j = -dt_j$. The effects on the respective real incomes of the two countries at each step will be

$$dR_i = v_i s_{ji} m_j M_j T_j - (v_i x_i - t_i) m_i M_i T_i, \qquad (3)$$

$$dR_j = v_j s_{ij} m_i M_i T_i - (v_j x_j - t_j) T_j, \qquad (4)$$

where t_i and t_j represent the tariff rates established at the termination of the previous step. Note that there must be some gain from non-discriminatory tariff reduction at the first step, because in each equation the first term on the right-hand side is positive, while at the beginning of negotiations the second term on the right-hand side is zero (by the maximization condition of eqn (2)).

The limits to which non-discriminatory reciprocal tariff reduction may go can be investigated by using equations (3) and (4) to define two 'boundary' loci of possible reciprocal tariff reductions, representing successive pairs of marginal tariff reductions that would leave one of the two countries no better off in terms of real income than it was initially. These loci, obtained by setting dR_i and dR_j, respectively, equal to zero, are

$$\frac{T_i}{T_j} = \frac{v_i s_{ji}}{v_i X_i - t_i} \frac{m_j M_j}{m_i M_i}, \qquad (5)$$

$$\frac{T_i}{T_j} = \frac{v_j x_j - t_j}{v_j s_{ij}} \frac{m_j M_j}{m_i M_i}. \qquad (6)$$

Reciprocal tariff reductions on a non-discriminatory basis that will benefit both countries will be possible only so long as the value of T_i/T_j given by equation (5) exceeds the value given by equation (6); that is, so long as

$$\frac{v_i s_{ji}}{v_i x_i - t_i} > \frac{v_j x_j - t_j}{v_j s_{ij}}. \qquad (7)$$

This condition must hold for the first step of tariff reductions from the initial level, since initially the denominator of the left-hand side and the numerator of the right-hand side are zero. Thereafter, however, the left-hand fraction falls and the right-hand fraction rises, as the tariff rates are reduced.

Will it be possible to reach free trade in the two countries by non-discriminatory reciprocal tariff-cutting? Substitution of $t_i = t_j = 0$ into equation (7) yields the necessary condition

$$\frac{s_{ji}s_{ij}}{x_i x_i} > 1. \tag{8}$$

This condition can be given an economic interpretation in several ways; the simplest approach is to express it in terms of conditions on the (geometric) average values of the parameters. Alternative statements of the condition can then be made as follows. Free trade on both sides is attainable through non-discriminatory reciprocal tariff reduction if:

(a) the average share of a country in the expansion of the other's imports exceeds the average proportion of the increase in a country's imports resulting from tariff reduction by which its domestic production of import substitutes is reduced ($s_{ji}s_{ij} > x_i x_j$), or

(b) on the average an increase in a country's imports reduces its domestic production by less than it increases the other country's exports ($[x_j/s_{ji}][x_i/s_{ij}] < 1$).

Version (b) amounts to the requirement that reciprocal tariff reduction must increase total industrial production in the negotiating countries, as stated in note 23. Note that this condition in incapable of fulfilment unless an expansion of imports involves some increase in total consumption, and does not merely replace domestic production (in the latter case, the condition reduces to $s_{ji}s_{ij} > 1$, which is by assumption impossible). In general terms, the condition implies that the possibility of reciprocal non-discriminatory tariff reduction proceeding to free trade will be greater, the larger the shares of the negotiating countries in each other's markets, and the more responsive their domestic demand and the less responsive their domestic supply of import substitutes to reduction in the landed price of imports.

Finally, the condition of equation (8) can be used to illustrate the proposition, presented in the text, that preferential arrangements may be more attractive than tariffs. By preferential arrangements, s_{ji} and s_{ij} can be made equal to or greater than unity, so that a free-trade area between the two countries would always be mutually beneficial.

This conclusion, however, is limited to this particular model: since exports are assumed to be in perfectly elastic supply, a country incurs no loss from trade diversion effected by preferential tariff reduction.

NOTES AND REFERENCES

[1] *Journal of Political Economy*, vol. LXVIII, August 1960, pp. 327–45.

[2] In R. E. Caves, H. G. Johnson, and P. B. Kenen (eds.), *Trade, Growth and the Balance of Payments: Essays in Honor of Gottfried Haberler*, Chicago: Rand McNally Co., 1965.

[3] J. E. Meade, *The Theory of International Economic Policy*, vol. I: *The Balance of Payments* London: Macmillan, 1951.

[4] The stimulus to develop this theory comes partly from my former colleague J. C. Knapp, of Manchester University, who has persistently posed the question why, if reduction of tariffs is economically beneficial, tariff negotiators always regard a tariff reduction as a concession that must be compensated by reciprocal tariff reductions by the other party to the bargain.

[5] See Anthony J. Downs, An economic theory of political action in a democracy, *Journal of Political Economy*, vol. LXV, April 1957, pp. 135–50, and his *An Economic Theory of Democracy*, New York: Harper & Bros, 1957; Gary S. Becker, *The Economics of Discrimination*, Chicago: University of Chicago Press, 1957; and Albert Breton, The economics of nationalism, *Journal of Political Economy*, vol. LXXII, August, 1964, pp. 376–87. From Downs I take the notion of government policy in a democracy as a rational response to the demands of the electorate; Becker's work contributed the notion (already present in my analysis of the scientific tariff) of conceptualizing 'irrational' behaviour as a preference and measuring it by the marginal premium (discount) individuals would pay (give) to gratify it; Breton's work contributed the notion of conceptualizing certain kinds of government policies as providing a collective consumption good. I have used these building blocks in an earlier and more general paper prepared for the University of Chicago Committee for the Comparative Study of New Nations Seminar on Nationalism and Economic Policy in Developing Nations ('A Model of economic Nationalism' [mimeo.]).

[6] The theory presented below is derived from the assumption of a 'preference for industrial production'; by extension, agricultural protectionism can be explained by an assumed 'preference for agricultural production'. Since industrial protectionism is a major common policy of less developed countries (which are predominantly agricultural in economic structure) and agricultural protectionism is a major common policy of advanced countries (which are predominantly industrial in economic structure), the two preferences could be synthesized in the concept of a 'preference for economic balance'. This concept was indeed suggested by R. A. Mundell, in discussion of an early draft of this article. Such a concept has the appeal of formal elegance and symmetry in explaining the commercial policies of countries at all stages of development. I have not pursued it, however, for two reasons: (1) policies of agricultural protection are implemented by different means than policies of industrial protectionism, and, more important, agricultural commodities are treated differently than industrial commodities under GATT; (2) advanced countries protect their industry or part of it as well as their agriculture, and do bargain over reductions of tariffs on industrial goods in a manner explained by the theory presented here.

[7] Downs (*Economic Theory of Democracy*) explains the dominance of pro-

ducer over consumer interests in a democracy by the costs of acquiring information and taking action, which generally exceed the potential benefits for the consumer, whose economic interests are diffuse, but not for the producer, whose economic interests are concentrated; the dominance of producer interests in political decisions is therefore a consequence of economic rationality.

[8] According to a well-known formula, the welfare cost of a small increase in the tariff rate, for a simple model ignoring cross-effects in production and consumption and input–output complications, may be written

$$-\frac{\mathrm{d}W}{\mathrm{d}t} = t\frac{P\mathrm{d}}{\mathrm{d}p} - t\frac{\mathrm{d}C}{\mathrm{d}p},$$

where t is the tariff rate, p the domestic price, P is domestic output of the protected good, and C domestic consumption of it (quantities being measured in unit values at free-trade prices, so that $\mathrm{d}p = \mathrm{d}\hat{p}$; the two terms on the right-hand side are, respectively, the marginal production and marginal consumption costs of protection ($\mathrm{d}C/\mathrm{d}p$ being negative). The present analysis, however, is concerned with the welfare cost, not of an increase in the tariff rate, but of an increase in protected output. Division of the foregoing expression by $\mathrm{d}P/\mathrm{d}p$ yields this welfare cost as

$$-\frac{\mathrm{d}W}{\mathrm{d}P} = t - t\left(\frac{\mathrm{d}C/\mathrm{d}p}{\mathrm{d}P/\mathrm{d}p}\right),$$

the second expression on the right-hand side being the marginal private consumption cost of protected industrial production. The ratio $[(\mathrm{d}C/\mathrm{d}p)/(\mathrm{d}P/\mathrm{d}p)]$ is a ratio of the price slopes of the demand and supply curves, referred to in the text as 'the relative price sensitivity of demand'. The marginal excess private cost of protected industrial production may also be expressed in terms of elasticities of supply and demand as

$$\frac{\mathrm{d}W}{\mathrm{d}P} = t\left(1 + \frac{P}{C}\frac{\eta}{\varepsilon}\right),$$

where η and ε are, respectively, the elasticities of consumption demand and domestic supply.

[9] An important implication of the theory is that inputs not counted as part of 'industrial production' will not be subject to protection. This implication is confirmed empirically by the escalation of tariff rates by stage of production typical of national tariff structures. On the protective effects of such escalation see my The theory of tariff structure, with special reference to world trade and development, in Harry G. Johnson and Peter B. Kenen, *Trade and Development*, Geneva: Études et Travaux de l'Institut Universitaire de Hautes Études Internationales, 1965.

[10] Using the mathematical expression of note 8, and the equality of the marginal degree of preference for industrial production v with its marginal private excess cost,

$$\frac{v}{t} = 1 - \left(\frac{\mathrm{d}C/\mathrm{d}p}{\mathrm{d}P/\mathrm{d}p}\right) = 1 + \frac{P}{C}\frac{\eta}{\varepsilon}.$$

If $-[(\mathrm{d}C/\mathrm{d}p)/(\mathrm{d}P/\mathrm{d}p)]$ is constant, v/t will be constant, and t will vary with v. If, on the other hand, η/ε is constant, v/t will decrease with P/C (which may be taken as an index of ability to compete with foreign producers). In both cases, differences in v due to differences in P/C must necessarily be accompanied by differences in t in the same direction. A decrease in t could accompany an increase in v only if the slope (elasticity) of the demand curve increased relatively to the slope (elasticity) of the supply curve as t (and P/C) increased.

[11] For simplicity, industrial products are here taken as *numéraire*, so that all terms of trade effects appear as changes in the prices of non-industrial goods.

[12] The orthodox optimum tariff formula for the two-commodity case may be derived as follows. Maximization of social welfare requires $U_m/U_x = dX/dM$, where X and M, respectively, represent export and import quantities and U_x and U_m the marginal utilities of X and M in domestic consumption. Here dX/dM is the marginal cost of additional imports, derived from the balance of trade equality $X = pM$ or $M = \pi X$ (where $p = 1/\pi$ is the price of M in terms of X) and the foreign supply of imports or demand for exports,

$$\frac{dX}{dM} = p\left(1+\frac{1}{\varepsilon}\right) = \frac{1}{\pi}\left(\frac{\eta}{\eta-1}\right),$$

where ε is the elasticity of foreign supply of imports and η the corresponding elasticity of foreign demand for exports as functions, respectively, of p and π. Welfare maximization requires the imposition of an import tariff such that

$$\frac{U_m}{U_x} = (1+t)\,p = \frac{dX}{dM}, \text{ that is,}$$

$$t = \frac{1}{\varepsilon} \quad \text{or} \quad t = \frac{1}{\eta-1}.$$

With a preference for industrial production, however, the loss of social utility from an additional unit of exports for the industrial exporter is not U_x but $U_x - vaU_x$, where v is the proportional marginal preference for industrial production and a is the proportion of the increase in exports effected by increased domestic industrial production; similarly, for the industrial importer, the gain in utility from an additional unit of imports is not U_m but $U_m - vbU_m$, where v is defined as before and b is the proportion of the increase in imports effected by decreased domestic industrial production. Substitution of these expressions yields the results $t = 1/\varepsilon - av(1+1/\varepsilon)$ for the industrial exporter, and $t = 1/(\eta-1)+bv$ for the industrial importer.

[13] The problem of many countries, which involves the possibility of preferential tariff reductions, is most conveniently dealt with in conjunction with differentiation of industrial production. It is difficult to deal with in the present model, since industrial exporting countries will have tariffs only if they possess monopoly–monopsony power, and this creates analytical complexities in a multicountry system.

The terminology of 'advanced' and 'less developed' employed in the text is, of course, misleading, since neither real product nor real income is necessarily higher for net industrial exporting than for net industrial importing nations; but the terminology does reflect a judgement that follows naturally from the preference for industrial production.

[14] The adjustment of the tariff of one country to changes in the other, based on the objective of maximizing national welfare, is to be distinguished from 'tariff retaliation' in the pure sense, which implies that a country derives utility by reducing the welfare of the other country through increasing its tariffs. The latter means that one country's welfare is a function of the other's, and introduces considerations that are excluded at this point, though they will be introduced briefly later in the argument.

[15] One country may possess sufficiently superior monopoly power to be better off when both follow optimum tariff policies than it would be under free trade; negotiation for reciprocal tariff reduction cannot bring such a country to practise free trade.

101

[16] Recall that the exercise of this monopoly–monopsony power is assumed to have already been tempered by the preference for industrial production.

[17] Both the theoretical conclusion and its application to the contemporary situation are strengthened if the less developed country of the analysis is assumed to derive positive disutility from its 'collective consumption' of the industrial production of the advanced country.

[18] Another way of making this point is to say that the marginal cost of protected industrial production in this case includes an additional element not encountered in the previous case, namely, the loss of utility from collective consumption of industrial production due to the decrease in industrial exports induced by protection.

[19] Outstanding examples are the adoption of free trade by Britain in the nineteenth century and her retreat into protectionism in the period after the First World War; the espousal of free trade by the United States and Canada in the period after the Second World War, and the growth of protectionism in both countries when they encountered difficulties in international industrial competition after 1957.

[20] The reduction in a country's industrial production will be less than the increase in its industrial imports to the extent that its consumption switches from non-industrial products to industrial imports, and that contraction of protected industrial production increases industrial production in the non-protected sector. Each country will therefore have an incentive to offer the other concessions on items that are close substitutes for non-industrial products in consumption and for non-protected industrial products in production, rather than on items that are close substitutes in consumption for its other industrial products and in production for its non-industrial products.

[21] At the margin, the marginal excess cost of protected industrial production is just equal to its marginal social utility; a small contraction of protected production occasions negligible loss, while an expansion of industrial exports yields a surplus of utility from collective consumption of industrial production.

[22] The relative magnitudes of the reduction in domestic production and the increase in imports will depend on the elasticities of demand and domestic supply of the good in question and the extent to which demand shifts from, and production shifts to, non-industrial production; the share of the increase in demand for imports that goes to the partner country depends on the magnitude of its elasticity of supply of exports relative to those of other countries; and the magnitude of the increase in the partner's industrial production relative to the increase in its exports depends on the relative magnitudes of the elasticities of domestic demand and supply of the commodity in the partner country. In all cases the elasticities have to be weighted appropriately by ratios of quantities initially produced, consumed, or traded.

[23] Suppose the value of the marginal utility of collective consumption of industrial production is a constant v, initially equal to the marginal excess cost of protected production e, and that for every unit reduction in protected industrial production through reduction of its own tariff the country receives an increase in its industrial exports equal to $1 - a > 0$, from the reduction in the partner country's tariff. Its net gain is initially $e - av > 0$; but it gains from further reciprocal tariff reduction only so long as e does not fall to av.

A simple mathematical model designed for analysis of the limits of non-discriminatory reciprocal tariff reduction is presented in the appendix. It is there shown that such tariff reduction can only reach free trade it if would increase industrial production in the two countries combined.

[24] J. M. Fleming, On making the best of balance of payments restrictions on

102

imports, *Economic Journal*, vol. LXI, March 1951, pp. 48–71, esp. 48–54. Fleming's problem is analytically both more interesting and more clear cut than the present one, since it explicitly comprehends discrimination among countries, and can use the equivalent of a single 'bargaining' rule, that the trade of all countries must always be exactly balanced.

[25] Though the argument is couched in terms of increased industrial production, it will be recalled from the preceding analysis that within limits a country could gain from reciprocal tariff reduction that reduced its aggregate industrial production, if the resulting increase in its real product exceeded the value of the corresponding loss of utility from collective consumption of industrial production.

[26] Trade diversion will be relatively still more attractive if the discriminating countries attach positive disutility to the industrial production of the countries discriminated against.

[27] Whether a country's real product rises or falls depends on the net outcome of the trade-creating and trade-diverting effects of the reciprocal tariff reductions, as the standard theory has demonstrated.

[28] In the real world, preferences have frequently been exchanged between industrially advanced countries and their less developed colonies or close political allies; these cases can be fitted into the argument by postulating that the advanced country includes the less developed territory in its concept of 'domestic'. Preferences given unilaterally to an industrially advanced country by its colonial dependencies of course fit perfectly into the theory presented here, which offers another way of looking at the phenomena of economic imperialism.

[29] A number of the propositions stated in this and the preceding three paragraphs have been arrived at independently by Benton F. Massell and Charles A. Cooper, A new look at customs union theory, RAND Paper, P-2972-2, available on request from the authors or RAND.

[30] These prerequisites are suggested by consideration of the determinants of the impact of customs union on trade – the initial individual country tariff levels and the industrial structures of the countries – and also by the necessity of the members agreeing on a common tariff level.

5

EUROPEAN ECONOMIC INTEGRATION AND THE UNITED STATES [1]*

LAWRENCE B. KRAUSE

The Brookings Institution

INTRODUCTION

For the second time in the twentieth century, a new area is dominating international trade. Just as the United States eclipsed Great Britain as the world's largest trading nation in the early part of the century, so is the European Economic Community outpacing the United States today. The exports and imports of the Common Market represent 24% of world trade (including intra-Community trade) while the U.S. percentage is only 16%. The members of the European Economic Community maintain their separate political identities, but for questions of international commerce they must be treated as a single unit, since they make unified decisions with respect to commercial policy. If all the countries currently applying for membership in the EEC were to be accepted, then the United States would be relatively small by comparison.

The formation of the European Economic Community has not only redefined trade statistics, it has and is changing the patterns of world trade. In 1958, the last year before tariff preferences were begun, less than 30% of the imports of the member countries originated in other member countries. In 1961, just three years later, 36% of the imports of the member countries came from other members. Looked at from the other side, exports of the EEC countries to non-members increased by only 29% between 1958 and 1961 while their exports to each other increased by 73%.

The economic success of the Common Market has been demonstrated, not only by the remarkable increases in trade, but also by the fact that the dismantling of internal restrictions to trade has been appreciably accelerated. With the reaching of an agreement on the

* *American Economic Review*, May 1963, 53, pp. 185–196.

beginning of a common agricultural policy, the EEC has moved into the second transitional stage of the Rome Treaty. Because of the very success of the Common Market in its economic objectives, it has become even more necessary to evaluate the EEC as to its effects on non-member countries.

THE EEC AS A POLITICAL MECHANISM

It has been a unanimous observation of all analysts of the EEC that the effects of European integration for non-members cannot be determined by studying the Rome Treaty alone. As much or more will depend on the administration of the provisions and subsequent policy decision that put its ideas into practice. Since these subsequent policy decisions while economic in character are determined within the particular political institutions of the EEC, some evaluation of the political mechanism is required to make judgements as to eventual outcomes.

It must be recalled that the determining motivations for the formation of a Common Market among the original six countries were primarily political in character. The desire to institutionalize the Franco-German *rapprochement*, the need to give an outlet to West German nationalism through the goal of wider European unity, and the attraction of combining the individual national powers into a large 'third force' that could stand on the same level and, independent of the United States and the Soviet Union, were probably much more important in bringing about the Rome Treaty than the expected economic gains of membership in an exclusive trading group. The vehicle chosen for furthering these political objectives was an economic union because of the willingness of the prospective member countries to accept this type of divestiture of national sovereignty as evidenced by the European Coal and Steel Community and corresponding reluctance to join a political union as indicated by the defeat of the European Defence Community.

Certain consequences follow directly from using economic means for political ends. When questions arise as to the treatment of non-member countries, there is always a political motive for discriminating against non-members even if no great economic interest is at stake, because the economic benefits of membership cannot be weakened without undermining the political unity that it is intended to cement. The common external tariff, for instance, is more than a means of protecting industry of the member countries from outside competition; it is the tie that binds the countries together. This suggests that the EEC may be unwilling to reduce their external tariffs to zero unless progress is made toward political unity through other means.

In sharp contrast to the substantial progress that the EEC has made on the economic front, the development of political unity has been minimal. The institutional framework provided for in the Rome Treaty is just sufficient to enable the customs union to operate, but nothing more. The centre of power rests in the Council of Ministers and the ministers are representatives of the member countries. Unanimous consent is required for practically all issues [2]. With such a system, implying as it does a veto power by all members, decision making is slow, very cumbersome, and extremely painful. An exact balance of national interests must be obtained before agreement can be reached on any issue. In the decision process, little if any weight is given to the interests of countries not represented at the bargaining table because of these difficulties. Problems of non-member countries that resulted from the creation of the EEC, therefore, are unlikely to receive attention by the Council of Ministers because nothing gets decided unless it poses a crisis for the Community itself or for one of the member countries. Furthermore, once agreement on an issue has been reached, it is next to impossible to get the Council of Ministers to reconsider their decision because they are unwilling to open old wounds. This is true despite some adverse consequences of the policy for non-member countries.

ECONOMIC IMPLICATIONS OF THE EEC FOR THE UNITED STATES

The importance of the political bias against the economic interest of non-member countries depends in part on what effects the Community is likely to have on excluded countries. For the United States, this question can be analysed by looking at the consequences of the EEC on the bilateral trade between the U.S. and the EEC and also at its consequences on our trade with third countries. For this purpose, United States exports to the Common Market can be divided into three groups: industrial products, agricultural products, and non-agricultural raw materials.

U.S. EXPORTS OF INDUSTRIAL PRODUCTS

Unlike trade in agricultural products, the Common Market has made relatively few changes in the institutional system whereby industrial goods are imported into member countries. A tariff is levied on industrial products when imported from non-members, but this has always been the case. The new element arises from the fact that goods coming from other member countries will not have to pay a tariff or be restricted in any way, and the tariff barrier to the outside world will be uniform regardless of which member country the import is sent [3]. The consequences of this system for non-members depend on how much protection the external tariff wall provides as compared to the previously existing national tariffs. The common external tariff was calculated by taking an unweighted average of the French, German, Italian, and Benelux tariffs (with some exceptions) [4]. The protectiveness of the tariff cannot be determined by merely comparing the resulting increases and decreases in tariffs required to reach the calculated level. For a producer within the Community that was previously protected by a high tariff, the most serious challenge to its competitive position will come from low-cost producers within the Community against which it will have no tariff protection. Unless the high-cost producers can bring their prices (and costs) down to the level of the low-cost producers within the EEC, they cannot stay in business. The essence of economic integration depends on this type of competition taking place. The prices of the large, low-cost producers within the Community will set the competitive level for the entire market. The common external tariff will be protective only to the extent that it protects the firms that can survive the internal competitive struggle.

An analysis of the protectiveness of the external tariff was made by estimating the amount of protection it affords the dominant low-cost suppliers within the EEC. The dominant suppliers were identified by looking at the trade flows among the member countries before the establishment of the Community. It was assumed that the dominant suppliers of a particular product class are to be found in the country which had the largest share of intra-Community trade in that product class. We can compare the level of the external tariff for each commodity class with the former national tariff of the country with the largest share of intra-Community trade. If the new tariff rate is higher than the old national rate, then the amount of protection it affords is greater than the rate needed to protect the industry previously. If the rate is the same as previously or lower, then we can say that the amount of protection has not been increased. We cannot definitely state that a reduced tariff will undermine a previously existing level of protection without knowing whether there was excess protection under the old national tariff rate.

Two further assumptions are required to make the comparison meaningful. It must be assumed that if the high-cost firms cannot meet the competition within the Community, then the low-cost producers can expand output without significantly changing their average costs. Further, it must be assumed that changes in the tariffs on imported raw materials will not greatly affect the competitive position of the dominant supplier. As to the first assumption, much of the literature of economic integration suggests that with the enlargement of market size, substantial economies of scale will be captured and thereby lower average costs. However, further economies of scale may be limited for producers which are already quite large and increases in cost with expansion may well offset them. With respect to the second assumption, the common external tariffs on industrial raw materials were purposely set quite low so as not to weaken the competitive position of processing industries and therefore this assumption seems quite reasonable.

TABLE 5·1. *Comparison of the new external tariff rate of the EEC on selected products with the old national tariff of the dominant supplier of each product*[a]

		Tariff comparisons[b]		
Types of products	Total	Plus	Even	Minus
Chemicals	12	10	0	2
Textile products	7	3	1	3
Manufactured products classified by material, other	19	14	3	2
Machinery and transport	11	11	0	0
Other manufactured products	12	8	1	3
Total	61	46	5	10

[a] Figures refer to number of products in category.
[b] Plus: tariff increased. Even: tariff unchanged. Minus: tariff declined.

Source: Post-Geneva weighted average *ad valorem* equivalent of duties, prepared by International Trade Analysis Division, U.S. Department of Commerce, March 1962, P.E.P. *Atlantic Tariffs and Trade*.

A comparison of the new EEC tariff for each of 61 three-digit SITC commodity classes with the former national tariff protecting the dominant suppliers gives the vivid impression that the protectiveness of the new tariff is much greater than that previously existing (Table 5·1). Our analysis shows that 75% of all manufactured products will have their protection raised and by large amounts. The size of the tariff reduction required to bring the new tariff down to the level of the old national tariff of the dominant supplier is over 50% for twenty-one out of the sixty-one classes, 26 to 50% for sixteen classes and less than 25% for only nine classes. Furthermore, for half of the ten classes for which tariff protection has been reduced, other methods of trade restrictions are commonly employed.

The impact of these higher EEC tariffs upon United States exports may well be substantial. Most of the industrial products which the United States exports to the EEC are concentrated in twenty-two of the sixty-one SITC classes analysed (Table 5·2). Substantial tariff reductions on these product classes will be required to bring the level of protection down to that previously granted to the dominant supplier. Up to now, the United States has benefited greatly from the rapid growth of the European economies and the pressures put on the German engineering industry in particular. We have been the residual supplier making the most of excess demand. However, this may not continue.

When Great Britain joins the Common Market, further difficulties will be created for American exports. As desirable as the union may be on other grounds, it will cause a twofold increase in the troubles facing U.S. exports. In the first place, as British exports cease to feel the discrimination of the EEC, an easy target for market dislodgement by the EEC and U.S. producers will be removed. Furthermore, the British themselves then may well become a serious competitor for existing American shares of the EEC market. In all the twenty-two product groups in which U.S. exports are concentrated, with the exception of paper and paperboard, the British also have a substantial position. In seven groups, the British share of the EEC market exceeds our own, and it is well above 5% for most of the others. This means that the British have a substantial base for expanding their exports if their competitive position improves. The competitive pressures arising from membership in the EEC and the tariff preferences gained thereby may be enough to transform the British into a fierce competitor. United States exports would become the prime

TABLE 5·2. *Imports of manufactured products by the EEC from the United States, 1961[a]*

Products	Value of imports (million dollars)	U.S. share of EEC imports (%)	Reduction of EEC tariff required to maintain protection (%)
Inorganic chemicals	47	19·7	49
Organic chemicals	142	31·8	50
Paints	9	13·6	48
Medicinal and pharmaceutical products	37	22·3	25
Miscellaneous chemicals	130	26·0	63
Paper, paperboard	31	6·9	10
Yarn and thread	21	4·9	20
Processed gems	14	7·1	0
Iron and steel	63	3·4	36
Manufacture of metals, n.e.c.	35	8·1	42
Power machines	104	27·1	68
Agricultural machinery	23	10·6	65
Office machines	79	28·2	4
Metal working machinery	99	28·0	65
Miscellaneous machinery	301	21·8	67
Electric machinery	199	16·2	48
Road motor vehicles	61	7·1	35
Aircraft	190	62·5	100 (if applied)
Apparel (non-fur)	13	3·7	0
Instruments	54	26·2	55
Musical instruments	13	11·9	26
Manufactured goods, n.e.s.	22	9·2	40
Total	1,687		

[a] Values will differ from U.S. exports of these items to the EEC because of the inclusion of transport costs and differences in accounting periods.
Source: U.N. *Commodity Trade Statistics*, 1961.

target under such circumstances and maintaining our market position in industrial products would not be easy.

U.S. AGRICULTURAL EXPORTS TO THE EUROPEAN ECONOMIC COMMUNITY [5]

The most serious challenge to United States exports arises from the adoption this year by the EEC of a common agricultural policy. [6] While many important aspects of the policy are yet to be determined, the major impact of the policy can be inferred from the mechanism that has been created. This development is of particular concern to the United States because Western Europe is such a large purchaser of U.S. agricultural products. During recent years the EEC countries alone absorbed over 20% of our agricultural exports and close to one-third of all such exports sold for hard currencies. The addition of the U.K. to the Common Market would increase the latter percentage to one-half and amounts to $1.5 thousand million.

The agricultural agreement of 14 January 1962, provides the initial steps for the integration of the agricultural sector of the EEC. The regulations found in the agreement differ substantially among the various products, but there are some common features. Existing restrictions of all kinds on imports are to be replaced by variable levies designed to offset the differences in market prices (after adjusting for transportation costs) in the EEC country importing and in the country of origin. The levies on imports from other EEC countries are to be gradually reduced until 1970, when a one-price system will emerge. The levies on imports from non-EEC countries are to be sufficiently high to ensure preference for imports from other EEC countries; they will not be reduced over time and might be increased if Community and world prices diverge further.

This system of variable levies will work in such a way that a chain of preference will be set up. Demands for agricultural products in any EEC country will be met first by domestic production. Should these supplies prove insufficient at existing support prices, then products from other EEC countries will be allowed into the market. Only if aggregate production within the Community is insufficient will imports be allowed from non-EEC countries, regardless of how competitively priced these goods may be.

Provision is also made in the agreement for export subsidies designed to offset differences in market prices which will enable a member country with an exportable surplus to export to another member country needing imports but having a lower price level. Subsidies on intra-Community trade will disappear by 1970. However, similar provisions are made for exports subsidies in the event that the Community as a whole experiences an exportable surplus to enable its products to compete in world markets and these provisions will not end with the transition period.

With imports determined solely as a residual between production and consumption of agricultural products within the Common Market, evaluation of the consequences of this policy depends on these magnitudes. Since the target level of price supports has not yet been agreed upon (nor pricing criteria), production cannot be estimated with certainty. The eventual agreement on price level will result from a compromise of the political requirements within the member countries. So far the West Germans have been particularly unwilling to consider a lowering of their price supports and German prices are the highest in the Community. In all likelihood, agreement can only be reached by substantially raising the average level of prices within the Community.

The implications for EEC imports of agricultural products from non-member countries are quite clear. With rising average prices, increases in production will exceed increases in consumption and an accelerated movement toward self-sufficiency for a wide range of products will occur. U.S. exports of wheat, coarse grains, and meat will be endangered, and these products make up a substantial portion of our exports. Some other U.S. exports will be undermined by the granting of tariff preferences to the products of the Associated Overseas Countries; namely, fats and oils and to a lesser extent tobacco and cotton.

Even with this over-all pessimistic expectation, the United States will probably fare better than most third country exporters of agricultural products because of the structure of our comparative advantage. The U.S. exports mainly coarse grains to Europe rather than wheat, poultry rather than beef or lamb, and oil seeds, cotton, and tobacco rather than cocoa, coffee, and sugar. The prospects are that other countries whose product structure is concentrated in the latter categories will be in a much worse position than the U.S.

The aggregate of unfortunate consequences for non-member countries of the common agricultural policy is greater than the sum of the losses in individual product markets. The agreement essentially removes the agricultural sector of the EEC from the resource allocating mechanism of world-market forces. If the EEC policy is pursued without moderation, bargaining for trade liberalization will be almost impossible because the mechanism ensures an absolute level of protection.

EXPORTS OF NON-AGRICULTURAL RAW MATERIALS

While the United States exports a considerable amount of non-agricultural crude materials to the Common Market ($750 million in 1960), the common external tariff is unlikely to interfere very greatly with this trade. Only for two commodity groups, petroleum products and aluminium, is the United States likely to suffer a trade loss. The loss may arise from the expansion of capacity that is induced by the tariff shelter. For most other products in this category, the external tariff is either zero or very low.

TRADE EFFECTS OF THE EEC VIA THIRD COUNTRIES

The commerce of the United States can be further affected by the Common Market even though American goods are not directly involved. If countries which normally spend a substantial portion of their foreign exchange earnings in the United States have their exports curtailed, then our balance of payments will subsequently suffer. This may well come about through tariff preferences granted the Associated Overseas Countries by the EEC.

The former French colonial areas of Africa are already substantial exporters of most tropical-zone agricultural products, and these compete with Latin-American exports to Europe. The common external tariff levied on Latin-American goods plus the marketing privileges offered African products gives a distinct competitive edge to the African suppliers. If there were a net shortage or balance of world supplies relative to demand at ruling prices, then the diversion of African supplies to Europe would leave other markets open to Latin America. Since, however, there are more than sufficient world supplies of coffee, cocoa, sugar, and tropical fruit (the principal products involved), the losses to Latin America of sales to Europe as a result of tariff discrimination cannot be made up elsewhere and are likely to lead to a substantial loss in foreign exchange for the Latin-Americans. Since the Latin-American countries buy from 48 to 64% of their total imports from the United States while the African countries buy only 4% of the total imports from us, the net loss to United States exports from the preferential position which the EEC affords African supplies could be substantial.

A further problem is created for the United States because another good customer of ours, Japan, is prevented from exporting to the EEC. All of the member countries discriminate against Japanese goods either by refusing to grant most-favoured-nations treatment or by more devious methods. This affects us in two ways. The Japanese are denied foreign exchange, a major part of which would have been spent in the United States, and the Japanese are forced to send a disproportionate share of their output to the U.S. because we have the only market that is even partially open to them. The problem promises to be more serious as Japanese development continues. Even though discriminations against the Japanese predate the Rome Treaty, they are aggravated by the EEC because the freedom of trans-shipment of goods within the EEC will limit the liberalization of their restrictions to the pace of the least liberal country. Since the EEC countries must liberalize jointly, the speed of the liberalization measures will be much slower than the pace some countries were prepared to undertake in its absence.

OFFSET: HIGHER RATES OF GROWTH OF THE EEC COUNTRIES

In discussions of the external impact of economic integration, the point is always made that the unfavourable impact of the formation of a customs union on non-member country exports will be offset in whole or in part by the increase in member country growth rates stimulated by the establishment of internal free trade. If the EEC has had or is likely to have a growth-stimulating effect, then it must be recognized that the beneficial consequences of this growth on the trade positions on non-member countries is not as great as one might expect at first glance. Since this growth is likely to be of an import-replacing character, the natural consequence of stimulating growth via exports induced by preferential tariffs, the quantity of additional imports demanded from non-member countries is likely to be less per unit of growth in income than could have been expected from past behaviour. It is not enough for the growth of income merely to lead to a slight increase in imports from non-members if the Community's extra exports to the rest of the world per unit of growth of income are not declining sufficiently fast to maintain balance.

In order to make the point somewhat differently, consider the EEC as if it were a single country. The character of the growth of this country is such that it is progressively requiring less imports per unit of output. If at the same time, the exports of the country are not also declining fast enough in relation to GNP, then other countries' balances of payments will be put under pressure. Merely to maintain the existing balance-of-payments positions of third countries, outsiders will have to improve their competitive position *vis-à-vis* the Common Market. Rapid growth within the EEC has not so far led to a deterioration in their competitive positions in third markets; in fact, the contrary may be true. As a result, rapid growth of the EEC has been combined with balance-of-payments surpluses.

SUMMARY AND CONCLUSIONS

As indicated previously, the consequences of the Common Market for non-member countries will depend as much or more on subsequent policy decisions of the Community as on the provisions of the Rome Treaty. This analysis suggests that at present non-member countries have been put in a disadvantageous position. Future developments will depend in large measure on the willingness of the EEC to recognize the interests of non-members in their deliberations or, to use the standard phraseology, whether the Common Market will be outward or inward looking. There is some evidence to indicate that up to now the Community has been looking a little in both directions.

One can get some comfort in the belief that the Common Market will be outward looking from the Rome Treaty itself. Article 110 indicates that the interests of the Community lie in expanding world trade. Furthermore, the influential leaders of the Commission of the EEC and Professor Hallstein in particular have continually supported this belief in public statements. Nor has the liberalism of the Common Market been confined to words alone. The first two internal tariff reductions were generalized to non-member countries (as long as the resulting tariff did not fall below the external target rate). Also, the Common Market was willing to enter negotiations through GATT in the so-called 'Dillon round' and eventually reached agreements with other countries through which their external tariff was reduced by almost 20%.

There is some indication, however, of less liberal tendencies within the EEC. The tariff reductions made so far by the Common Market have been relatively painless in that they have merely removed some but not most of the excess protection created by the common external tariff. The common agricultural policy, however, has not only raised new barriers to trade, it has established a system that guarantees perfect protection. This policy can only be considered as extremely protectionist from the point of view of agricultural exporting countries.

Policy formation within the Common Market, of course, is not created in a vacuum. If the United States moves toward greater trade restrictions through actions such as raising tariffs on carpets and glass, then we strengthen the protectionist forces within the EEC and bring forth retaliatory restrictions to an excessive degree such as did occur. With the passage of the Trade Expansion Act, the United States has taken the first step toward leadership in the liberal direction. It is now up to the Common Market to indicate its willingness to proceed along this road.

Unfortunately, the immediate response in Europe to the American overture seems far from enthusiastic. While there is little question as to the willingness of the EEC to take part in another tariff negotiation, the hoped for major reduction in tariffs that is possible under the American law has little chance of acceptance according to some EEC spokesmen [7]. If a negotiated tariff reduction seems difficult, then a unilateral reduction by the EEC of their tariffs seems remote indeed. Yet according to this analysis, a unilateral reduction by the EEC is called for to satisfy the spirit, if not the letter, of the GATT requirement that protection not be increased through the formation of a customs union.

The economic size and power of the European Economic Community has cast it in a leadership role in the world. This power, unfortunately, can be used to further the narrow self-interest of the member countries as they conceive it to be. A continuance of existing political institutions almost assures that the power will be used in this way. On the other hand, responsible exercise of this power is possible with the development of greater political unity. Many difficult decisions would have to be made in exercising enlightened leadership, such as inducing major shifts of resources out of agriculture, and this is possible only with a strong sense of unity among the members.

Political unity may, but need not, mean a single federal state. Certainly many transitional stages would be gone through even if a single state was the ultimate goal. Fortunately, responsible leadership need not depend on reaching this particular ideal of unity. Progress toward majority rule and closer coordination of national policies may well be sufficient. From this point of view, the accession of Great Britain to the Rome Treaty would be the most important single step toward bringing about a more outward looking Community. British membership would add greater balance to the Community and would assure members and nonmembers alike as to the permanence of European unity and thus responsibility would follow.

NOTES AND REFERENCES

[1] Research for this paper was undertaken while the author was on leave from Yale University on fellowship grants jointly given by the Social Science Research Council and the Brookings Institution.

[2] The Rome Treaty provides that some issues are to be settled through qualified majority voting in the Council of Members and the number of issues so determined are to increase with successive stages within the transitional period. So far, no issue of any consequence has been determined by majority voting.

[3] During the transitional period, existing barriers on intra-Community trade will be gradually reduced and finally eliminated.

[4] This average led to tariffs somewhat on the high side because of the un-weighted feature and also because the national tariffs used in the calculation were above those actually in force on 1 January 1958. The German tariff which was averaged excluded the 25% tariff reduction of August 1957. The rate chosen for Italy excluded the tariff reductions of 1951. Also a Benelux tariff on most chemicals of 12% was averaged in, although no such tariff was in force. Rome Treaty, Article 19(2), Article 19(3)(d) and List E.

[5] A more extensive treatment of this subject can be found in my paper published by the Joint Economic Committee, *Factors Affecting the United States Balance of Payments*, Part 2, The Common Market: New Challenges to U.S. Exports, 1962.

[6] See Chapter 14 of this volume.

[7] Speech by M. Couve de Murville on 20 February 1962, before the American Club of Paris; speech by Valery Giscard d'Estaing on 27 March 1962, at the opening of the Lyon Trade Fair; and speech by Michel Maurice Bokanowski on 25 October 1962, to the American Chamber of Commerce in Paris.

6

THE IMPACT OF CUSTOMS UNIONS ON TRADE IN MANUFACTURES [1]*

JOHN WILLIAMSON

University of Warwick

ANTHONY BOTTRILL

1. INTRODUCTION

Both the EEC and EFTA were founded over a decade ago and have now established internal free trade in industrial products. One would therefore expect to be able to reach a reasonably well-informed judgement of their effects on trade flows. There are a number of studies that have reported on attempts to construct such estimates. Individually the various methods must be judged unreliable, and the same is true of a new method developed in the present paper. But collectively the available evidence is capable of indicating conclusions of about the same degree of reliability as is customary in applied economics. That is to say, there is a wide margin of uncertainty about the correct figure, but the order of magnitude can be established with reasonable confidence.

The plan of the present paper is as follows. Section 2 develops an analytical framework to clarify precisely what it is that one wishes to measure. Section 3 contains a critical survey of the principal previous published studies and a collation of their results. Section 4 describes the new approach and section 5 presents the results that it has yielded. A concluding section is devoted to utilizing the assembled evidence to form a judgement of the effects that the EEC and EFTA have had on trade flows.

2. AN ANALYTICAL FRAMEWORK

The world is divided into three mutually exclusive and collectively exhaustive blocs: the EEC, EFTA, and the rest of the world (ROW).

* Oxford Economic Papers, November 1971, pp. 323–351.

118

The object of the exercise is to contrast the world trade matrix Y as it appears in year t (indicated by a superscript) with the situation that would have materialized in year t if the EEC and EFTA had not been formed. The latter is referred to as the 'anti-monde'. The differences between this hypothetical anti-monde and the actual position can be attributed to:

(a) trade creation; i.e. the replacement of domestic production by imports from a partner country;

(b) trade diversion; i.e. the replacement of imports from non-partners by imports from a partner country;

(c) external trade creation; i.e. the replacement of domestic production by imports from a non-partner country (on account of a change in the external tariff);

(d) supply-side diversion; i.e. the replacement of exports to non-partners by exports to partners; and

(e) balance-of-payments reactions induced by attempts to adjust the payments imbalances caused by the foregoing changes.

We adopt the following notation:

c_{ii} = intra-ith bloc trade creation;

d_{ij} = diversion of the ith bloc's imports from bloc j;

$d_{ii} = \sum_{j \neq i} d_{ij}$ = diversion of ith bloc's imports (to bloc i);

e_{ij} = increase in i's imports from j caused by external trade creation;

$e_i = \sum_j e_{ij}$ = total external trade creation of bloc i;

r_{ij} = increase in i's imports from j caused by payments reactions;

s_{ij} = reduction in j's exports to i caused by supply constraints;

x_{ij} = (hypothetical) imports of bloc i from bloc j in the anti-monde;

$x_i = \sum_j x_{ij}$ = (hypothetical) imports of bloc i in the anti-monde;

y_{ij} = actual imports of bloc i from bloc j;

$y_i = \sum_j y_{ij}$ = actual imports of bloc i.

The world trade matrix Y is:

| | Exports by | | | |
	EEC	EFTA	ROW	Total
EEC	y_{11}	y_{12}	y_{13}	y_1
Imports of EFTA	y_{21}	y_{22}	y_{23}	y_2
ROW	y_{31}	y_{32}	y_{33}	y_3

This matrix can be broken down to exhibit the various changes that followed the creation of the EEC and EFTA. Both these blocs produced internal trade creation and both diverted imports from non-member countries. In addition, the EEC may have been responsible for external trade creation in those members that levelled their tariffs down to the common external tariff, and for its converse (external trade destruction) in the former low-tariff members who raised their external tariffs to the common level. The attractions of partners' markets may have directed some EEC and EFTA exports away from non-partners' markets, but this effect may have been partially, wholly, or more than fully offset by the greater competitiveness of exports from these blocs resulting from the advantages of a larger 'home' market. Finally, every flow in the matrix may have been affected by reaction designed to re-equilibrate payments positions. A breakdown of the Y matrix designed to show all these effects would be as follows:

$$
\begin{bmatrix}
y_{11} & y_{12} & y_{13} \\
y_{21} & y_{22} & y_{23} \\
y_{31} & y_{32} & y_{33}
\end{bmatrix}
$$

$$
= \begin{bmatrix}
x_{11}+c_{11}+d_{11}+r_{11} & x_{12}-d_{12}+e_{12}-s_{12}+r_{12} & x_{13}-d_{13}+e_{13}+r_{13} \\
x_{21}-d_{21}-s_{21}+r_{21} & x_{22}+c_{22}+d_{22}+r_{22} & x_{23}-d_{23}+r_{23} \\
x_{31}-s_{31}+r_{31} & x_{32}-s_{32}+r_{32} & x_{33}+r_{33}
\end{bmatrix}. \quad (1)
$$

Most investigators have implicitly assumed quite a few of these effects to be zero. Perhaps the most difficult problem is posed by supply constraints. It is possible that the fast growth of EEC and EFTA intra-trade in the years immediately following their formation (and also of EEC intra-trade in 1969) was partially at the expense of slower growth in exports to the ROW [2]. There is no conclusive evidence as to whether this was an important factor. In the longer run, however, one would expect supply bottlenecks to be overcome, and one might also expect their effect to be counteracted by the greater competitive strength resulting from a larger 'home market'. We therefore follow a well-established precedent in assuming $s_{ij} = 0$. The possibility that payments-induced adjustment measures might introduce distortions does not seem to have been recognized in previous work. For the time being we join previous authors in postulating $r_{ij} = 0$, and in due course (section 5) we present evidence to justify this assumption. We therefore adopt the simplified framework (2) in place of (1):

$$\begin{bmatrix} y_{11} & y_{12} & y_{13} \\ y_{21} & y_{22} & y_{23} \\ y_{31} & y_{32} & y_{33} \end{bmatrix} = \begin{bmatrix} x_{11}+c_{11}+d_{11} & x_{12}-d_{12}+e_{12} & x_{13}-d_{13}+e_{13} \\ x_{21}-d_{21} & x_{22}+c_{22}+d_{22} & x_{23}-d_{23} \\ x_{31} & x_{32} & x_{33} \end{bmatrix}. \quad (2)$$

This implies, of course: $y_i = x_i + c_{ii} + e_i$.

3. A SURVEY OF PREVIOUS STUDIES

The problem is to estimate the various flows distinguished on the right-hand side of (2). The most interesting magnitudes are the total sizes of creation, diversion, and external creation (i.e. c_{11}, d_{11}, e_1, c_{22}, and d_{22}), but there is also a certain interest in the geographical impact of diversion and external trade creation (i.e. d_{ij}, e_{ij}, for $j \neq i$).

Perhaps the most general distinction between alternative approaches to the estimation of integration-induced changes in trade flows is the *ex ante/ex post* dichotomy. *Ex ante* estimates are those that rely solely on the sort of *a priori* knowledge that a planner might command before integration commenced, while *ex post* estimates are based on some form of analysis of the historical experience of integration. The most important recent study to have utilized *ex ante* methods is that of Krause [3], who predicted the trade diversion that would be caused by the EEC and EFTA on the basis of assumptions about demand elasticities. This type of approach is of rather limited interest, however, because it does not provide a method of enabling one to improve previous estimates on the basis of new historical experience. For that, one must use *ex post* estimates. The major problem this poses is to construct an anti-monde (the X matrix). The published studies discussed below are grouped according to the assumptions they employ for this purpose.

(a) *Shares analyses*
An early attempt to measure the impact of the Common Market on trade was made by Major [4] in 1962. The method consisted of an inspection of changes in market shares over the period 1958–61. It concluded that the EEC did not have much effect during this early period.

Major's analysis of market shares was subsequently developed by Verdoorn and Meyer zu Schlochtern [5]. In terms of the present notation, their measure of the 'Apparent Effect of Integration', A_{ij}, in year t, was:

$$A_{ij} = \frac{(2 - y_{ij}^0/y_i^0 - y_{ij}^0/y_j^0)y_{ij}^t/y_{ij}^0}{(1 - y_{ij}^0/y_j^0)y_i^t/y_i^0 + (1 - y_{ij}^0/y_i^0)y_j^t/y_j^0}$$

where y_j^t = total exports of bloc j in year t and where year zero is a preintegration base year. If imports of i from j develop in a manner that is typical of i and j's total trade, then A_{ij} will approximate unity; while if this trade develops particularly rapidly (slowly), A_{ij} will exceed (fall short of) unity. It seems that, for example, $(A_{11} - 1)$ is interpreted as a measure of the trade creation attributable to the EEC. In Table 6·1 this has been taken as their estimate of c_{11}/x_{11}. Similarly, $(1 - A_{12})$ is taken to be a measure of EEC trade diversion from EFTA as a proportion of hypothetical EEC imports from EFTA (d_{12}/x_{12}). But it is not at all certain that this is a correct interpretation, and there are passages in their text that suggest these understate their actual estimates. More serious, the formula for A_{ij} does not seem to be based on any coherent theory of the anti-monde. And a high value for A_{ii} could in fact reflect trade diversion rather than creation. We would hazard the guess that A_{ij} gives a good ordinal ranking of the importance of integration effects in total but a poor cardinal measure of either creation or diversion.

Waelbroeck [6] used two methods to estimate the impact of the EEC on trade. The first method assumed that the total imports and exports of each bloc were unchanged by integration; it was acknowledged that this is strictly valid only if there is no trade creation. It was also assumed that in the anti-monde the world trade matrix would have changed through time only as a result of different rates of change in the imports and exports of different blocs, and an algorithm developed by Stone and Brown was used to calculate the implied X-matrix. The results are shown in Table 6·1 as though the only EEC effect were trade diversion, although Waelbroeck did not imply that this was the case. The obvious criticisms of the method are that it is strictly valid only in the limiting case where only diversion occurs, and that it does not enable one to distinguish creation from diversion. In addition, it treats imports and exports with a symmetry which is highly questionable.

A less formal, but (in the view of the authors) more valuable, approach is that originally pioneered by Lamfalussy [7]. He assumed that in the anti-monde all exporting blocs would have increased their share of the EEC market in the same proportion that they actually increased their share in third markets. This approach suggested that the effect of the EEC was negligible up to 1960, but indicated a small gain in the years 1960–2. The principal inadequacy of this analysis is the implicit assumption that the total volume of imports was un-

TABLE 6.1. Estimates of integration effects

Trade bloc	Year	Author	Source (footnote number)	Trade creation c_{11} ($b)	c_{11}/y_{11}	c_{11}/x_{11}	Trade diversion d_{11} ($b)	d_{11}/y_{11}	d_{11}/x_{11}	External creation e_1 ($b)	$(c_{11}+d_{11})/x_{11}$
EEC	1962	Lamfalussy	[7], p. 15								0·05
		Verdoorn and Schloctern	[5], p. 105		0·18	0·22	0·54	0·05	0·05		0·27
		Waelbroeck, Method I	[6], pp. 153–6								0·05
		,, Method II[a]	[6], p. 162								0·08
	1962/3	Trappeniers[a b]	[15], p. 153	1·01		0·23 (max)			0·14 (max)		0·14–0·23
	1963	Walter[a b]	[8], p. 86		0·07	0·08	0·49	0·04	0·05		0·43
	1964	Truman, aggregated[a] 1958 base	[9], p. 222	4·93	0·36	0·57	0	0	0	1·73	0·57
		aggregated[a] 1960 base	ditto	2·93	0·21	0·27	0	0	0	0·13	0·27
		disaggregated, 1958 base	[9], p. 224	4·54	0·33	0·51	0·18	0·01	0·02	1·76	0·53
		disaggregated, 1960 base	ditto	2·60	0·19	0·25	0·63	0·05	0·06	0·97	0·31
	1965	Balassa, aggregated[a b]	[12], p. 8	1·90	0·12	0·14	0	0	0	0·91	0·14
		disaggregated[a b]	ditto		0·12	0·15	1·13	0·07	0·09		0·24
	1966	Clavaux disaggregated[b]	[13], p. 612	5	0·29	0·41	0	0	0	1·06	0·41
	1968	Major and Hays updating of Truman: aggregated 1958 base	[11], p. 33	10·77	0·50	0·98	0	0	0	2·89	0·98
		aggregated 1960 base	Correspondence	7·96	0·37	0·60	0	0	0	0·85	0·60
				c_{22}	c_{22}/y_{22}	c_{22}/x_{22}	d_{22}	d_{22}/y_{22}	d_{22}/x_{22}		$(c_{22}+d_{22})/x_{22}$
EFTA	1962	Waelbroeck, Method I	[6], pp. 153–6	0·75	0·13	0·15	0·24	0·08	0·08		0·15
		Method II[a]	[6], p. 162	0·37	0·07	0·08	0·46	0·08	0·10		0·18
	1965	EFTA Secretariat	[14], p. 23								0·08

[a] Indicates total trade, rather than just manufactures.   [b] Indicates constant-price calculation.

affected by formation of the EEC, which amounts to treating the total impact on trade as diversion.

(b) *Import propensity*

Walter [8] calculated a value of x_{11} by assuming that each member's hypothetical import propensity from its partners in 1963 could have been inferred from the actual behaviour of its import propensity over the years 1953–7. A first calculation took the hypothetical 1963 propensity as equal to the average of that actually recorded in the years 1955–7. Since this assumed that the volume of imports can normally be expected to rise at the same rate as the volume of GNP, it is not surprising that this method yielded a very large EEC effect. A second calculation estimated the hypothetical 1963 propensity by extrapolating the 1953–7 trend in the propensity. This still gave a large EEC effect, this is recorded in Table 6·1. (It should be noted that Walter's calculation covered total trade rather than only manufactures.)

(c) *Share in total apparent consumption*

One of the more detailed analyses has been developed by Truman [9]. His fundamental assumption is that in the absence of the EEC the shares in total apparent consumption of domestic production, imports from the rest of the EEC, and imports from the rest of the world would have been constant. He found that the share of imports from non-EEC sources had risen (though not as much as that from EEC sources): this was interpreted as the result of external trade creation, itself the result of tariff-cutting by the former high-tariff countries to the level of the common external tariff, exceeding trade diversion, which occurred largely in the former low-tariff countries. The calculations were performed for individual member countries using both aggregate data for all manufacturing and data disaggregated by broad industry groups, and taking both 1958 and 1960 as base years to compare with the 'final' year of 1964. Truman's principal results are presented in Table 6·1.

The biggest doubt aroused by Truman's work is the basic assumption that the share of imports in total apparent consumption would remain unchanged in the absence of tariff changes. This is, seemingly, strongly at variance with the general belief that income-elasticities of demand for imports are typically well above unity. Truman himself challenges this belief, citing Maizels's study [10] which suggested that the long-run trend in the ratio of imports to domestic production is downward. In fact Truman's assumption is consistent with an aggregate income elasticity above one to the extent that imports constitute an above-average proportion of the total supply of income-elastic products. Despite this, there must remain a strong suspicion that his estimates for trade creation are biased upwards. This is especially true of external trade creation, since Truman attributes all the increase in share of extra-EEC imports to the levelling toward the common external tariff. In fact, the dollar liberalization of the late fifties and early sixties and the Dillon Round must have been significant contributory factors, and these are not genuine 'EEC effects'. But one should also note that his estimates of both trade diversion and external trade creation must be subject to an (equal) downward bias caused by offsetting changes within aggregates. Finally, Truman himself judges that the use of 1938 as base year tends to overstate trade creation as a result of the fact that 1958 was a recession year which depressed imports more than production, while the 1960 base may have underestimated trade creation. These considerations suggest that the most reliable of Truman's estimates are those using disaggregated data and 1960 as base year, but that even this basis substantially overestimates EEC-induced external trade creation.

A recent updating of some of Truman's calculations to 1968 has been done by Major and Hays [11]. Their work shows that the share of non-EEC sources in total apparent consumption has risen relatively little (from 7·2% to 7·9%) since 1964, which suggests that there has not been much additional external trade creation. In contrast, the share of EEC intra-trade has continued to rise strongly, from 6·2% in 1958 to 9·9% in 1964 and to 12·3% in 1968. If one follows Truman's assumption that the total rise in consumption shares can be attributed to the EEC, this provides two estimates for 1968 corresponding to Truman's aggregate estimates for 1964. These are shown in Table 6·1.

(d) *Constant import elasticities*

There are several ways of overcoming the fundamental defect of Truman's approach: the assumption that the share of imports in total apparent consumption would show no tendency to increase through time in the absence of customs unions. The first is to assume that the income elasticity of demand for imports would be constant through

125

time if there were no integration, even though it may exceed unity. This approach has been explored by Balassa [12] who calculated *ex post* income elasticities over the periods 1953–9 and 1959–65 for intra-EEC and extra-EEC imports. If these elasticities would have remained unchanged in the absence of integration, it follows that:

(i) A rise in the total import elasticity is evidence of trade creation.

(ii) A rise in the intra-elasticity offset by a fall in the extra-elasticity is evidence of trade diversion.

(iii) A rise in the extra-elasticity indicates external trade creation.

Balassa did not go beyond calculating the changes in income elasticities, so that it has been necessary to infer the trade changes shown in Table 6·1. The aggregate figure (for total trade, not manufactures) was calculated by assuming that the recorded rise in the intra-elasticity from 2·4 to 2·8 was caused by the Common Market, while the rise in the extra elasticity from 1·6 to 1·7 reflected external trade creation. The figure for manufactures was constructed from Balassa's elasticities for 1-digit SITC manufacturing industries by assuming that in each case the elasticity would have remained the same in the second period as it was in the first in the absence of the EEC.

It has been argued by Clavaux [13] that there are compelling reasons for believing that the procedure used by Balassa produces unduly conservative estimates. The main source of downward bias arises from the fact that the intra-EEC elasticity for the early 1950s was boosted by the liberalization of intra-European trade. On sub-dividing the period 1952–9 he found that the intra-EEC elasticity fell from 2·6 in the years 1952–5 to 1·9 during 1956–9. He argues that the latter is a more reasonable estimate of the elasticity that could have been expected in the absence of the EEC. That would imply that the trade creation attributable to the EEC needs to be revised upwards from Balassa's $2 thousand millions to some $5 thousand millions by 1966.

(e) *Extrapolation*

An alternative way of overcoming the central weakness in Truman's approach is to extrapolate the rate of change of share of imports in total apparent consumption that was observed prior to the start of integration in order to construct the anti-monde. This approach has been used by the EFTA Secretariat in order to form an estimate of the effects that EFTA has had on its members' trade [14]. This study disaggregated to a 2-digit SITC level and made free use of supplementary information regarding particular commodities, as well as changing the estimation technique where the standard procedure led to *a priori* absurd results. No doubt there are dangers of bias in such *ad hoc* procedures, but they would seem to be worth accepting in order to get the best possible estimate of the hypothetical position. A more serious criticism is that extrapolation of the import share change in the base period (1954–9) may overestimate X and therefore underestimate the effects of EFTA since the base period was one which included substantial liberalization. There is also the disadvantage that the method makes no attempt (other than *ad hoc* corrections) to normalize for exogenous changes that could be expected to alter past trends, e.g. changes in competitiveness that were not maintained throughout the period 1954–65. Nevertheless, the thoroughness of this study means that it provides a valuable addition to knowledge.

Extrapolation of a rather different sort was used by Trappeniers in an early study [15]. He extrapolated the rate of growth of the share of imports bought from partners, and took the excess of the actual over the extrapolated share as a measure of the EEC effect. About half the increased share of partners was estimated to be a consequence of the EEC. Unfortunately Trappeniers then erred in assuming that this implied that half the growth in imports from the EEC was an EEC effect, which is untrue because the bulk of the growth in imports from the EEC was paralleled by an increase from other sources. After correcting for this error, one reaches an estimated 14% EEC effect if there is no trade creation or 23% if there is no diversion, as against Trappeniers's figure of 65%, for 1962–3.

(f) *Import functions*

In principle a very appealing way of constructing the hypothetical position is to estimate a set of import functions, which could then be used to generate predictions of the X-matric. (This requires the assumption that the feedback effect of integration-induced trade on growth is a second-order effect that can be ignored, so that observed values of income can be inserted in the estimated functions.) Unfortunately, the only study that has exploited this possibility carries very little conviction. Kreinen [16] calculated import functions for the EEC and EFTA countries over the period 1953–61. The volumes of total (not manufactured) imports from partner and non-partner countries were made separate functions of real income and relative prices. The estimated equations were strikingly unsatisfactory: for example, no less than twenty-three of the fifty-one price elasticities have the wrong sign. And the use of data from as late as 1961 to estimate a hypothetical position is more than questionable (see Fig. 6·1 below). Most important, it is not clear that the price variable ('the ratio of the import price index to the domestic wholesale price index . . . in logarithm form', p. 275) was handled appropriately. Unless tariff changes were reflected in the import price index, it is likely that the effects of intra-European liberalization during the base period were absorbed in the income term. And if they were reflected there, then it would have been necessary to use separate import price indices for partners and non-partners in the post-integration period and to have calculated an anti-monde price index for imports from partners. Since there is no indication that this was done, Kreinin's results must be heavily discounted. For this reason they are not shown in Table 6·1. (All Kreinin's estimates are of negligible effects, under $100 million.)

(g) *Import and export elasticities*

Waelbroeck's second method [6] utilizes a formula originally developed by the Finnish economists Pöyhönen and Pulliainen to explain the world trade matrix. It is assumed that in the anti-monde exports from i to j would have increased in proportion to $Y_i^a Y_j^b$ (where Y is GNP) with constant tariffs. The empirical estimates used in applying the formula are $a = 0·84$ and $b = 0·75$. Mechanical application of this formula would have yielded an estimate of trade creation of some $4 thousand millions by 1962, but Waelbroeck argues that on the basis of previous trends some 75% of this creation would have occurred in the anti-monde. The figure shown in Table 6·1 is therefore only a quarter of the total estimate in the EEC case (although the whole estimate is included in the EFTA case).

4. A NEW SHARES ANALYSIS

It was argued in the previous section that little confidence can be placed in the results of the best-known existing share analysis [5], because of its apparent lack of a coherent theoretical basis. Nevertheless, the idea of using share performance to estimate what trade would have been in the absence of integration remains attractive.

This is partly because there is some evidence to indicate that, in the absence of preferential tariff changes, shares tend to display a useful degree of constancy [17]; and partly because the use of share performance automatically normalizes for changes in competitiveness and income. The present section therefore explores, from first principles, the possibilities of utilizing data on trade shares. We are mainly interested in estimating trade creation (c_{11} and c_{22}), total trade diversion (d_{11} and d_{22}), and the EEC's external creation (e_1). A subsidiary problem to which we return subsequently is whether we can also break down diversion and external creation between the two other blocs of suppliers.

In addition to the previous notation, define:

$u_{ij} = x_{ij}/x_i =$ (hypothetical) share of bloc j in i's imports in the anti-monde;

$v_{ij} = y_{ij}/y_i =$ actual share of bloc j in i's imports.

If one were able to estimate the hypothetical shares, u_{ij}, this would be a major step toward constructing the X-matrix. It would not suffice, because $x_i = y_i$ only if $c_{ii} + e_i = 0$; but the area of ignorance would be substantially narrowed. It is therefore natural to inquire as to how one might plausibly estimate u_{ij}.

We believe that the most promising hypothesis is that originally introduced by Lamfalussy [7]. According to this, the share performance of the jth supplier in markets where he neither gains nor loses preferential advantages gives a good indication of his hypothetical performance in markets which were in fact being affected by integration. In terms of the present analysis, the rest of the world provides a control which indicates what share performance would have been in EEC and EFTA markets if those two organizations had not been formed. For example, the actual change in v_{31} (the EEC's share in ROW imports) over some period indicates the simultaneous change in u_{11} (the share of intra-trade in EEC imports) that could have been expected in the anti-monde. A rough idea of the reliability of this hypothesis can be gained by inspecting Fig. 6·1, which compares the values of u_{11} predicted from v_{31} with actual values of v_{11}. Prior to 1961 the differences were relatively small and unsystematic; since then, of course, the effects of the EEC have led to a large and growing divergence.

A more systematic examination of the hypothesis is undertaken in Appendix 6·1. This appendix also compares the merits of different

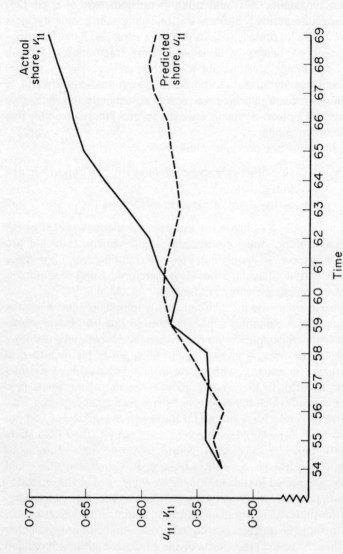

FIG. 6·1. The actual and predicted shares of intra-EEC imports in total EEC imports.

ways of formalizing the assumption that u_{ij} moves in a similar way to v_{3j}, on the basis of their success in predicting share changes between 1954 and 1959. Eventually two methods were selected. One is an *a priori* formula [18] for u_{ij}:

$$u_{ij}^t = v_{ij}^0 + \frac{v_{ij}^0(1-v_{ij}^0)}{v_{3j}^0(1-v_{3j}^0)} (v_{3j}^t - v_{3j}^0).$$ (3)

This formula ensures that the predicted gain in market share will be small if the previous market share was either very small (suggesting a low level of potential trade between the two blocs) or very large (suggesting that there is little scope for gaining share at the expense of other blocs). It has the disadvantage that the predicted shares may not sum to unity, but this was overcome by multiplying the u_{ij} given by (3) by $1/\sum_j u_{ij}$, so as to constrain the predicted shares to sum to one.

The second method of predicting u_{ij} was to regress u_{ij} on v_{3j} over the years 1954–9, and then to use the resulting equations to predict the u_{ij} during the 1960s. It was again decided to constrain $\sum_j u_{ij}$ to sum to unity.

A third set of calculations were also performed, based on the assumption that in the absence of integration the shares would have remained as they were in 1959 throughout the 1960s. This is a somewhat crude hypothesis, but it provides a check that our results are not due to spurious fluctuations in third markets or to supply constraints [19].

As already noted, the construction of the U-matrix does not enable one to proceed directly to the estimation of trade creation and diversion. In the EEC case, one has two independent equations that will assist in the estimation of c_{11}, d_{11}, and e_1:

$$y_{11} = x_{11} + c_{11} + d_{11} = u_{11} x_1 + c_{11} + d_{11};$$ (4)

$$y_1 = x_1 + c_{11} + e_1.$$ (5)

These two equations contain a fourth unknown, x_1. The matrix equation (2) yields two further equations containing x_1, d_{1j}, and e_{1j}, but since these introduce a further two unknowns (the geographical breakdown of diversion and external creation) they are of no assistance in solving the primary problem. A solution therefore requires the introduction of two further assumptions or relationships.

We believe that the best available way of completing the system is to draw on existing estimates of the *relative* size of creation, diversion, and external creation. This has the disadvantage that our method is unable to cast new light on this important aspect of the problem. Hence the method's value is confined to estimating the total size of integration effects, for a given assumption about their composition. At this stage we simply specify that we close the system by postulating:

$$d_{11} = \alpha c_{11}, \tag{6}$$

$$e_1 = \beta c_{11}. \tag{7}$$

Substitution in (4) and (5) then yields:

$$c_{11} = \frac{y_{11} - u_{11} y_1}{1 + \alpha - u_{11}(1 + \beta)}. \tag{8}$$

(6) and (7) can then be solved for d_{11} and e_1.

The two independent equations for EFTA are:

$$y_{22} = x_{22} + c_{22} + d_{22} = u_{22} x_2 + c_{22} + d_{22}, \qquad y_2 = x_2 + c_{22}.$$

These contain only three unknowns (c_{22}, d_{22}, and x_2), so it is only necessary to introduce one additional assumption. We again select the size of diversion relative to creation:

$$d_{22} = \gamma c_{22}.$$

This enables one to solve for c_{22} (and hence d_{22}):

$$c_{22} = \frac{y_{22} - u_{22} y_2}{1 + \gamma - u_{22}}. \tag{9}$$

Having thus solved the problems of primary interest, one may proceed to the secondary problem of splitting the diversion and external creation caused by one bloc between the other two blocs. This is simple in the EFTA case, since there is no external creation. Since x_2 is determined simultaneously with c_{22} ($x_2 = y_2 - c_{22}$), (2) gives immediately:

$$d_{21} = u_{21} x_2 - y_{21}, \tag{10}$$

$$d_{23} = u_{23} x_2 - y_{23}. \tag{11}$$

Similar extraction of the EEC equations from the first row of (2) yields only:

$$d_{12} - e_{12} = u_{12} x_1 - y_{12}; \tag{12}$$

$$d_{13} - e_{13} = u_{13} x_1 - y_{13}. \tag{13}$$

An additional assumption would therefore be required to obtain the geographical breakdown of gross trade diversion and external trade creation for the EEC [20]. The results given by (12) and (13) are, however, adequate for the purpose of relaxing the assumption that $r_{ij} = 0$, which is a subject taken up at the end of the next section.

5. THE RESULTS OF THE NEW ANALYSIS

The foregoing analysis was initially applied by using the data on exports of manufactures periodically published (for example) by the Department of Trade and Industry [21] and by the UN [22]. While in any one of these publications the series contained are, so far as possible, on consistent definitions and coverage and are also without any significant element of estimation, the extraction of a long series spanning a period from 1954 to 1969 from a sequence of publications reveals important discontinuities. The analysis was therefore repeated using a specially constructed series prepared by the Department of Trade and Industry. This series is presented and briefly discussed in Appendix 6·3. (Use of the original uncorrected data results in somewhat lower estimates of integration effects, but the general picture is not changed.) The base year (year zero) used in applying (3) was 1959.

We first present (Table 6·2) the hypothetical shares given by our two approaches for the years 1954–69. This will permit the reader to insert his own preferred assumptions about the relative importance of creation and diversion, rather than being tied to our assumptions. Examination of Table 6·2 reveals that the hypothetical shares of both EEC and EFTA intra-trade began lagging behind their actual shares from 1961 on. The effect grew fairly steadily and is pronounced in recent years.

In order to translate these share changes into estimates of creation and diversion, it is necessary to select values for α, β, and γ. The only studies that have attempted the necessary sub-division of integration effects are the disaggregated studies of Truman and Balassa (for α and β) and that of the EFTA Secretariat (for γ). Bearing in mind the probable overestimation of external trade creation in Truman's results (see section 3 above), the orders of magnitude suggested by these studies are:

Truman: $\alpha = \beta = 0.25$,
Balassa: $\alpha = \beta = 0.5$,
EFTA Secretariat: $\gamma = 1.25$.

TABLE 6·2. Predicted and actual shares 1954–69

Series		1954 base						1959 base									
		1954	1955	1956	1957	1958	1959	1960	1961	1962	1963	1964	1965	1966	1967	1968	1969
u_{11} Formula	ROW (3)	0·526	0·535	0·527	0·539	0·563	0·571	0·580	0·580	0·571	0·567	0·569	0·575	0·580	0·592	0·595	0·589
v_{11} Actual	ROW (3)		0·542	0·543	0·539	0·543	0·573	0·569	0·585	0·594	0·615	0·635	0·655	0·663	0·670	0·679	0·687
u_{11} Regression	ROW (T)	0·473	0·488	0·486	0·491	0·495	0·519	0·511	0·509	0·502	0·499	0·500	0·503	0·506	0·512	0·514	0·510
v_{11} Actual	ROW (T)	0·298	0·292	0·288	0·277	0·273	0·269	0·518	0·536	0·549	0·571	0·590	0·602	0·605	0·613	0·618	0·625
u_{12} Formula	ROW (3)	0·269	0·280	0·286	0·281	0·274	0·268	0·262	0·260	0·258	0·260	0·245	0·241	0·234	0·222	0·214	0·217
v_{12} Regression	ROW (T)	0·176	0·252	0·256	0·256	0·250	0·243	0·240	0·242	0·237	0·226	0·215	0·206	0·198	0·189	0·179	0·174
v_{12} Actual	ROW (T)	0·258	0·173	0·185	0·184	0·165	0·159	0·242	0·239	0·237	0·237	0·227	0·225	0·220	0·212	0·208	0·209
u_{13} Formula	ROW (3)		0·178	0·171	0·180	0·183	0·158	0·218	0·222	0·219	0·210	0·200	0·191	0·180	0·172	0·163	0·158
v_{13} Actual	ROW (3)		0·260	0·258	0·253	0·255	0·239	0·158	0·160	0·171	0·174	0·186	0·184	0·186	0·186	0·191	0·195
u_{13} Regression	ROW (T)	0·517	0·526	0·519	0·530	0·554	0·563	0·191	0·173	0·169	0·159	0·150	0·139	0·139	0·141	0·142	0·139
v_{13} Actual	ROW (T)	0·443	0·514	0·529	0·536	0·551	0·556	0·247	0·252	0·261	0·264	0·273	0·272	0·275	0·275	0·278	0·281
u_{21} Formula	ROW (3)	0·316	0·440	0·454	0·470	0·488	0·487	0·264	0·242	0·232	0·219	0·210	0·207	0·215	0·219	0·219	0·217
v_{21} Actual	ROW (3)	0·271	0·310	0·306	0·295	0·290	0·286	0·563	0·563	0·554	0·549	0·551	0·558	0·563	0·576	0·579	0·572
u_{21} Regression	ROW (T)	0·167	0·293	0·293	0·285	0·288	0·283	0·541	0·553	0·549	0·537	0·517	0·515	0·503	0·481	0·480	0·484
v_{21} Actual	ROW (T)		0·251	0·251	0·250	0·255	0·248	0·491	0·485	0·471	0·473	0·461	0·465	0·466	0·473	0·474	0·468
u_{22} Formula	ROW (3)	0·287	0·164	0·176	1·075	0·156	0·151	0·480	0·491	0·487	0·473	0·457	0·454	0·440	0·425	0·419	0·427
v_{22} Regression	ROW (T)	0·265	0·192	0·178	0·179	0·161	0·161	0·277	0·275	0·273	0·274	0·260	0·255	0·248	0·235	0·227	0·230
v_{22} Actual	ROW (T)	0·236	0·309	0·295	0·280	0·256	0·265	0·262	0·281	0·289	0·303	0·302	0·311	0·323	0·336	0·332	0·345
u_{23} Formula	ROW (3)	0·292	0·274	0·264	0·274	0·301	0·310	0·242	0·238	0·235	0·234	0·223	0·221	0·215	0·208	0·203	0·204
v_{23} Actual	ROW (3)	0·260	0·244	0·235	0·244	0·269	0·277	0·232	0·249	0·256	0·267	0·267	0·274	0·283	0·297	0·290	0·304
u_{23} Regression	ROW (T)		0·287	0·280	0·270	0·271	0·269	0·160	0·162	0·173	0·161	0·189	0·187	0·189	0·189	0·194	0·198
v_{23} Actual	ROW (T)		0·256	0·249	0·240	0·242	0·240	0·197	0·166	0·162	0·300	0·181	0·175	0·174	0·182	0·188	0·170
u_{23} Regression	ROW (T)	0·443	0·439	0·456	0·456	0·428	0·420	0·267	0·277	0·294	0·261	0·316	0·314	0·319	0·319	0·323	0·328
v_{23} Actual	ROW (T)	0·504	0·500	0·516	0·516	0·489	0·482	0·288	0·259	0·257	0·298	0·276	0·272	0·277	0·279	0·291	0·269
v_{31} Actual	ROW (3)							0·317	0·316	0·304	0·255	0·295	0·302	0·306	0·317	0·318	0·310
v_{21} Actual	ROW (3)							0·281	0·275	0·261	0·257	0·251	0·256	0·257	0·266	0·267	0·260
v_{22} Actual	ROW (3)							0·264	0·261	0·257	0·220	0·241	0·237	0·230	0·219	0·210	0·212
v_{23} Actual	ROW (3)							0·233	0·227	0·221	0·440	0·204	0·201	0·193	0·183	0·176	0·177
v_{32} Actual	ROW (3)							0·419	0·423	0·440	0·525	0·464	0·460	0·464	0·464	0·472	0·478
v_{33} Actual	ROW (3)							0·486	0·498	0·518		0·545	0·543	0·550	0·551	0·556	0·562

TABLE 6·3. *New estimates of integration effects, 1960–9 ($ billions or ratio)*

Year, area, and assumptions	Method 1: Formula D, ROW (3) to ROW (inc. OSA)					Method 2: Linear regression, ROW (T) to ROW (inc. OSA)					Method 3: $u_{ij}^{t}=v_{ij}^{59}$, ROW (T) to ROW (inc. OSA)				
	c_{11}	c_{11}/x_{11}	$d_{11}(=e_1)$	d_{11}/x_{11}	$\frac{c_{11}+d_{11}}{x_{11}}$	c_{11}	c_{11}/x_{11}	$d_{11}(=e_1)$	d_{11}/x_{11}	$\frac{c_{11}-d_{11}}{x_{11}}$	c_{11}	c_{11}/x_{11}	$d_{11}(=e_1)$	d_{11}/x_{11}	$\frac{c_{11}+d_{11}}{x_{11}}$
1960 EEC: $\alpha = \beta = 0.25$	—	—	—	—	—	—	—	—	—	—	—	—	—	—	—
1961	0.1	0.02	—	—	0.02	0.7	0.09	0.2	0.02	0.11	0.4	0.06	0.1	0.01	0.07
1962	0.7	0.08	0.2	0.02	0.10	1.3	0.17	0.3	0.04	0.21	0.9	0.10	0.2	0.03	0.13
1963	1.7	0.17	0.4	0.04	0.21	2.3	0.27	0.6	0.07	0.34	1.8	0.19	0.4	0.05	0.24
1964	2.6	0.25	0.7	0.06	0.31	3.3	0.38	0.8	0.09	0.47	2.7	0.27	0.7	0.07	0.34
1965	3.4	0.31	0.9	0.08	0.39	4.0	0.39	1.0	0.10	0.49	3.5	0.32	0.9	0.08	0.40
1966	4.2	0.32	1.0	0.08	0.40	4.6	0.41	1.2	0.11	0.49	4.1	0.33	1.0	0.08	0.41
1967	4.2	0.34	1.2	0.10	0.44	4.9	0.42	1.2	0.10	0.51	4.7	0.37	1.4	0.09	0.46
1968	5.3	0.35	1.3	0.09	0.44	6.0	0.42	1.5	0.11	0.53	5.8	0.40	1.7	0.10	0.50
1969	7.7	0.42	1.9	0.11	0.53	8.3	0.48	2.1	0.12	0.60	7.8	0.44	2.0	0.11	0.55
1960 EEC: $\alpha = \beta = 0.5$	—	—	—	—	—	—	—	—	—	—	—	—	—	—	—
1961	0.1	0.01	0.1	0.01	0.02	0.6	0.08	0.3	0.04	0.12	0.4	0.05	0.2	0.02	0.07
1962	0.6	0.07	0.3	0.03	0.10	1.1	0.14	0.6	0.07	0.21	0.7	0.09	0.4	0.04	0.13
1963	1.4	0.14	0.7	0.07	0.21	1.9	0.22	1.0	0.11	0.33	1.5	0.15	0.7	0.08	0.23
1964	2.2	0.21	1.1	0.11	0.32	2.8	0.29	1.4	0.15	0.44	2.3	0.22	1.1	0.11	0.33
1965	2.9	0.26	1.4	0.13	0.39	3.4	0.33	1.7	0.16	0.49	2.9	0.27	1.5	0.13	0.40
1966	3.5	0.29	1.7	0.14	0.43	3.8	0.33	1.9	0.16	0.49	3.4	0.28	1.7	0.14	0.42
1967	3.5	0.27	1.7	0.13	0.40	4.1	0.34	2.1	0.17	0.51	3.9	0.31	2.1	0.16	0.47
1968	4.4	0.29	2.2	0.15	0.44	5.0	0.35	2.5	0.18	0.53	4.8	0.33	2.4	0.17	0.50
1969	6.4	0.35	3.2	0.18	0.53	6.9	0.40	3.5	0.20	0.60	6.5	0.37	3.3	0.18	0.55
1960 EFTA: $\gamma = 1.25$	—	—	—	—	—	—	—	—	—	—	—	—	—	—	—
1961	0.1	0.01	0.1	0.01	0.02	0.1	0.01	0.1	0.03	0.05	0.1	0.02	0.1	0.02	0.04
1962	0.1	0.03	0.3	0.04	0.07	0.1	0.02	0.2	0.05	0.11	0.1	0.04	0.2	0.05	0.09
1963	0.2	0.05	0.4	0.07	0.12	0.2	0.05	0.3	0.07	0.16	0.2	0.04	0.3	0.05	0.09
1964	0.3	0.08	0.5	0.11	0.19	0.3	0.07	0.4	0.10	0.23	0.3	0.07	0.4	0.07	0.12
1965	0.4	0.11	0.8	0.14	0.25	0.5	0.12	0.8	0.16	0.27	0.5	0.10	0.6	0.09	0.16
1966	0.6	0.16	1.1	0.20	0.36	0.6	0.16	1.1	0.22	0.36	0.6	0.13	0.9	0.13	0.23
1967	0.9	0.23	1.3	0.28	0.51	0.9	0.22	1.2	0.27	0.49	0.9	0.20	1.1	0.11	0.27
1968	1.0	0.24	1.3	0.30	0.54	0.9	0.22	1.2	0.27	0.49	0.9	0.20	1.3	0.15	0.30
1969	1.3	0.26	1.6	0.33	0.59	1.2	0.25	1.6	0.32	0.57	1.2	0.27	1.5	0.15	0.35
(area 2 labels)	c_{22}	c_{22}/x_{22}	d_{22}	d_{22}/x_{22}	$\frac{c_{22}+d_{22}}{x_{22}}$	c_{22}	c_{22}/x_{22}	d_{22}	d_{22}/x_{22}	$\frac{c_{22}+d_{22}}{x_{22}}$	c_{22}	c_{22}/x_{22}	d_{22}	d_{22}/x_{22}	$\frac{c_{22}+d_{22}}{x_{22}}$

Table 6·3 shows the estimates of creation and diversion that result from inserting these values, and the figures for u_{ij} from Table 6·2, into equations (8) and (9). So far as the EEC is concerned, the first thing to note is that the 'total EEC effect on intra-trade' (i.e. $(c_{11} + d_{11})/x_{11}$) is virtually unaffected by the values chosen for α and β, so long as they are assumed to be equal. Second, and equally reassuring, is that the results do not vary greatly with the chosen method of estimating hypothetical shares: the total EEC effect only varies between 53% and 60% in 1969. One may therefore use the *a priori* preferred approach, Method 1, without the fear that the results would be drastically different if one had chosen some alternative method. Unfortunately there is a third consideration that is not illustrated in Table 6·3: the fact that the total EEC effect is fairly sensitive to *differential* changes in α and β. (Increases in α tend to decrease the total EEC effect and increases in β to raise it.) For example, a value for α of 0·5 and for β of 0·25 reduces the total EEC effect for 1969 estimated by Method 1 from 53 to 39%. Values of $\alpha = 0·25$ and $\beta = 0$ give a total EEC effect of 36%. Given the lack of evidence that diversion has greatly outweighed external creation, it is difficult to attach much weight to these lower estimates. But there must remain a significant element of doubt until such time as a more satisfactory study of the relative sizes of the different EEC effects becomes available. (The EFTA Secretariat are working on an extension of their published study that will also cover the EEC, so this may well solve the problem in due course.)

In contrast to the EEC case, the EFTA results do depend significantly on the method of prediction that is chosen. Specifically, the assumption that shares would have remained unchanged in the absence of integration yields markedly lower estimated integration effects, since EFTA was tending to lose ground in ROW markets during the 1960s. The first two methods take this as evidence that EFTA's share of EFTA markets would also have declined in the absence of integration, while the third method ignores it. EFTA experience during the 1950s, and the superior performance of Method 1 to Method 3 reported in Appendix 6·1, suggest that the first approach is to be preferred. Method 1 is again adopted as the preferred estimate: the similarity of the results yielded by Method 2 is reassuring.

Table 6·3 does not show the effect of varying γ, because the published evidence only provides a single estimate. However, we have recently learned of the *preliminary* results of the revised EFTA Secretariat study [23]. The latest estimates indicate a larger EFTA effect in 1965, principally as a result of more trade creation, so that γ may be close to one. This would imply a total EFTA effect, $(c_{22} + d_{22})/x_{22}$, of 26%, only 1% larger than that with $\gamma = 1.25$. The preliminary results for 1967 suggest that γ may have been falling over time, perhaps to a figure in the region of 0.7. That would imply a total EFTA effect of 53%, as against the 51% with $\gamma = 1.25$. Since the size of the total EFTA effect is so insensitive to large changes in y, one may place reasonable confidence in the results in the final column of Table 6.3.

TABLE 6.4. *The geographical breakdown of net trade diversion ($ millions)*

| Year | EEC, $\alpha = \beta$ | | | | EFTA, $\gamma = 1.25$ | | | |
| | Method 1 | | Method 2 | | Method 1 | | Method 2 | |
	$d_{12}-e_{12}$	$d_{13}-e_{13}$	$d_{12}-e_{12}$	$d_{13}-e_{13}$	d_{21}	d_{23}	d_{21}	d_{23}
1960	—	—	280	−290	—	—	—	—
1961	210	−210	60	−60	90	−50	−110	190
1962	120	−120	−70	80	10	100	−260	420
1963	100	−80	−140	140	50	150	−190	460
1964	−170	170	−320	320	310	60	−90	520
1965	−240	240	−280	280	430	110	−10	580
1966	−280	280	−130	150	640	130	190	590
1967	−250	250	−130	100	1170	−50	560	530
1968	−310	310	0	0	1340	−90	760	410
1969	−340	380	70	−80	1230	370	470	1090

At the end of section 4, equations (10) to (13) showed how it should be possible to utilize the hypothetical shares to estimate the geographical breakdown of net trade diversion. The results of solving these equations with the figures presented in Tables 6.2 and 6.3 are shown in Table 6.4 So far as the EEC is concerned, the *assumption* that $\alpha = \beta$ implies that net trade diversion for EFTA and the ROW together is zero; what one bloc gains, the other loses, and the only problems are to decide which bloc is the gainer and what is the extent of its gain. According to the results of Method 1, EFTA was the loser in the early years but became a substantial net gainer from the mid-1960s onwards. According to Method 2, EFTA's early losses were converted to a gain during the mid-1960s, which has recently been lost again to the ROW. The results for EFTA are even less consistent.

Not only do both methods yield negative trade diversion in some years (which is implausible with EFTA since there is no external trade creation), but Method 2 contradicts the conventional wisdom that the EEC has been the major sufferer from EFTA-induced trade diversion, while Method 1 supports it. The inconsistency of these results is not such as to inspire confidence, and it would seem impossible to utilize them at the present juncture.

It remains to consider whether significant distortions in the estimates might be produced by the repercussions of attempts to neutralize the balance-of-payments impacts of integration. The previous section concluded that diversion and external creation had been roughly equal for the EEC, so that their net effect on the balance of payments was zero. Hence both the EEC and the ROW experienced a payments change only to the extent that they suffered from the effects of EFTA diversion. Clearly these effects were proportionately far smaller than they were for EFTA, so one may concentrate on studying the effects on EFTA itself. According to our estimate, EFTA's trade balance in 1969 was something over $1 billion stronger than it would have been in the anti-monde. Suppose that $400 millions of this increase were neutralized by lesser exports, $400 millions by higher imports, and the remainder by capital movements or reserve changes. If the effects on exports and imports were distributed in proportion to the value of trade with each region, r_{22} would be close to zero since the increased imports would cancel out the fall in exports. The value of r_{22} would be about $- \$200$ millions. This would mean that $x_{32} > y_{32}$, so that the use of v_{32} in predicting u_{22} would bias u_{22} down and therefore bias c_{22} and d_{22} upwards. But the effect is quantitatively trivial: substitution of the amended value of x_{32} merely increased u_{32} from 0·212 to 0·213. Since this is the largest repercussion that one could expect to find, one may safely follow the custom of ignoring balance-of-payments reactions.

6. THE STYLIZED FACTS

It is of interest to compare the results of our method shown in Table 6·3 with those of previous studies that were shown in Table 6·1. (The following comparison is confined to $(c_{11} + d_{11})/x_{11}$ and to the results of Method 1.) A noticeable EEC effect seems to have first appeared in 1962, with the Verdoorn–Schloctern study giving substantially higher estimates than the 5 to 10% of the other methods: the latter

would seem to be more reliable in view of the criticisms of the
Verdoorn approach discussed in section 3. By 1963 the effect seems
to have grown substantially – to around 20%, if one ignores Walter's
very high estimate of 43%. This is in fact the most puzzling discrepancy, since there is no obvious explanation. It is true that Walter
worked in volume terms, whereas our analysis is conducted in value
terms, and he included total trade, whereas our analysis is restricted
to manufactures. In view of the small movements in the prices of
internationally traded manufactures during the 1960s, it is difficult
to attach much significance to the first of these differences; and since
the common agricultural policy had not been launched by 1963,
there is no obvious reason as to why the second difference should
produce a larger EEC effect. This discrepancy therefore remains an
unsolved problem. Fortunately there is much better agreement with
the other studies. Our estimate agrees with Truman's preferred estimate of 31% in 1964. Balassa's results appear unduly conservative,
which accords with the *a priori* expectation. Clavaux's figure is in
close agreement. The figures produced by Major and Hay's updating
of Truman's estimates are far too large, but this is to be expected in
view of the ever-growing upward bias implicit in Truman's assumption that the share of imports in total apparent consumption would
not grow in the absence of integration.

Despite the vast range of variation in the results of published
studies, the previous paragraph suggests that there is only one study
(that of Walter) whose inconsistency with our results is at all disturbing. Once allowance is made for their inadequacies, the other
studies tend to confirm our own results. Hence we conclude that
intra-EEC trade in 1969 was something like 50% greater than it
would have been if the EEC had not been created. Most of this rise
appears to be attributable to trade creation rather than diversion,
while the harm done to other countries' exports by diversion was
largely offset by positive external trade creation.

Although our figure of a 25% EFTA effect in 1965 is greater than
the 18% of the EFTA Secretariat reported in Table 6·1, it is probable
that the difference will be much reduced when the revised study by
the EFTA Secretariat becomes available. If, as expected, this leads to
an increase in the ratio of creation to diversion in EFTA, one would
expect to end up with a total EFTA effect rather higher than the
EEC effect, say 60%, as a result of a higher rate of trade diversion
coupled with a rate of trade creation only marginally less.

139

APPENDIX 6·1: ALTERNATIVE FORMULATIONS
OF THE SHARE HYPOTHESIS

The hypothesis to be formalized is that the share performance of the jth supplier in markets where there are no preferential tariff changes gives a good indication of the jth supplier's hypothetical performance in markets that were in fact being affected by integration. Four formulae were considered.

$$u_{ij}^t = \frac{v_{3j}^t}{v_{3j}^0} \, v_{ij}^0. \tag{1}$$

This says that if the actual proportion of ROW imports supplied by bloc j rose by 10% of its initial level (e.g. from 0·2 to 0·22), then the hypothetical proportion of i's imports supplied by j would also have risen by 10% of its initial value. A disadvantage of the formula is that it gives implausible results when v_{ij} is large, since there is then little scope for j to expand its sales in the ith market.

$$\frac{(1-u_{ij}^t)}{(1-v_{ij}^0)} = \frac{(1-v_{3j}^t)}{(1-v_{3j}^0)}. \tag{2}$$

This says that if bloc j gains 10% of the potential market share it could gain in the ROW, one would also expect it to gain 10% of that part of the bloc i market that it does not already supply. This rectifies the defect in formula (1), but at the cost of giving implausible values when v_{3j} is small. For example, suppose that j initially had only 1% of the ROW market. A doubling of that market share would suggest a stronger performance than implied by the gain of 1·01% of the potential market, which is what formula (2) takes to be the relevant figure.

$$u_{ij}^t = v_{ij}^0 + (v_{3j}^t - v_{3j}^0). \tag{3}$$

A possible compromise between (1) and (2) is to assume that a gain of 1% of the absolute market share in the ROW would indicate a hypothetical gain of 1% of the absolute market share in bloc i.

$$u_{ij}^t = v_{ij}^0 + \frac{v_{ij}^0(1-v_{ij}^0)}{v_{3j}^0(1-v_{3j}^0)} \, (v_{3j}^t - v_{3j}^0). \tag{4}$$

This is an alternative compromise between formulae (1) and (2). It involves weighing the observed change in share in ROW imports so as to reduce the predicted share in the ith bloc's imports if v_{ij} is either very large or very small, while magnifying the effect if v_{3j} is either very large or very small.

Of these four formulae, only (3) gives predicted shares which in general sum to unity. It was therefore decided to see whether constraining the shares given by the other formulae so that they summed to one would improve performance. This was found to result in a definite improvement, so all shares were constrained.

The data used are shown in Appendix 6·3. There is a certain amount of freedom about how one should choose to interpret 'the ROW'. In particular, it seems reasonable to consider excluding OSA imports from ROW imports, on the grounds that the Sterling Area is a former preferential trading bloc which was rapidly eroding during the period under study. However, data limitations prevent one extracting the OSA unless one also restricts the coverage of ROW exports to those originating from the U.S.A., Canada, and Japan (designated 'ROW (3)').

Hypothetical shares were calculated by all four methods for 1958 and 1959 on a 1954 base (see Table 6·5). There were three objects in mind in studying how well the technique would have performed if it had been used to predict trade developments in the 1950s. The first was to assess whether the general approach is of significant predictive value. The second was to determine which of the four formulae gave the best predictions. The third was to assess which of the three alternative data sets enabled the best predictions to be made. (The first data set takes ROW (3) as the ROW for purposes of exports and includes the OSA in ROW on the import side; the second takes ROW (3) on the export side but excludes OSA imports from the analysis altogether; the third takes the total ROW on both export and import sides.)

In order to answer these questions it is helpful to develop measures of the size of the prediction errors. Two *ad hoc* measures were devised. The first was called the 'proportionate error', PE, and is defined as $(u_{ij}^t/v_{ij}^t - 1) \times 100$. The second was called the 'absolute error', AE, and is defined as $(u_{ij}^t - v_{ij}^t) \times 100$. The absolute values of these two measures were summed over the six u_{ij} cases involved in each prediction (i.e. each application of one of the formulae to a particular data set for a particular year). The results are displayed in Table 6·5 in the rows labelled 'sum of $|PE|$' and 'sum of $|AE|$'.

To assess whether the approach is of significant predictive value it is possible to observe that the errors did not seem to be unreason-

TABLE 6·5. A comparison between actual and predicted share performance

Data set		1954 v_{IJ}	1958 A	B	C	D	v_{IJ}	1959 A	B	C	D
ROW (3) to ROW	u_{11}	0·526	0·572	0·560	0·562	0·563	0·573	0·582	0·570	0·571	0·571
(inc. OSA)	u_{12}	0·298	0·265	0·283	0·277	0·273	0·268	0·260	0·283	0·276	0·269
	u_{13}	0·176	0·163	0·157	0·161	0·165	0·158	0·158	0·146	0·153	0·159
	u_{21}	0·517	0·563	0·551	0·553	0·554	0·556	0·573	0·561	0·562	0·563
	u_{22}	0·316	0·282	0·301	0·295	0·290	0·283	0·276	0·302	0·293	0·286
	u_{23}	0·167	0·155	0·148	0·152	0·156	0·161	0·150	0·137	0·144	0·151
Sum of $|PE|$		35·2	27·5	33·2	23·0	18·2	53·1	17·0	35·4	21·9	9·9
Sum of $|AE|$		11·6	8·2	7·8	6·2	4·9	17·3	5·2	7·8	4·8	2·4
ROW (3) to ROW	u_{11}	0·526	0·552	0·562	0·554	0·549	0·573	0·557	0·581	0·566	0·555
(exc. OSA)	u_{12}	0·298	0·290	0·310	0·301	0·296	0·268	0·295	0·324	0·310	0·304
	u_{13}	0·176	0·158	0·128	0·145	0·155	0·158	0·148	0·094	0·125	0·141
	u_{21}	0·517	0·543	0·553	0·545	0·540	0·556	0·547	0·573	0·557	0·545
	u_{22}	0·316	0·307	0·329	0·319	0·313	0·283	0·313	0·343	0·328	0·321
	u_{23}	0·167	0·150	0·118	0·136	0·147	0·161	0·140	0·084	0·116	0·134
Sum of $|PE|$		35·2	36·1	88·0	63·3	43·8	53·1	44·7	134·8	82·9	59·5
Sum of $|AE|$		11·6	8·8	16·4	13·8	10·6	17·3	11·3	28·2	17·3	14·7
ROW (T) to ROW	u_{11}	0·473	0·518	0·504	0·506	0·510	0·519	0·529	0·513	0·514	0·519
(inc. OSA)	u_{12}	0·269	0·240	0·255	0·250	0·246	0·243	0·226	0·255	0·249	0·244
	u_{13}	0·258	0·241	0·241	0·244	0·243	0·239	0·235	0·232	0·237	0·237
	u_{21}	0·443	0·487	0·473	0·475	0·480	0·487	0·497	0·482	0·484	0·490
	u_{22}	0·271	0·243	0·256	0·252	0·248	0·248	0·240	0·256	0·251	0·246
	u_{23}	0·287	0·269	0·270	0·272	0·271	0·265	0·263	0·261	0·265	0·264
Sum of $|PE|$		40·8	24·1	22·6	16·7	19·5	55·1	55·6	44·1	39·1	46·0
Sum of $|AE|$		13·6	7·3	5·8	5·4	6·1	18·0	19·6	15·1	12·0	16·2

ably large and that there was no indication that they were systematically increasing as the year being predicted was pushed further back from the base year (see Fig. 6·1). A more systematic procedure is to calculate the errors that would have occurred if one had adopted the naive hypothesis that 1954 shares could have been expected to remain unchanged. This hypothesis produced errors that are shown in the appropriate rows of Table 6·1 and in the columns headed 'v_{ij}'. It will be found that the naive hypothesis produced unambiguously larger errors in sixteen of the twenty-four cases, while in a further three cases the comparison was ambiguous since the PE and AE comparisons showed opposite results. There were five cases where the naive hypothesis performed better. Since the naive method is itself one that can be defended as a plausible first approximation (see section 4), these results are not discouraging.

Of the four formulae, it is clear that (2) performed least well. There is little to choose between the other three, but (4) appears to be marginally preferable. Since this also appears the most attractive on *a priori* grounds, it was adopted for the work reported in the main paper.

Of the three data sets, the first gave the best predictions. The work reported in the text therefore restricts the ROW on the export side to the three major countries of the U.S.A., Canada, and Japan, but the OSA countries were not extracted from the ROW on the import side. Our work did not suggest that the results are particularly sensitive to the data set employed.

Regression analysis
An alternative way of formalizing the hypothesis that u_{ij} varies with v_{3j} is to calculate a regression equation using the data from the years 1954–9. Each equation is based on only six observations, which means that the results cannot command great confidence and are quite likely to be less reliable than those based on the *a priori* approach; but, at the very least, this alternative approach provides a useful check.

Six sets of equations were calculated, based on the three sets of data and utilizing both log and linear forms. The results are shown in Table 6·6. The values of the various statistical measures calculated did not suggest that there was a lot to choose between the alternative specifications. In fact the linear regression employing data from ROW (T) to ROW (inc. OSA) was chosen, partly on the grounds that

TABLE 6.6. Alternative regression equations

Data set	Dependent variable	Log regressions						Linear regressions						Independent variable
		Constant term	Coefficient of y_{3j}	SE	t-value	Correlation coefficient	SE estimate	Constant term	Coefficient of y_{3j}	SE	t-value	Correlation coefficient	SE estimate	
ROW (3) to ROW (inc. OSA)	y_{11}	−0.087	0.322	0.130	2.47	0.78	0.009	0.369	0.624	2.248	2.52	0.78	0.011	y_{31}
	y_{12}	−0.084	0.841	0.312	2.69	0.80	0.011	0.044	0.853	0.314	2.71	0.81	0.007	y_{32}
	y_{13}	−0.520	0.670	0.720	0.93	0.42	0.023	0.066	0.245	0.281	0.87	0.40	0.009	y_{33}
	y_{21}	−0.045	0.412	0.120	3.45	0.87	0.008	0.316	0.776	0.218	3.57	0.88	0.009	y_{31}
	y_{22}	−0.026	1.006	0.275	3.66	0.88	0.009	−0.006	1.076	0.297	3.62	0.88	0.006	y_{32}
	y_{23}	−0.306	1.283	0.831	1.54	0.61	0.027	−0.043	0.491	0.339	1.45	0.59	0.011	y_{33}
ROW (3) to ROW (exc. OSA)	y_{11}	−0.102	0.317	0.158	2.00	0.71	0.010	0.368	0.574	0.275	2.09	0.72	0.012	y_{31}
	y_{12}	−1.242	−0.975	0.622	1.57	0.62	0.014	0.552	−1.386	0.898	1.54	0.61	0.009	y_{32}
	y_{13}	−0.561	0.651	0.494	1.32	0.55	0.021	0.068	0.215	0.175	1.23	0.52	0.009	y_{33}
	y_{21}	−0.085	0.366	0.182	2.01	0.71	0.011	0.336	0.645	0.305	2.11	0.73	0.013	y_{31}
	y_{22}	−1.220	−0.968	0.717	1.35	0.56	0.016	0.578	−1.459	1.096	1.33	0.55	0.011	y_{32}
	y_{23}	−0.469	0.966	0.616	1.57	0.62	0.027	0.007	0.334	0.225	1.49	0.60	0.011	y_{33}
ROW (T) to ROW (inc. OSA)	y_{11}	−0.079	0.380	0.110	3.47	0.87	0.007	0.306	0.742	0.211	3.51	0.87	0.008	y_{31}
	y_{12}	−0.183	0.680	0.348	1.95	0.70	0.012	0.080	0.704	0.356	1.98	0.70	0.007	y_{32}
	y_{13}	−0.390	0.686	0.437	1.57	0.62	0.012	0.085	0.336	0.219	1.53	0.61	0.007	y_{33}
	y_{21}	−0.005	0.565	0.169	3.34	0.86	0.011	0.205	1.033	0.301	3.43	0.86	0.012	y_{31}
	y_{22}	−0.206	0.642	0.344	1.87	0.68	0.012	0.087	0.674	0.357	1.89	0.69	0.007	y_{32}
	y_{23}	−0.101	1.499	0.994	1.51	0.60	0.027	−0.127	0.817	0.569	1.44	0.58	0.018	y_{33}

this had all the t-values close to being significant and partly so as to provide an additional check on the previous results by using a different data set.

The assumption that export performance in third markets permits a prediction of hypothetical trade performance at unchanging levels of preference can also be used to analyse the recent performance of U.K. exports. We adopt the following notation, which is consistent with that used previously:

	U.K. exports	Total imports	U.K. share	U.K. exports	Total imports
EEC	y_{14}	y_1	v_{14}	$x_{14}-d_{14}+e_{14}$	$x_1+c_{11}+e_1$
Cont. EFTA	y_{54}	y_5	v_{54}	$x_{54}+c_{54}+d_{54}$	x_5+c_5
OSA	y_{64}	y_6	v_{64}	$x_{64}-d_{64}$	x_6
ROW	y_{74}	y_7	v_{74}	x_{74}	x_7

It has to be admitted that the use of the ROW (excluding the OSA) as a control group gives extremely bad predictions of the changes that were actually realized during the 1950s. The U.K. share in this market actually rose (from 11·1 to 12·2%) between 1954 and 1959, while it fell substantially in the EEC (from 14·4 to 11·9%), EFTA (from 18·9 to 14·5%), and the OSA (from 56·6 to 47·3%). One gets much better predictions if one uses the ROW *including* the OSA as the control group. Nevertheless, it was decided to use the ROW excluding the OSA as the control group for the calculations. This is partly because we wished to obtain an estimate of the effect of the erosion of Commonwealth ties on exports to the OSA, but primarily we judged that the contradictory performance of U.K. exports to the ROW and elsewhere during the 1950s was a fluke.

Since the application of the analysis to a single country's exports does not permit one to constrain the shares to sum to unity, it was decided to predict the hypothetical share vector (u_{14}) by formula (3).

In order to close the system, it is again necessary to introduce certain additional assumptions. The following were chosen:

$c_{11}+e_1$ = EEC trade creation;
= the estimates given by Method 1, $\alpha = \beta = 0.25$, of Table 6·3;

c_5 = increase in continental EFTA imports caused by trade creation;

= $0.8c_{22}$ (since the U.K. has only 72/373 of the EFTA trade creation in Table VI of [14]; and where c_{22} is given by Method 1 of Table 6·3).

TABLE 6·7. *Estimated effects of preferential tariff changes on U.K. exports* ($ *billions*)

		1966	1967	1968	1969
Loss of exports to EEC caused by net trade diversion	$d_{14}-e_{14}$	0·01	−0·05	0·07	0·10
Additional exports to EFTA caused by trade creation and diversion	$c_{54}+d_{54}$	0·15	0·22	0·12	0·24
Loss of exports to OSA caused by post-1959 erosion of Commonwealth preference and other ties	d_{64}	1·47	1·82	2·22	2·38
Ditto, using Method A	d_{64}	1·05	1·13	1·47	1·58

The results of these calculations are shown in Table 6·7. The first row suggests that EEC diversion was slightly greater than external creation in recent years, but that in comparison to the anti-monde the loss of exports has been modest. This is consistent with the apparent experience of extra-EEC imports as a whole. The second row suggests that the effects of EFTA in stimulating exports to continental EFTA have been rather less than would be indicated by the preceding analysis, [27] although the discrepancy is marked only for the post-devaluation year of 1968. The third row suggests that there has been a striking export loss in the OSA. The size of this loss may well have been exaggerated by the use of Method C (in view of the fact that the initial share in OSA markets was several times that in the control group), so the loss was recalculated using Method A (row 4). The loss is still very substantial.

A decade ago, Major concluded [24]: 'Britain's falling share in world trade in manufactures is not explained, to any great extent, by changes in the pattern of world trade; . . . a good deal of it is due to her falling share in sterling markets; and . . . this has probably been associated . . . with the reduced protection which she has enjoyed in these markets.'

The present analysis suggests that the second of these conclusions remained valid throughout the 1960s, and that it is a factor of considerable force. In contrast, the view is sometimes expressed that 'geographical factors' account for very little of the slow growth of U.K. exports [25]. This conclusion comes from automatically assuming that it is reasonable to expect the U.K. to maintain a constant share in OSA markets. In fact, given the very high initial share of the U.K. and the erosion of the preferences and historical ties that were responsible for that share performance, it is entirely natural for the British share to decline. In this sense, the geographical distribution of U.K. exports was a major determinant of their slow growth during the 1960s.

It is only proper to stress that the poor predictive performance of the underlying hypothesis during the 1950s means that these results should be treated with considerable caution.

APPENDIX 6·3: THE DATA [26]

While efforts are usually made to ensure that significant discontinuities of definition and coverage are removed from series published at any one time, it is likely that there will be discontinuities if a long series has to be compiled from a sequence of publications issued at different dates. The final estimates were therefore based upon a special series, which is shown below, in which adjustments were made to eliminate so far as possible the effects of the discontinuities.

Trade flows cover SITC 5–8 and are measured from the export side. Blocs are defined as follows:

(a) The EEC consists of all EEC countries.

(b) EFTA consists of all EFTA countries (including Finland) except Iceland, except that exports from the ROW to Finland are not included in y_{23}.

(c) ROW 3 consists of U.S.A., Canada, and Japan.

(d) The ROW covers all non-EEC, non-EFTA countries, except that intra-trade of the Sino-Soviet bloc and the estimated effects of the U.S.–Canadian automotive agreement are excluded so far as possible from y_{33}.

(e) The OSA consists of the non-OECD Sterling Area, in which Rhodesia is included only for 1954–65.

These data differ from series compiled from a sequence of the annual articles on world trade in manufactures published by the

TABLE 6.8. *World exports of manufactures, 1954–69 ($ millions)*

			Exports from			Of which
		EEC	EFTA	ROW	Total	ROW 3
1954	EEC	2,832	1,607	1,544	5,983	947
to	EFTA	2,489	1,523	1,612	5,624	804
	ROW	5,677	6,252	12,100	24,029	9,479
of which, OSA		828	3,126	—	—	1,109
1955		3,512	1,819	1,873	7,204	1,154
		2,936	1,675	2,060	6,671	1,097
		6,560	6,882	13,444	26,836	10,504
		1,005	3,377	—	—	1,418
1956		4,114	2,166	2,186	8,466	1,298
		3,272	1,810	2,130	7,212	1,101
		7,202	7,641	15,849	30,692	12,448
		1,184	3,445	—	—	1,549
1957		4,585	2,390	2,364	9,339	1,535
		3,649	1,943	2,179	7,771	1,222
		8,288	8,167	17,569	34,024	13,779
		1,360	3,617	—	—	1,735
1958		4,550	2,299	2,342	9,191	1,535
		3,740	1,956	1,962	7,658	1,094
		8,894	8,002	16,192	33,088	12,653
		1,405	3,536	—	—	1,561
1959	EEC	5,454	2,553	2,510	10,517	1,505
to	EFTA	4,293	2,184	2,331	8,808	1,240
	ROW	9,675	8,391	16,834	34,900	13,095
of which, OSA		1,386	3,397	—	—	1,736
1960		7,055	2,972	3,605	13,632	2,374
		5,320	2,574	3,199	11,093	1,942
		10,699	8,889	18,554	38,142	14,145
		1,643	3,666	—	—	2,364
1961		8,403	3,479	3,800	15,682	2,486
		5,851	2,969	3,088	11,968	1,755
		10,790	8,907	19,513	39,210	14,415
		1,564	3,581	—	—	2,255
1962		9,779	3,898	4,134	17,811	2,788
		6,064	3,195	3,205	12,464	1,792
		10,745	9,087	21,338	41,170	15,566
		1,608	3,444	—	—	2,749
1963		11,648	4,291	4,478	20,417	3,022
		6,324	3,567	3,489	13,380	1,896
		11,196	9,661	23,059	43,916	16,683
		1,777	3,715	—	—	3,250
1964		13,627	4,625	4,848	23,100	3,214
		7,191	4,209	4,350	15,750	2,515
		12,577	10,255	27,315	50,147	19,750
		2,058	3,956	—	—	4,036

		Exports from			Of which
	EEC	EFTA	ROW	Total	ROW 3
1965	15,335	4,873	5,281	25,489	3,304
	7,873	4,756	4,726	17,355	2,673
	14,488	11,365	30,674	56,527	22,043
	2,448	4,269	—	—	4,317
1966	17,434	5,204	6,201	28,839	3,640
	8,251	5,297	5,185	18,733	2,852
	16,308	12,280	34,934	63,522	24,755
	2,517	4,143	—	—	4,266
1967	18,311	5,151	6,418	29,880	3,857
	8,586	5,994	5,635	20,215	3,253
	18,011	12,414	37,302	67,727	26,382
	2,706	3,925	—	—	4,687
1968	21,716	5,744	7,686	35,146	4,544
	9,269	6,411	6,423	22,103	3,641
	20,652	13,622	42,930	77,204	30,640
	2,815	3,862	—	—	5,226
1969	27,677	7,001	9,587	44,265	5,616
	10,851	7,733	6,840	25,424	3,815
	22,716	15,493	49,114	87,323	35,007
	3,088	4,340	—	—	5,702

Department of Trade and Industry (for example, in [20]) in the following ways:

(a) Several minor discontinuities have been eliminated. For instance, estimates of trade in pearls and diamonds have been included in, and re-exports excluded from, the U.K. export series throughout.

(b) Finland is included with EFTA throughout.

(c) Approximate estimates of the effects of the U.S.–Canadian automotive agreement have been applied to the original published data to obtain the corrected value of y_{33}.

(d) An approximate adjustment has been made to the figures of ROW exports from 1954 to 1961 in order to remove as far as possible the discontinuity due to the change in the treatment of U.S. special category exports. The adjustment is somewhat uncertain on the limited statistical information available.

(e) The exporting countries have been supplemented to include all EFTA countries instead of simply the U.K., Sweden, and Switzerland, and the coverage of exporting countries in the ROW has been extended from the three countries included in ROW 3. (Some of the minor trade flows in the extended ROW data have been partially estimated for 1969, since full data were not available.)

NOTES AND REFERENCES

[1] This paper arose from work undertaken while both authors were members of the Government Economic Service. They wish to express their appreciation to H.M. Treasury and to the Department of Trade and Industry for permission to draw on this work in writing the present paper. They are greatly indebted to several members of the Government Economic and Statistical Services for valuable help and criticism. It remains the case that judgements and opinions are strictly the responsibility of the authors alone.

[2] This would be particularly serious in the method developed in section 4 of the present paper, since exports to the ROW are used as a control to estimate the anti-monde. Supply constraints which depressed these shares would therefore result in some over-estimation of the integration-induced growth in intra-trade.

[3] L. B. Krause, *European Economic Integration and the United States*, Washington D.C., 1968.

[4] R. L. Major, The Common Market: production and trade, *National Institute Economic Review*, Aug. 1962.

[5] P. J. Verdoorn and F. J. M. Meyer zu Schloctern, Trade creation and trade diversion in the Common market, in Collége d'Europe, *Intégration européenne et réalité économique*, Bruges, 1964.

[6] J. Waelbroeck, Le commerce de la communauté européenne avec les pays tiers, in *Integration Européenne*.

[7] A. Lamfalussy, Intra-European trade and the competitive position of the EEC, *Manchester Statistical Society Transactions*, March 1963.

[8] I. Walter, *The European Common Market*, New York, 1967.

[9] E. M. Truman, The EEC: trade creation and trade diversion, *Yale Economic Essays*, Spring 1969.

[10] A. Maizels, *Industrial Growth and World Trade*, Cambridge University Press, 1963.

[11] R. L. Major and S. Hays, 'Another look at the Common Market', *National Institute Economic Review*, Nov. 1970.

[12] B. Balassa, Trade creation and trade diversion in the European Common Market, *Economic Journal*, March 1967.

[13] F. J. Clavaux, The import elasticity as a yardstick for measuring trade creation, *Economia Internazionale*, Nov. 1969.

[14] EFTA Secretariat, *The Effects of EFTA*, Geneva, 1969.

[15] F. Trappeniers, The structure of the Common Market, in *The Market Economy in Western European Integration*, Louvain, 1963.

[16] M. E. Kreinen, Trade creation and diversion by the EEC and EFTA, *Economica Internazionale*, May 1969.

[17] P. Uribe, H. Theil, and C. G. de Leeuw, The information approach to the prediction of interregional trade flows, *Review of Economic Studies*, July 1966.

[18] We are indebted to Professor A. B. Atkinson for suggesting this formula.

[19] We also considered adding a fourth set of calculations, based on the assumption that $u^t{}_{ij}$ could be predicted by extrapolating the change in v_{ij} between 1954 and 1959. However, we previously argued that share changes during the 1950s were strongly influenced by differential trade liberalization, and

so this approach would tend to reproduce the errors for which we criticized Balassa and Kreinin.

[20] The reader may be tempted to try further substitutions to solve these equations. There are insufficient degrees of freedom to permit this: further manipulations only lead to identities.

[21] *Board of Trade Journal*, 30 Sept. 1970 (now renamed *Department of Trade and Industry Journal*).

[22] *UN Monthly Bulletin of Statistics*, March 1970.

[23] We are indebted to Mr J. Lanner and the EFTA Secretariat for permission to quote these *very preliminary* results of their revised study.

[24] R. L. Major, World trade in manufactures. *National Institute Economic Review*, July 1960, p. 27.

[25] H. B. Junz and R. R. Rhomberg, Prices and export performance of industrial countries, 1953–63. *IMF Staff Papers*, Nov. 1963. See Table I and the comments to it.

[26] We are extremely grateful to the Department of Trade and Industry for permission to use and publish the adjusted series given in this Appendix.

PART TWO

MONETARY UNION

7

THE BALANCE-OF-PAYMENTS PROBLEMS OF A EUROPEAN FREE-TRADE AREA [1]*

J. E. MEADE

Cambridge University

I do not propose to inquire into the effect of the institution of a free-trade area in Western Europe upon productivity, standards of living and so on. I propose only to raise some of the financial issues which are involved. Is it possible in Western Europe to combine free trade with full employment and balance-of-payments equilibrium?

Balance-of-payments problems as between the members of a European free-trade area can be avoided if each member takes steps to keep its own overall balance of payments in equilibrium. It will not matter if France, for example, is in deficit with the rest of the free-trade areas provided she is in overall balance, i.e. in equal surplus with outside countries. She can then use the outside currencies which she earns to pay her debts within the free-trade area. And these outside currencies will be needed by the other members of the free-trade area; for if France is in deficit inside the free-trade area, some other member or members (say, Germany) must be in equal surplus within the free-trade area. But if Germany is also in overall balance, then the German surplus in the free-trade area must be matched by an equal German deficit with outside countries. If France has no overall deficit on her balance of payments, she can pay Germany with her earnings of outside currencies; and if Germany has no overall surplus on her balance of payments, she will need these outside countries to pay her debts to the outside world.

This multilateral principle is well illustrated by the history of Benelux. Within Benelux the natural structure of trade and other transactions is such that the Netherlands is practically always in bilateral deficit with the Belgium–Luxemburg Economic Union. In the early post-war years the Dutch balance of payments was in over-

* *Economic Journal*, September 1957, 67, pp. 379–396.

all deficit; and in these conditions the finance of her bilateral deficit with Belgium gave rise to problems which could be solved only by restricting Dutch imports from her partner. But from 1951 onwards the Dutch international payments regained an overall balance; and the Dutch were earning a surplus with outside countries which matched their deficit with the Belgium–Luxemburg Economic Union. The Dutch could pay the Belgians with the currencies of third countries.

Consideration of the payments problems of Benelux suggests that the maintenance of overall equilibrium in the balance of payments of each partner country is not merely a possible, but also the only acceptable, method of dealing with payments between the partners. Consider the alternative principle that each parter should keep its payments with the other members of the union (rather than with all the other countries of the world) in balance. This result could be achieved in Benelux without restrictions on intra-Benelux trade if there were a very great rise in Belgian prices and costs (brought about by inflation in Belgium or by an appreciation of the Belgian franc) so as to cause an increase in Belgian purchases from, and a decrease in Belgian sales to, the Dutch on a sufficient scale to bring the bilateral Belgian–Dutch balance of payments into equilibrium. But this would have threatened to put the Belgian overall balance of payments into serious deficit, since the rise in Belgian prices and costs would have increased Belgian imports from, and would have decreased her exports to, the rest of the world as well. Belgium would have had to impose strict controls over payments to other countries. Or if the Dutch–Belgian balance of payments were put into bilateral balance by such a deflation in the Netherlands as to reduce Dutch purchases from, and to increase Dutch sales to, Belgium to the required extent, then this would have caused a great decrease in Dutch imports from, and an increase in Dutch exports to, the outside world as well. The Dutch would have to deal with a large undesired surplus in their overall balance of payments [2]. In conditions in which the structure of trade and payments is such that some members of a free-trade area naturally have deficits with their partners matched by surpluses with outside countries, while other members are in the opposite situation, the principle that each member should be primarily concerned with its overall balance of payments is the only acceptable one.

Our first and basic principle is, therefore, that each member of the free-trade area should maintain equilibrium in its overall balance of payments. But before proceeding further I would like to make two comments on this general principle.

First, the maintenance of overall equilibrium in a country's balance of payments is nothing like so precise a criterion as might at first sight appear. Obviously, since some countries will naturally and properly be lending abroad or borrowing from abroad for ordinary commercial and developmental purposes, by equilibrium in the balance of payments we do not mean an equality between current payments and current receipts. We are concerned with the balance of all normal current and capital payments and receipts. Even so, we cannot make an exact equality between payments and receipts our criterion. A country which has very inadequate reserves of gold and dollars may probably aim at some surplus of normal receipts over payments which will enable it to bring its reserves to a reasonable level. We can only lay down a general principle that it is the duty of each member of the free-trade area to avoid a continuing deficit or surplus on its overall balance of payments which threatens to result in the unreasonable accumulation or loss of its reserves.

Second, we must allow for the fact that not all outside currencies are convertible into each other. To return to my Benelux example, suppose that the Netherlands and Belgium are both in overall equilibrium, but that the Belgians have a deficit with the outside world and a surplus with the Netherlands, while the Dutch have a deficit with Belgium but a surplus with the outside world. If the outside currency which the Dutch are earning is a 'hard' currency which is convertible into the outside currency which the Belgians are spending, all is well. The Dutch can pay the Belgians with this currency, and the Belgians can use it to finance their outside debts.

But trouble might arise if Benelux as a whole, while it is in overall balance, has an outside surplus of 'soft' currencies and an outside deficit of 'hard' currencies. The Netherlands might be earning a surplus of outside 'soft' currencies which were not convertible into the 'hard' currencies needed by Belgium for the finance of her outside deficit.

There are in fact two very different types of case in which a European free-trade area as a whole might be earning a surplus of 'soft' currencies.

In the first case the surplus earnings of the free-trade area may be in terms of a currency which is not freely convertible into other outside currencies but is more or less freely convertible into the currency of one of the members of the free-trade area. The outstanding example of this is, of course, the overseas members of the sterling area. Suppose that in the European free-trade area the Germans have a dollar deficit and that the French are in debt to the Germans but are earning a surplus in Australian pounds, which are freely convertible into United Kingdom pounds, the United Kingdom being a member and Australia not a member of the free-trade area. If sterling is not freely convertible into dollars, the French cannot pay the Germans in an outside currency which the Germans need. The basic cure in this type of case is, of course, that the sterling area as a whole, rather than just the United Kingdom, should be in overall balance. If the free-trade area (excluding the United Kingdom) has a surplus with the sterling area, then the sterling area (including the United Kingdom) will be in overall balance only if it has a surplus with some country outside the free-trade area and the sterling area, e.g. with the dollar world. Once again the circle is closed. France can pay Germany with her sterling earnings and, since the sterling area has a dollar surplus, Germany can convert this sterling into dollars for the finance of her dollar deficit without putting a strain on the sterling area's dollar reserves.

The basic balance-of-payments rule for the free-trade area must thus be modified to the effect that each national government undertakes to maintain overall equilibrium in the balance of payments of the monetary area of which it is the centre rather than merely overall equilibrium in its own national balance of payments. This puts the United Kingdom in a special position which has become a familiar problem in the European Payments Union and the Organization for European Economic Co-operation. The United Kingdom, as banker for the sterling area, has cleared all sterling-area payments through EPU, but in the adjustment of the OEEC trade liberalization programme to maintain balance-of-payments equilibrium she has been able to enter into commercial-policy commitments only for the United Kingdom and not for the other members of the sterling area such as Australia.

A different type of problem might arise if the outside deficits of the free-trade area were in dollars and the outside surpluses were in some currency like the Brazilian cruzeiro, which is convertible neither into other outside currencies (such as the dollar) nor into the currency of a member country (such as sterling). But the countries of Western

Europe are now in a sufficiently strong position to deal with this type of problem in a simple but decisive manner. If the monetary authority of each European country does not undertake to exchange into its own European currency any Brazilian cruzeiros which its exporters may earn, then in self-defence the individual European exporters to Brazil will demand from the Brazilian importers to be paid in their own European currencies or in other acceptable convertible currencies. This means that the Brazilian authorities have to take steps to see that their importers do not purchase more from Western Europe as a whole than Brazil can finance out of the proceeds of her exports or other earnings. Immediately after the War each country of Europe dealt with this problem by a separate bilateral payments arrangement with Brazil or with similar 'soft' currency countries. This is now unnecessary; and, through the so-called Hague Club, arrangements are now being made whereby the Brazilians can transfer any earnings which they may obtain in one European currency into another European currency for the purchase of goods from that second European country. In these conditions while one European country alone may have an excess of exports to Brazil and another an excess of imports from Brazil, there can be no problem of an excess of earnings of the 'soft' Brazilian currency by the free-trade area as a whole.

But let me return to my main problem. By what means can each member of the free-trade area keep its overall balance of payments in equilibrium? There are at least five possible lines of approach to this problem which I shall call the liquidity approach, the gold-standard approach, the integration approach, the direct-control approach and the exchange-rate approach.

By the *liquidity approach* I mean that steps might be taken to increase the availability of liquid reserves to the European countries which are in overall deficit so that they can thereby tide over temporary balance-of-payments difficulties. This cannot, of course, provide a full cure for lasting and permanent balance-of-payment deficits. But it can deal with temporary balance-of-payments problems and, above all, it can provide a buffer which will enable other measures for dealing with permanent difficulties to have time to work out their effects. Reserves of some European countries and particularly of the United Kingdom are still lamentably low. An increase in liquidity is an essential ingredient in a satisfactory solution of our problem.

How can this best be achieved? One's thoughts naturally turn to the European Payments Union, which provides a mechanism whereby, according to the credit element in the monthly settlements, European countries with a surplus in their payments to other European countries automatically provide credit, and so liquidity, to those European countries which have a deficit in their payments with other European countries. Could the European liquidity problem be solved by a development of this European instrument whereby European surplus countries provide credits to European deficit countries?

There are two serious objections to reliance upon an EPU type of mechanism.

In the first place there may well be times when the European free-trade area as a whole is in deficit with the outside world. This means that the overall deficits of the European deficit countries are greater than the overall surpluses of the European surplus countries. In such circumstances, it is impossible to cover the deficits of the deficit members by the surpluses of the surplus members. For this reason it would be much more satisfactory to proceed by means of a more 'universal' approach (such as an extension of drawing rights with the International Monetary Fund) which would give each European country, regardless of the position of its European partners, greater international liquidity to deal with its own overall balance-of-payments problems.

If, however, this more 'universal' approach is for any reason ruled out, it is possible to do something by methods whereby European surplus countries lend temporarily to European deficit countries. But there is now a second objection to an EPU type of mechanism. My basic theme has been that if each member is in overall balance-of-payments equilibrium, then the settlement of payments within the free-trade area should be possible. Suppose that the Netherlands has a dollar surplus matched by a deficit with Belgium, while Belgium has a dollar deficit matched by its surplus with the Netherlands; it should be possible for the Dutch to pay the Belgians with dollars. But with the EPU arrangements the Netherlands will continuously pile up reserves of gold and dollars, since their surplus is earned wholly in that form, while their deficit is payable through the EPU partly in book credit. But Belgium will run out of gold and dollar reserves, since her dollar deficit must be financed wholly in that form while her surplus is with EPU and will be financed partly by a book credit with

EPU. This difficulty is avoided if settlements through EPU are 100% in gold; but in this case EPU does not fulfil the function of providing additional credit by overall surplus to overall deficit members.

It is, of course, possible to devise methods for European surplus countries to lend to European deficit countries, which are not open to this objection. This might be done merely by arrangements between the exchange equalization accounts or similar authorities of the members to the effect that the authorities of an overall surplus member would hold more of the currencies of an overall deficit member. Or it might be rather more institutionalized in the form of a European Monetary Fund into which all members paid certain amounts of their own currencies, and possibly also of their reserves of gold and dollars, and from which members with overall deficits were able to make temporary drawings. Or it might take the extreme form of the payment of all the gold and dollars of all the members into a common single pool, payments between members being financed by the transfer of claims on this pool, and payments to the outside world by drawings from the pool. This last system would, of course, have special implications for the United Kingdom, since it would mean pooling with the Europeans the reserves held against the claims of the whole Sterling Area; and although there is nothing inherently illogical (indeed there is much positively desirable) in extending the payments mechanism to cover a wider region than the commercial free-trade area, the political difficulties involved are obviously very great.

In any case an increase in international liquidity for European countries is not a complete cure for our problem. What methods could be used to deal with persistent balance-of-payments problems in the European free-trade area? Let us consider first what I have called the *gold-standard approach*.

By this I mean the application of the principles of the old gold standard as they are expounded in the text-books. Any member of the free-trade area which is in overall deficit will lose reserves of foreign exchange; it should allow this to lead to a restriction of the domestic supply of its money until its domestic money incomes, prices and costs are so deflated that it has put its overall balance of payments into equilibrium by buying less imports and supplying more and cheaper products for export. Simultaneously any surplus member of the free-trade area should allow its receipt of foreign-exchange reserves to cause a monetary inflation domestically, which should lead to an increase in its imports and a decrease in its exports. This solution is dangerous. It requires that each European national government should devise its domestic monetary and budgetary policies essentially with regard to its balance-of-payments situation and with little or no thought for its domestic situation. Financial policies to prevent domestic inflations or to preserve full employment must be more or less abandoned.

This would mean that Germany, so long as she has an overall balance-of-payments surplus, must inflate her domestic money incomes, prices and costs. But Germany, with her memories of past hyper-inflation, is very unwilling to do this. And, as recent events show, a surplus country like Germany is always able to restrain an inflation; she can, through restrictive domestic monetary and budgetary policies, offset the domestic inflationary effects of a balance-of-payments surplus and continue to pile up balances of gold and foreign currencies. But this means that a potentially deficit member of the free-trade area such as France might have to make an undue share of the adjustment by a domestic deflation of its money incomes, prices and costs; for it cannot indefinitely postpone the adjustment, since its stock of gold and foreign currencies is limited and exhaustible. It might have to abandon a domestic financial policy of expansion for full employment just at the time that the structural adjustments of its industries due to the removal of trade barriers within the free-trade area may be causing some redundancy of labour in its less efficient industries, so that it was especially desirable to have a domestic background of financial expansion to ease the development of its more efficient industries. Governments are nowadays so wedded (and, in my opinion, rightly so wedded) to the idea that it is one of their duties to preserve full employment that the probable outcome of this solution would in fact be the breakdown of the free-trade-area arrangements.

Many who accept these criticisms of the gold-standard approach may ask whether we could not get rid of payments difficulties, at least within the free-trade area, by combining with the building of a free-trade area in Western Europe the integration of European financial arrangements so as to make it as easy for a Frenchman to pay a German within Europe as it is for a Welshman to pay an Englishman within the United Kingdom.

The logic of this *integration approach* is unassailable. But it is not, I think, always realized how far-reaching this proposal is. This we can best see by asking why it is that the adjustment of payments between England and Wales is so much easier than that between Germany and France. There are at least five elements to the answer.

In the first place, the fact that goods, labour and capital can move freely between England and Wales makes adjustment easier. Suppose Wales is in economic difficulty. A deflation of prices and incomes in Wales relatively to prices and incomes in England will have more effect in inducing consumers to buy Welsh rather than English products and in inducing workers to work in England rather than Wales, because there are no restrictions on the movement of goods or workers from Wales to England. Moreover, any rise in interest rates in Wales caused by a scarcity of money capital due to the deflation of money supplies in Wales would have more effect in attracting new capital funds from England because there are no barriers to the movement of capital within the United Kingdom. Indeed, the Welsh and the English share in common the London capital market. A complete common market for goods, labour and capital throughout Western Europe would similarly make the mechanism of adjustment of payments easier. There is some truth in the contention that the gold-standard approach is less dangerous when it is applied to the payments between the members of an economic union than when it is applied to payments between national States which maintain impediments to the movement of goods and services between them.

But this is not the whole of the story. A second reason why the adjustment of payments between England and Wales is much easier than between Germany and France is because the United Kingdom has, while Western Europe has not, got a single common currency and banking system. If the Welsh balance of payments with England is £1 million in deficit, then this means that £1 million of currency or bank deposits passes from the ownership of Welshmen to that of Englishmen. This deflation of £1 million in Wales and inflation of £1 million in England is the end of the direct monetary adjustment. But if the French balance of payments with Germany is 1 million francs in deficit, then the French central bank loses 1 million francs of foreign-exchange reserves and the German central bank gains an equivalent amount of reserves. There are many reasons why a change of 1 million in a country's foreign-exchange reserves may cause a change of many millions in its total domestic supply of money. In particular, if France has only a small proportion of her total domestic supply of money covered by foreign-exchange reserves, she may have to deflate her domestic supply of money by many times any loss of her reserves, in order to prevent a dangerous fall in her foreign-exchange reserve ratio. In other words, the absence of a single money means that the abruptness and speed of adjustment in France and Germany may have to be much greater than in Wales and England. Much of this problem would, of course, be solved by sufficiently far-reaching arrangements for increasing international liquidity between the members of the European free-trade area. In the example just given, if France had foreign-exchange reserves equal to 100% of her domestic money supply, then any given loss of reserves would no longer make it necessary for her to deflate her domestic money supply by many times that loss of reserves.

Thirdly, England and Wales have a single national government which by the adoption of a stricter or easier central-banking monetary policy or by running a budget surplus or deficit can pump monetary purchasing power out of or into the system as a whole. This means that there can be an effective anti-inflation or anti-deflation financial policy for the United Kingdom as a whole which can take into account the interest both of Wales and of England. Trouble with the Welsh balance of payments need not be intensified by a failure of monetary demand in England to expand sufficiently. This is a most far-reaching difference between interregional and international payments. In Europe at present it is the function of each national government by control of its central bank's monetary policy and through its own budgetary policy to prevent undesirable domestic inflations and deflations. Free trade combined with fixed exchange rates (the gold-standard approach) would prevent European governments from devising their domestic financial policy for the purpose of preserving domestic stability. But the prevention of widespread booms and slumps is an essential feature of modern government. To entrust this task to a supra-national European authority would require a very far-reaching surrender of powers by the national governments to ensure a single central-bank policy and a single budgetary policy for Western Europe as a whole.

Fourthly, suppose that the balance-of-payments deficit of Wales is greater than the balance-of-payments surplus of England, so that the United Kingdom as a whole has a deficit with the outside world. There exist central authorities for the United Kingdom which will then do something to correct the United Kingdom balance of payments. Restrictions on imports into the United Kingdom as a

whole world cause consumers in the surplus area, England, to purchase from the deficit area, Wales, goods which could no longer be
procured from abroad. Similarly, a depreciation of the pound would
cause outside goods to rise in price relatively to goods inside the
United Kingdom, and England would buy more from Wales and less
from outside countries and would sell more to outside countries and
less to Wales. This also is a very far-reaching point. A European
supra-national authority with extensive governmental powers would
be needed to devise and administer a single programme of control
over imports into the free-trade from outside (we shall return to this
problem at a later stage) and to decide upon any changes in the
exchange-rate between all European currencies, on the one hand, and
all outside currencies, on the other.

Fifthly, if in the United Kingdom (in spite of the factors which we
have just mentioned) some economic adjustment does bring concentrated depression in a single region (like South Wales in the 1930s),
then the central government in London exists to take special measures
to bring new investment and enterprise to South Wales and to help
to move labour out of South Wales. No such supranational authority
exists to take such 'special-area' action on the part of Western Europe
as a whole for the promotion of economic development in, say, a
particular region of Europe, like Southern Italy.

The integration approach thus involves – in addition to the formation of a common market for goods and for factors of production
and the provision of much greater international liquidity for European monetary authorities – a very extensive range of powers for
what would amount to a single European government. Such a
government would have to be able to control central-bank monetary
policy and governmental budgetary policy throughout Europe, to
determine a single European commercial and exchange-rate policy
vis-à-vis third countries, and to carry out an effective special-area
policy for depressed regions in Europe.

This is in my opinion ultimately desirable; let us hope that it will
prove ultimately practicable; but it is not a starter at the moment,
and it would be a great shame to sacrifice the present real political
possibilities of building a commercial free-trade area to this ideal of
simultaneous monetary and budgetary integration.

Let us consider next the possibility of dealing with a deficit in a
country's balance of payments by imposing restrictions on imports
from abroad or on payments to other countries. This *direct-control*

approach is more desirable than sole reliance on the gold-standard approach, with its potential threat to full employment; and it is more practicable than the integration approach with its very far-reaching political implications. But in so far as it involves a deficit member of the European free-trade area restricting imports from another member of that area, it cuts deeply into the idea of a true free-trade area. Its interference with the free-trade principle is not to be measured merely by the amount of restriction of imports which actually exists at any one moment of time. The mere knowledge that trade may be restricted in this way in the future will discourage the large-scale investments that may be necessary to build up localized specialized mass production for the whole European market. The mass production of motor cars in Detroit in the United States involves the investment of huge sums of capital in plant and equipment in Detroit, which is undertaken because the producer knows for certain that the whole United States market will always be freely open to him.

If restrictions on trade between the members of a European free-trade area are to be avoided, it must, of course, be possible for traders to make payments for such purposes. This does not in itself imply the absence of all exchange controls over the currencies of the countries concerned. Thus any one member country, say France, could maintain strict exchange controls; every Frenchman who wanted a foreign currency, say, German marks, to purchase goods from Germany, might be required to obtain the currency from a central French exchange-control authority or its agent; and every Frenchman who acquired any foreign currency, say, German marks from the sale of French products to Germany, might be required to surrender the currency to the central French exchange-control authority or its agent in exchange for francs. All that is necessary to ensure the free entry of German products into France is that the French exchange-control authority should in fact always grant a Frenchman's request for foreign currency if he can show that it is required to finance the import of German products into France.

But the problem is very different if it is intended that there should be freedom of capital movements between the member countries. Full freedom of movement of capital funds from France to Germany, for example, means that the Frenchman must be free to buy German marks for all purposes, capital as well as current. But suppose that the German exchange control differs from the French, the French forbidding and the German allowing the movement of capital funds into dollars. If the Frenchman is free to lend to the German, and the German is then free to lend to the American, it does not require great ingenuity on the part of financiers (who are not conspicuously lacking in that quality) to devise means whereby in effect the Frenchman is lending his money to the American by way of a German intermediary. The control of the movement of capital from France to the United States will become much less effective if there is freedom of movement of capital funds from France to Germany and the German mark is fully convertible. To make one member's control over exports of capital to countries outside the free-trade area effective, the exchange-control regulations of all the members must be harmonized, if freedom of capital movement within the free-trade area is to be maintained. This is a very difficult operation. If it should prove too difficult, then freedom of movement of capital funds cannot be allowed in Europe so long as some members are in heavy deficit and need to control the outflow of capital at least to the outside world, while others are in strong surplus and wish to make their currencies convertible into outside currencies.

But let us return to the problem of trade controls. Is it possible for a member of the European free-trade area to deal with a deficit in its overall balance of payments by restricting imports from outside countries without restricting imports from the other members of the free-trade area? [3]

The use by the members of the European free-trade area on balance-of-payments grounds of restrictions on imports from third countries can be organized in either of two ways which I will call the *national* and the *supra-national* methods respectively. By the national method I mean simply that each individual member of the free-trade area might restrict imports from outside countries into its own national markets as an aid to the preservation of equilibrium in its own overall balance of payments. By the supra-national method I mean that the members of the free-trade area should set up some joint authority which would determine the total amount of outside goods which could be imported into the free-trade area as a whole, using this instrument to preserve equilibrium in the balance of payments of the area as a whole with the outside world.

There can, I think, be little doubt that in the circumstances of the European free-trade area it is the national method which must be employed, at least until there is some further movement towards

167

extensive European integration. There is great difficulty in the supranational method. Suppose that Germany is in overall surplus and France in overall deficit, but that France's deficit is greater than Germany's surplus and the area as a whole is in deficit. To get a single joint programme of control of imports into the area from outside agreement has got to be reached on at least three basic points. First, how severe should the total restrictions be? Germany may want the problem solved mainly by deflation or depreciation by France with little common import restriction, and France may want it solved mainly by inflation or appreciation by Germany with much import restriction. With the supranational method this choice would have to be made by common agreement. Second, given the degree of total restriction, which particular imports should be restricted? France may want severe restrictions on the import of wheat which she produces, but not on chemicals which she does not produce; and Germany may want the opposite type of import programme. Thirdly, given the degree of restriction of each particular import, how many of the import licences should be given to German and how many to French importers? If we may draw any conclusions from the history of the Benelux economic union, we can safely conclude that the formation of a common programme of restriction of imports from third countries is one of the most difficult things to achieve even when there are only two trading partners to be considered.

Let us then consider the case of a member of the European free-trade area which is in an overall balance-of-payments deficit and which is trying to deal with this by restricting imports from outside countries without restricting imports from the other members of the free-trade area. In these conditions too much reliance cannot be placed upon the weapon of import control. In any free-trade area comprising the main countries of Western Europe each individual member would in fact purchase a large proportion of its total imports from other members of the area. In 1955 the United Kingdom purchased 28%, Western Germany 51%, France 33%, Italy 46%, the Belgium-Luxemburg Economic Union 59% and the Netherlands 59% of its imports from other countries of Western Europe. Import restrictions which were confined to imports from other sources would thus be limited in their scope.

Moreover, the limitation of this weapon is rather greater than these crude figures suggest. For the imports of the typical Western

European country from outside Europe consist very largely of raw materials and foodstuffs which are less easily dispensable than many manufactured goods which it imports from its Western European partners.

There is a further reason why restrictions on imports from outside countries imposed on what I have called the national as opposed to the supranational principle may in certain circumstances prove a rather weak weapon of control. Suppose that France restricts imports of United States products because she is in deficit, but that Germany does not do so because she is in surplus. Then if United States products can move freely from Germany to France, the French restrictions become very ineffective. Indeed, for the system to have any sense at all it must be open to France to restrict the import of United States produce whether it comes into France directly or via Germany. But even if this is done, French restrictions on some United States products (say, motor cars) may mean that more such cars are imported into Germany, thereby releasing for export to France some German cars which would have been wanted in the German market if Germany had also been restricting the import of United States cars. The national method will, because of such substitutabilities, be somewhat less effective a device for causing a net reduction in total imports than the supranational method. France will have to rely rather more on disinflation or depreciation than would otherwise be the case, when France is in deficit and Germany in surplus.

But when all the members of the free-trade area are simultaneously in overall deficit, when – that is to say – the free-trade area is in deficit because the outside world is in surplus with all the individual members, then the national method will work very effectively. If Germany is restricting the import of United States cars because she (Germany) is in overall deficit, then the restrictions which France is putting on the import of United States cars will not be offset by the increased import of German cars which are being replaced by United States cars in the German market. If and when developments in the outside world (and, of course, in particular in the United States) impose an almost universal strain on European balances of payments, then the national method will automatically regain its full effectiveness. I personally regard the fact that it will be rather an ineffective tool, except in circumstances such as these, as a strong recommendation of it.

Because of the difficulties involved in operating the supranational method, even the six countries forming the full European customs union would probably have to operate their restrictions on imports from outside countries by the national method. They would then have to maintain a customs control at their common frontiers to prevent the products of outside countries from entering a member country with severe import restrictions indirectly via a member country with lax restrictions on the products of outside countries. But the experience of Benelux suggests that, unless they are successful not only in imposing a single tariff of duties on imports from outside countries, but also in unifying all domestic excise duties and turnover taxes and in removing all their domestic agricultural support policies, they will in any case have to maintain customs controls at their common frontier.

But whatever the members of the full customs union may do, the United Kingdom must employ the national method for her restrictions on imports from outside countries. She will wish as far as possible to avoid discriminating against the products of Commonwealth countries, particularly if they are members of the sterling area; but if she joined in any common European supranational import-control plan, she might be forced to restrict imports from sterling-area-commonwealth countries, even though she had to admit similar European products without restriction.

Incidentally, because of this special relationship both to Europe and to the sterling-area countries the United Kingdom will find restrictions on imports from outside countries a particularly weak weapon. In 1955 the United Kingdom purchased 28% of her imports from Western Europe and 38% from the Sterling Area, leaving only 34% from other sources for restriction; and much of this 34% consists of basic materials and foodstuffs which it would be undesirable to restrict.

There remains the *exchange-rate approach* to the problem. A simple process of elimination leads inevitably to the conclusion that if the European national governments are going to use monetary and budgetary policies for purposes of domestic stabilization – if, for example, in their present situation of balance-of-payments surplus the German authorities are nevertheless going to use their monetary policy to prevent a domestic inflation – and if it is desired to avoid the use of quantitative import restrictions on trade within the free-trade area, a greater use of the weapon of exchange-rate variations

170

will have to be made. Some re-alignment of exchange rates may be particularly necessary during the initial stages of building the free-trade area. The removal of trade barriers of varying degrees of severity and the consequential development of import and export trades of varying degrees of expansibility may leave some members in deficit and others in surplus. The correction of this initial structural disturbance may require some exchange-rate adjustments quite apart from any need for exchange-rate variations to maintain equilibrium when once it has been achieved. Members of the free-trade area with a persistent surplus in their overall balance of payments will have to be ready to appreciate, and those with a persistent deficit will have to be ready to depreciate, the foreign-exchange values of their currencies.

This question is a difficult and controversial one, and it is not possible to discuss it at length in this lecture [4]. There are, of course, serious disadvantages in variations of exchange-rates. There is the possibility that anti-social speculative movements of funds will be generated by the expectation of depreciations. There is the danger that a depreciation by raising the price of imports and so the cost of living will itself cause a rise of wage-rates which, by making exports more costly, will give rise to yet a further depreciation.

These dangers will be much less if the European governments adopt effective domestic measures to prevent domestic inflations as well as to prevent domestic deflations. Speculation against a currency is most serious and dangerous when speculators think that a depreciation may set in motion the vicious inflationary spiral of higher import prices, higher wage-rates, higher money costs, more depreciation and so on without end. Exchange-rate variations are certainly not a substitute for sensible and effective domestic policies to prevent inflation; on the contrary, they can be expected to work only if they are accompanied by such domestic policies.

The governments of all the countries of Western Europe are nowadays technically and politically in a position to control the total money demand within their countries by means of suitable budgetary and banking policies. What is much less certain is their ability to cope with inflation arising on the side of costs. If the institutions for the fixing of wage-rates are such that, so long as there is reasonably full employment, money wage-rates are pushed up more quickly than output per head, the European governments will be faced by an unhappy dilemma: through their control over banking and budgetary policies either they must allow an increase in the total money demand for goods and services which will provide employment for all workers at the higher money wage-rates (in which case prices will rise as rapidly as costs) or else they must restrict monetary demand so as to prevent domestic purchasers from offering higher prices for the country's output (in which case higher money costs are likely to lead to unemployment). Only if suitable wage-fixing arrangements can be devised will the European governments be able to use their control over banking and budgetary policies in such a way as to combine full employment with sufficient stability of prices to reassure their own citizens and foreign holders of their money that it is not necessary perpetually to speculate against a further loss of value and depreciation of the national currency concerned.

This problem of control of inflation from the cost side as well as the demand side is perhaps the most important economic issue which now faces the governments of Europe. In present circumstances it can be tackled only on a national basis, since trade unions are national organizations and wage-fixing methods and habits vary widely from country to country. There are sure to be some divergences in its treatment; and differences in the annual percentage rate of change of prices and costs in different European countries, though very moderate in amount, could give rise to serious balance-of-payments problems as they accumulate at compound interest over a period of years. For this reason, if for no other, rates of exchange between the European currencies must be variable, if it is desired to avoid more or less permanent restrictions on imports from being used as the way of meeting a growing divergence in levels of prices and costs.

But while exchange-rate variations are a necessary weapon in the armoury, it is of the utmost importance that they should not be regarded merely as another name for exchange-rate depreciations. Strong currencies should be expected to go up as much as weak currencies to go down. In order to establish this principle, it is especially important to initiate the use of this weapon in Europe with the appreciation of a strong currency rather than with the depreciation of a weak currency. There should probably be some depreciation of the French franc; but first and foremost at this moment there should be a substantial appreciation of the German mark.

I think that my attitude to exchange-rate variations is very much like Sir Winston Churchill's attitude to democracy, which he once described as the worst of all possible forms of government except the others. And I am reminded, too, that Mr E. M. Forster once wrote a book entitled *Two Cheers for Democracy*, so I ask you to join with me in giving one cheer for a depreciation of the French franc and two cheers for an appreciation of the German mark.

I will conclude by outlining my own tentative conclusions on this difficult problem.

Full employment is more important than free trade for Europe; and financial policies to prevent booms and slumps must for some time remain primarily the function of the European national governments. In order to ensure that they could not be forced to abandon their full-employment policies on balance-of-payments grounds they should for the time being be able to restrict imports even from their partners in the free-trade area, until experience has shown that alternative balance-of-payments arrangements can be made to work. But such restrictions are a serious derogation of the principle of European free trade; they should be used only as a very last resort; and their imposition and use should be subject to the close supervision of an appropriate European authority.

A workable positive arrangement which would enable full employment to be maintained without restrictions on intra-European trade could meanwhile be worked out on the basis of three main principles. First, the European national governments must carry out effective domestic stabilization policies, the surplus countries putting the emphasis on the avoidance of deflation, and the deficit countries on the avoidance of inflation. Second, the foreign-exchange values of the currencies of countries in a persistent balance-of-payments surplus must be appreciated and of those in a persistent balance-of-payments deficit must be depreciated. Thirdly, greater foreign-exchange reserves must be extended to the deficit countries to tide over the process of readjustment.

There are many ways of implementing these three general principles; but by way of illustration I will tentatively recommend one particular method.

As I have said, domestic monetary stabilization would remain essentially the concern of the national governments; but something can be done to encourage suitable national action by international discussion and cooperation. Each member of the free-trade area should formally recognize that its partners had a legitimate interest in the successful stabilization of its own domestic incomes, prices and costs, and, in particular, in the avoidance of deflations by surplus members and of inflations by deficit members. There should be some European institution like the Organization for European Economic Co-operation at which the national governments would regularly consult each other about their domestic financial policies.

Against a background of domestic stability the exchange rates of the national currencies of the members of the free-trade area should be allowed to float in a more or less free foreign-exchange market. This suggestion is liable to raise up a picture of wildly fluctuating European currencies, many of them losing their value completely. If reasonable domestic policies for domestic stabilization are applied, nothing could be more absurd; and unless such policies can be applied, no sensible balance-of-payments policies for a true free-trade area can be devised. If reasonable domestic policies for domestic stabilization are applied, there will still be some moderate external disturbances or some moderate divergences in price and cost levels requiring adjustment. To meet these, exchange rates will float moderately upwards or downwards; and every encouragement should be given for the development of a free market in forward exchange, so that the moderate inconveniences and uncertainties for traders resulting from these moderate fluctuations in exchange-rates may be minimized.

In such circumstances there should be no essential difficulty for the countries of continental Europe in allowing their exchange rates to float. There would be more difficulty in the case of sterling, which is a currency used extensively by traders in other countries, held in large amounts by residents in other countries, and backed by inadequate reserves. There are, therefore, much greater possibilities of speculation by non-resident holders against sterling than against other currencies. But this is a difference of degree rather than of kind. It means that it is more important for the United Kingdom to obtain greater reserves or a greater degree of international liquidity by one means or another; and it means that it is especially important for the United Kingdom to devise an effective domestic policy for the avoidance of inflation from the cost as well as from the demand sides. In such conditions the pound could be confidently expected to float up as often as to float down; and there is no reason why in such circumstances a floating pound should not continue to be used as an international currency.

But what would be the use of a country's international reserves of gold and foreign-exchange in such a system, in which its currency was allowed freely to find its own level in the foreign-exchange markets? The foreign-exchange markets, though in general free, might be subject to the intervention of the exchange equalization account or similar authority of each member country, the authority selling some of its reserves of foreign-exchange for its own domestic currency to mitigate what it considered an unreasonable speculation against its currency, or vice versa. Cushioned in this way by the use of a country's reserves, the necessary fluctuations in a country's exchange rate could be taken at a very moderate speed.

Such a system is, of course, open to misuse if the authority in one country attempts to manipulate the exchange rate between its currency and the currencies of its partners to obtain some commercial or other advantage which its balance-of-payments position does not really need. Partly to avoid this danger and partly to provide greater liquidity for European countries there might be instituted a European Monetary Fund into which each member would pay an amount of its own national currency. This fund would be under some form of independent 'supranational' management of a technical banking character; and its management would be empowered on its own initiative to buy and sell the currencies in the fund to ease the balance-of-payments adjustments of the members. This fund would also provide a forum at which the policies of the fund itself and of the national exchange equalization funds could be continuously discussed and integrated. To avoid speculation such integration would, of course, have to take the form of secret discussions between the central monetary authorities of the member countries. Such a system would be capable of almost indefinite development. As an integrated Europe became more and more of a reality, so the member States could pay greater and greater sums of their own currencies into the European Fund and could start also to pay into it part of their reserves of gold and dollars as well, until finally the supranational fund had superseded the national exchange equalization funds. And as their domestic financial policies became more and more harmonized and integrated, so smaller and smaller fluctuations in exchange-rates need be permitted, until finally the conditions for what I have called the integration approach to the balance-of-payments problems have been fully met and exchange-rate variations can be abandoned.

The proposals which I have just made are, or course, riddled with difficulties and imperfections. I put them forward only as a challenge to others to produce something which is simpler, but equally effective, for dealing with European balances of payments without preventing European free trade or destroying European full employment.

NOTES AND REFERENCES

[1] Presidential Address to Section F of the British Association, delivered on 5 September 1957 at Dublin.

[2] Suppose that the Netherlands were in overall surplus (its deficit with Belgium being less than its surplus with the outside world), while Belgium were in overall deficit (her surplus with the Netherlands being less than her deficit with the outside world). Suppose then that the Dutch inflate and the Belgians deflate. The Dutch will get rid of their overall surplus by decreasing their surplus with the outside world but *increasing their deficit with Belgium*, while the Belgians will get rid of their overall deficit by decreasing their deficit with the outside world and *increasing their surplus with the Netherlands*. The solution of a balance-of-payments problem of a free-trade area may thus well involve the increase of the deficits and surpluses within the area itself.

[3] I do not propose to consider on this occasion which, if any, of the systems of import control discussed below would require a special waiver under the General Agreement on Tariffs and Trade.

[4] For my own views on the subject, see J. E. Meade, The case for variable exchange rates, *The Three Banks Review*, September 1955.

8

A THEORY OF OPTIMUM
CURRENCY AREAS*

R. A. MUNDELL

University of Waterloo

It is patently obvious that periodic balance-of-payments crises will remain an integral feature of the international economic system as long as fixed exchange rates and rigid wage and price levels prevent the terms of trade from fulfilling a natural role in the adjustment process. It is, however, far easier to pose the problem and to criticize the alternatives than it is to offer constructive and feasible suggestions for the elimination of what has become an international disequilibrium system [1]. The present paper, unfortunately, illustrates that proposition by cautioning against the practicability, in certain cases, of the most plausible alternative: a system of national currencies connected by flexible exchange rates.

A system of flexible exchange rates is usually presented, by its proponents [2], as a device whereby depreciation can take the place of unemployment when the external balance is in deficit, and appreciation can replace inflation when it is in surplus. But the question then arises whether all existing national currencies should be flexible. Should the Ghanaian pound be freed to fluctuate against all currencies or ought the present sterling-area currencies remain pegged to the pound sterling? Or, supposing that the Common Market countries proceed with their plans for economic union, should these countries allow each national currency to fluctuate, or would a single currency area be preferable?

The problem can be posed in a general and more revealing way by defining a currency area as a domain within which exchange rates are fixed and asking: What is the appropriate domain of a currency area? It might seem at first that the question is purely academic since it hardly appears within the realm of political feasibility that national currencies would ever be abandoned in favour of any other arrangement. To this, three answers can be given: (1) Certain parts of the

* *American Economic Review*, September 1961, 51, pp. 657–664.

world are undergoing processes of economic integration and dis-integration, new experiments are being made, and a conception of what constitutes an optimum currency area can clarify the meaning of these experiments. (2) Those countries, like Canada, which have experimented with flexible exchange rates are likely to face particular problems which the theory of *optimum* currency areas can elucidate if the national currency area does not coincide with the optimum currency area. (3) The idea can be used to illustrate certain functions of currencies which have been inadequately treated in the economic literature and which are sometimes neglected in the consideration of problems of economic policy.

I. CURRENCY AREAS AND COMMON CURRENCIES

A single currency implies a single central bank (with note-issuing powers) and therefore a potentially elastic supply of interregional means of payments. But in a currency area comprising more than one currency the supply of international means of payment is con-ditional upon the cooperation of many central banks; no central bank can expand its own liabilities much faster than other central banks without losing reserves and impairing convertibility [3]. This means that there will be a major difference between adjustment within a currency area which has a single currency and a currency area involving more than one currency; in other words there will be a difference between interregional adjustment and international adjust-ment even though exchange rates, in the latter case, are fixed.

To illustrate this difference consider a simple model of two entities (regions or countries), initially in full employment and balance-of-payments equilibrium, and see what happens when this equilibrium is disturbed by a shift of demand from the goods of entity B to the goods of entity A. Assume that money wages and prices cannot be reduced in the short run without causing unemployment, and that monetary authorities act to prevent inflation.

Suppose first that the entities are countries with national cur-rencies. The shift of demand from B to A causes unemployment in B and inflationary pressure in A [4]. To the extent that prices are allowed to rise in A the change in the terms of trade will relieve B of some of the burden of adjustment. But if A tightens credit restrictions to prevent prices from rising all the burden of adjustment is thrust onto country B; what is needed is a reduction in B's real income and if this cannot be effected by a change in the terms of trade – because B cannot lower, and A will not raise, prices – it must be accomplished by a decline in B's output and employment. The policy of surplus countries in restraining prices therefore imparts a recessive tendency to the world economy on fixed exchange rates or (more generally) to a currency area with many separate currencies [5].

Contrast this situation with that where the entities are regions within a closed economy lubricated by a common currency; and suppose now that the national government pursues a full-employment policy. The shift of demand from B to A causes unemployment in region B and inflationary pressure in region A, and a surplus in A's balance of payments [6]. To correct the unemployment in B the monetary authorities increase the money supply. The monetary expansion, however, aggravates inflationary pressure in region A: indeed, the principal way in which the monetary policy is effective in correcting full employment in the deficit region is by raising prices in the surplus region, turning the terms of trade against B. Full employment thus imparts an inflationary bias to the multiregional economy or (more generally) to a currency area with common currency.

In a currency area comprising different countries with national currencies the pace of employment in deficit countries is set by the willingness of surplus countries to inflate. But in a currency area comprising many regions and a single currency, the pace of inflation is set by the willingness of central authorities to allow unemployment in deficit regions.

The two systems could be brought closer together by an institutional change: unemployment could be avoided in the world economy if central banks agreed that the burden of international adjustment should fall on surplus countries, which would then inflate until unemployment in deficit countries is eliminated; or a world central bank could be established with power to create an international means of payment. But a currency area of either type cannot prevent both unemployment and inflation among its members. The fault lies not with the type of currency area, but with the domain of the currency area. The optimum currency area is not the world.

II. NATIONAL CURRENCIES AND FLEXIBLE EXCHANGE RATES

The existence of more than one currency area in the world implies (by definition) variable exchange rates. In the international trade example, if demand shifts from the products of country B to the products of country A, a depreciation by country B or an appreciation by country A would correct the external imbalance and also relieve unemployment in country B and restrain inflation in country A. This is the most favourable case for flexible rates based on national currencies.

Other examples, however, might be equally relevant. Suppose that the world consists of two countries, Canada and the United States, each of which has separate currencies. Also assume that the continent is divided into two regions which do not correspond to national boundaries – the East, which produces goods like cars, and the West, which produces goods like lumber products. To test the flexible-exchange-rate-argument in this example assume that the United States dollar fluctuates relative to the Canadian dollar, and that an increase in productivity (say) in the automobile industry causes an excess demand for lumber products and an excess supply of cars.

The immediate impact of the shift in demand is to cause unemployment in the East and inflationary pressure in the West, and a flow of bank reserves from the East to the West because of the former's regional balance-of-payments deficit. To relieve the unemployment in the East the central banks in both countries would have to expand the national money supplies, or to prevent inflation in the West, contract the national money supplied. (Meanwhile the Canada–United states exchange rate would move to preserve equilibrium in the national balances.) Thus, unemployment can be prevented in both countries, but only at the expense of inflation; or, inflation can be restrained in both countries but at the expense of unemployment; or, finally, the burden of adjustment can be shared between East and West with some unemployment in the East and some inflation in the West. But both unemployment and inflation cannot be escaped. The flexible exchange rate system does not serve to correct the balance-of-payments situation between the two regions (which is the essential problem) although it will do so between the two countries; it is therefore not necessarily preferable to a common currency or national currencies connected by fixed exchange rates.

III. REGIONAL CURRENCY AREAS AND FLEXIBLE EXCHANGE RATES

The preceding example does not destroy the argument for flexible exchange rates, but it might severely impair the relevance of the argument if it is applied to national currencies. The logic of the argument can in fact be rescued if national currencies are abandoned in favour of regional currencies.

To see this suppose that the 'world' reorganizes currencies so that Eastern and Western dollars replace Canadian and United States dollars. Now if the exchange rate between the East and the West were pegged, a dilemma would arise similar to that discussed in the first section. But if the East–West exchange rate were flexible, then an excess demand for lumber products need cause neither inflation nor unemployment in either region. The Western dollar appreciates relative to the Eastern dollar thus assuring balance-of-payments equilibrium, while the Eastern and Western central banks adopt monetary policies to ensure constancy of effective demand in terms of the regional currencies, and therefore stables prices and employment.

The same argument could be approached from another direction. A system of flexible exchange rates was originally propounded as an alternative to the gold-standard mechanism which many economists blamed for the world-wide spread of depression after 1929. But if the arguments against the gold standard were correct, then why should a similar argument not apply against a common currency system in a multiregional country? Under the gold standard depression in one country would be transmitted, through the foreign-trade multiplier, to foreign countries. Similarly, under a common currency, depression in one region would be transmitted to other regions for precisely the same reasons. If the gold standard imposed a harsh discipline on the national economy and induced the transmission of economic fluctuations, then a common currency would be guilty of the same charges; interregional balance-of-payments problems are invisible, so to speak, precisely because there is no escape from the self-adjusting effects of interregional money flows. (It is true, of course, that interregional liquidity can always be supplied by the national central bank, whereas the gold standard and even the gold-exchange standard were hampered, on occasion, by periodic scarcities of internationally liquid assets; but the basic argument against the gold standard was essentially distinct from the liquidity problem.)

Today, if the case for flexible exchange rates is a strong one, it is, in logic, a case for flexible exchange rates based on *regional* currencies, not on national currencies. The optimum currency area is the region.

IV. A PRACTICAL APPLICATION

The theory of international trade was developed on the Ricardian assumption that factors of production are mobile internally but immobile internationally. Williams, Ohlin, Iversen and others, however, protested that this assumption was invalid and showed how its relaxation would affect the real theory of trade. I have tried to show that its relaxation has important consequences also for the monetary theory of trade and especially the theory of flexible exchange rates. The argument for flexible exchange rates based on national currencies is only as valid as the Ricardian assumption about factor mobility. If factor mobility is high internally and low internationally a system of flexible exchange rates based on national currencies might work effectively enough. But if regions cut across national boundaries or if countries are multiregional then the argument for flexible exchange rates is only valid if currencies are reorganized on a regional basis.

In the real world, of course, currencies are mainly an expression of national sovereignty, so that actual currency reorganization would be feasible only if it were accompanied by profound political changes. The concept of an optimum currency area therefore has direct practical applicability only in areas where political organization is in a state of flux, such as in ex-colonial areas and in Western Europe.

In Western Europe the creation of the Common Market is regarded by many as an important step toward eventual political union, and the subject of a common currency for the six countries has been much discussed. One can cite the well-known position of J. E. Meade [7], who argues that the conditions for a common currency in Western Europe do not exist, and that, especially because of the lack of labour mobility, a system of flexible exchange rates would be more effective in promoting balance-of-payments equilibrium and internal stability; and the apparently opposite view of Tibor Scitovsky [8, 9] who favours a common currency because he believes that it would induce a greater degree of capital mobility, but further adds that steps must be taken to make labour more mobile and to facilitate supranational employment policies. In terms of the language of this paper Meade favours national currency areas while Scitovsky gives qualified approval to the idea of a single currency area in Western Europe.

In spite of the apparent contradiction between these two views, the concept of optimum currency areas helps us to see that the conflict reduces to an empirical rather than a theoretical question. In both cases it is implied that an essential ingredient of a common currency, or a single currency area, is a high degree of factor mobility; but Meade believes that the necessary factor mobility does not exist, while Scitovsky argues that labour mobility must be improved and that the creation of a common currency would itself stimulate capital mobility. In other words neither writer disputes that the optimum currency area is the region – defined in terms of internal factor mobility and external factor immobility – but there is an implicit difference in views on the precise degree of factor mobility required to delineate a region. The question thus reduces to whether or not Western Europe can be considered a single region, and this is essentially an empirical problem.

V. UPPER LIMITS ON THE NUMBER OF CURRENCIES AND CURRENCY AREAS

A dilemma now arises: Factor mobility (and hence the delineation of regions) is most usefully considered a relative rather than an absolute concept, with both geographical and industrial dimensions, and it is likely to change over time with alterations in political and economic conditions. If, then, the goals of internal stability are to be rigidly pursued, it follows that the greater is the number of separate currency areas in the world, the more successfully will these goals be attained (assuming, as always, that the basic argument for flexible exchange rates *per se* is valid). But this seems to imply that regions ought to be defined so narrowly as to count every minor pocket of unemployment arising from labour immobility as a separate region, each of which should apparently have a separate currency!

Such an arrangement hardly appeals to common sense. The suggestion reflects the fact that we have, thus far, considered the reasons for keeping currency areas small, not the reasons for maintaining or increasing their size. In other words we have discussed only the stabilization argument, to which end it is preferable to have many currency areas, and not the increasing costs which are likely to be associated with the maintenance of many currency areas.

It will be recalled that the older economists of the nineteenth century were internationalists and generally favoured a world currency. Thus, John Stuart Mill wrote [10, p. 176]:

'. . . So much of barbarism, however, still remains in the transactions of most civilised nations, that almost all independent countries choose to assert their nationality by having, to their own inconvenience and that of their neighbours, a peculiar currency of their own.'

Mill, like Bagehot and others, was concerned with the costs of valuation and money-changing, not stabilization policy, and it is readily seen that these costs tend to increase with the number of currencies. Any given money *qua* numeraire or unit of account fulfils this function less adequately if the prices of foreign goods are expressed in terms of foreign currency and must then be translated into domestic currency prices. Similarly, money in its role of medium of exchange is less useful if there are many currencies; although the costs of currency conversion are always present, they loom exceptionally large under inconvertibility or flexible exchange rates. (Indeed, in a hypothetical world in which the number of currencies equalled the number of commodities, the usefulness of money in its roles of unit of account and medium of exchange would disappear, and trade might just as well be conducted in terms of pure barter.) Money is a convenience and this restricts the optimum number of currencies. In terms of this argument alone the optimum currency area is the world, regardless of the number of regions of which it is composed.

There are two other factors which would inhibit the creation of an arbitrarily large number of currency areas. In the first place markets for foreign exchange must not be so thin that any single speculator (perhaps excepting central banks) can affect the market price; otherwise the speculation argument against flexible exchange rates would assume weighty dimensions. The other argument limiting 'Balkanization' concerns the very pillar on which the flexible exchange-rate argument rests. The thesis of those who favour flexible exchange rates is that the community in question is not willing to accept variations in its real income through adjustments in its money wage rate of price level, but that it is willing to accept virtually the same changes in its real income through variations in the rate of exchange. In other words it is assumed that unions bargain for a money rather than a real wage, and adjust their wage demands to changes in the cost of living, if at all, only if the cost-of-living index excludes imports. Now as the currency area grows smaller and the proportion of imports in total consumption grows, this assumption becomes increasingly unlikely. It may not be implausible to suppose that there is some degree of money illusion in the bargaining process between unions and management (or frictions and lags having the same effects), but it is unrealistic to assume the extreme degree of money illusion that would have to exist in small currency areas. Since the necessary degree of money illusion becomes greater the smaller are currency areas, it is plausible to conclude that this also imposes an upper limit on the number of currency areas.

VI. CONCLUDING ARGUMENT

The subject of flexible exchange rates can logically be separated into two distinct questions. The first is whether a system of flexible exchange rates can work effectively and efficiently in the modern world economy. For this to be possible it must be demonstrated that: (1) an international price system based on flexible exchange rates is dynamically stable after taking speculative demands into account; (2) the exchange rate changes necessary to eliminate normal disturbances to dynamic equilibrium are not so large as to cause violent and reversible shifts between export and import-competing industries (this is not ruled out by stability); (3) the risks created by variable exchange rates can be covered at reasonable costs in the forward markets; (4) central banks will refrain from monopolistic speculation; (5) monetary discipline will be maintained by the unfavourable political consequences of continuing depreciation, as it is to some extent maintained today by threats to the levels of foreign exchange reserves; (6) reasonable protection of debtors and creditors can be assured to maintain an increasing flow of long-term capital movements; and (7) wages and profits are not tied to a price index in which import goods are heavily weighted. I have not explicitly discussed these issues in my paper.

The second question concerns how the world should be divided into currency areas. I have argued that the stabilization argument for flexible exchange rates is valid only if it is based on regional currency areas. If the world can be divided into regions within each of which there is factor mobility and between which there is factor immobility, then each of these regions should have a separate currency which fluctuates relative to all other currencies. This carried the argument for flexible exchange rates to its logical conclusion.

But a region is an economic unit while a currency domain is partly an expression of national sovereignty. Except in areas where national

185

sovereignty is being given up it is not feasible to suggest that currencies should be reorganized; the validity of the argument for flexible exchange rates therefore hinges on the closeness with which nations correspond to regions. The argument works best if each nation (and currency) has internal factor mobility and external factor immobility. But if labour and capital are insufficiently mobile within a country then flexibility of the external price of the national currency cannot be expected to perform the stabilization function attributed to it, and one could expect varying rates of unemployment or inflation in the different regions. Similarly, if factors are mobile across national boundaries then a flexible exchange system becomes unnecessary, and may even be positively harmful, as I have suggested elsewhere [11].

Canada provides the only modern example where an advanced country has experimented with flexible exchange rates. According to my argument the experiment should be largely unsuccessful as far as stabilization is concerned. Because of the factor immobility between regions an increase in foreign demand for the products of one of the regions would cause an appreciation of the exchange rate and therefore increased unemployment in the remaining regions, a process which could be corrected by a monetary policy which aggravated inflationary pressures in the first region; every change in demand for the products in one region is likely to induce opposite changes in other regions which cannot be entirely modified by national stabilization policies. Similarly the high degree of external capital mobility is likely to interfere with stabilization policy for completely different reasons: to achieve internal stability the central bank can alter credit conditions but it is the change in the exchange rate rather than the alteration in the interest rate which produces the stabilizing effect; this indirectness conduces to a cyclical approach to equilibrium. Although an explicit empirical study would be necessary to verify that the Canadian experiment has not fulfilled the claims made for flexible exchange rates, the prima facie evidence indicates that it has not. It must be emphasized, though, that a failure of the Canadian experiment would cast doubt only on the effectiveness of a flexible exchange system in a multiregional country, not on a flexible exchange system in a unitary country [12].

NOTES AND REFERENCES

[1] I have analysed this system in some detail in R. A. Mundell, The international disequilibrium system, *Kyklos*, 1961 (2), **14**, 153–72.

[2] See, for example, Milton Friedman, The case of flexible exchange rates, *Essays in Positive Economics*. Chicago, 1953; J. E. Meade, The case for variable exchange rates, *Three Banks Review*, Sept. 1955; F. L. Lutz, The case for flexible exchange rates, Banca Naz. del Lavoro, Dec. 1954.

[3] More exactly, the rates at which central banks can expand monetary liabilities depend on income elasticities of demand and output elasticities of supply.

[4] For present purposes inflation is defined as a rise in the prices of home-produced goods.

[5] The tendency of surplus countries to control (what is, from a national point of view) inflation can be amply documented from United States and French policy in the 1920s and West Germany policy today. But it is unfortunate that a simple change in world relative prices is interpreted, in the surplus countries, as inflation.

[6] Instructive examples of balance-of-payments problems between different regions of the United States can be found in S. E. Harris, *Interregional and International Economics*. New York, 1957, Chapter 14. For purposes of this paper regions are defined as areas within which there is factor mobility, but between which there is factor immobility.

[7] J. E. Meade, The balance of payments problems of a free trade area, *Econ. Jour.*, Sept. 1957, **67**, 379–96. Especially pp. 385–86.

[8] Tibor Scitovsky, *Economic Theory and Western European Integration*. Stanford, 1958, Chapter 2.

[9] These statements of course cannot do full justice to the arguments of Meade and Scitovsky.

[10] J. S. Mill, *Principles of Political Economy*, Vol. II. New York, 1894.

[11] In my paper, The monetary dynamics of international adjustment under fixed and flexible exchange rates, *Quarterly Journal of the Economics Society*, May 1960, **74**, 227–57, I advanced the argument that stabilization policy would be more difficult under fixed exchange rates if short-term capital were immobile than if it were mobile, and more difficult under flexible exchange rates if capital were mobile than if it were immobile. Although the method of analysis was fundamentally different the conclusions support the hypothesis of this paper that the fixed-exchange-rate system is better within areas where factors are mobile and the flexible-exchange-rate system is better for areas between which factors are immobile. The argument of my other paper imposes an additional argument against increasing the number of currencies.

[12] Other economists have advanced arguments in favour of Balkanization of multiregional countries (see for example, A. D. Scott, A note on grants in federal countries, *Economica*, Nov. 1950, **17**, (n.s.), 416–22) and the argument for regional currency areas adds to the list; but, as Scott is careful to emphasize, no country can make such decisions on purely economic grounds.

9

PROBLEMS OF EUROPEAN
MONETARY UNION*

HARRY G. JOHNSON

The rapid development of the commitment of the six members of the
European Communities to the establishment of a common currency
as the next essential step in the evolution towards European economic
and political integration is in some ways surprising, given the recent
troubles of the Communities. But it is understandable, and can indeed
be viewed as virtually inevitable, in the light of the political dynamics
of relations within the Community and between the Community and
the United States.

TWO REASONS FOR CURRENCY UNION

Within the Community, the disruption of previously agreed arrangements by the events leading up to and including the devaluation of
the franc and the appreciation of the mark in 1969 obviously
required a major effort at patching up the Community and trying to
arrange matters so that the events of 1969 could not be repeated.
Apart from this holding operation, the strategy of the proponents of
European political union has always been to try to persuade the
governments to accept a seemingly rather innocuous economic
objective, symbolic of unity, in the hope that acceptance of the
commitment would force them to take the ancillary steps towards
economic unification and especially harmonization of economic
policies that would pave the way for political unification. Before
the events of 1968–9, it was widely asserted by the 'Europeans' that
the adoption of the Common Agricultural Policy ruled out forever
any change in the rates of exchange among the European currencies.
This assertion assumed that the European governments would be
forced by commitment to the Common Agricultural Policy to follow
domestic policies consistent with the maintenance of rigid exchange
rates. In fact, persistent German efforts to curb inflation on the one
hand, and General de Gaulle's concession of a wage rise inconsistent

* *Journal of World Trade Law*, July: August 1971, 5, pp. 377–87.

with the maintenance of the value of the franc as a result of the events of May 1968 on the other, made changes in the exchange values of the franc and the mark in the long run inevitable. When the chips were down, it was the Common Agricultural Policy and not the members' autonomy in domestic policy that had to give way. Having failed once, the 'Europeans' were naturally inclined, not to question their concept of effective strategy, but to try the same strategy again on an altogether more ambitious scale. If the commitment to the Common Agricultural Policy was not enough to ensure a commitment to fixed exchange rates and therefore to the policy harmonization required to maintain fixed exchange rates, the members had to be committed directly and explicitly to the maintenance of fixed exchange rates, to induce them to accept the need for policy harmonization and therefore for the economic prerequisites to political unification. As before, the strategy rests on the belief that economic policy autonomy can be forced to be sacrificed by a sufficiently strong political commitment to achieving an ideological symbol of political unity.

The other political dynamics concerns the relation between Europe and the United States in the international monetary system. Until 1965, the Six had been gradually accepting the idea that the United States had a special central position in the international monetary system, which obliged it to move cautiously in its efforts to correct its balance-of-payments deficit. The escalation of the war in Vietnam, without the necessary steps to finance it by increased domestic taxation, meant inflation in the United States that would inevitably spread to the rest of the fixed-exchange-rate world via enlarged U.S. balance-of-payments deficits, and face Europe in particular with the choice between accepting the inflation and protecting itself against it by appreciating its currencies against the dollar. In addition, there was the growing private use of the U.S. dollar in international trade and finance, and European fears of 'dollar imperialism' or 'dollar domination', expressed in complaints about the restriction of national monetary autonomy by the growth of the Euro-dollar market and about 'Americans buying us out with our own money'. There has been little recognition in Europe that the Common Market tariff itself encourages American firms to establish production facilities in Europe rather than export to the European market from the United States, or that the efforts of European central banks to preserve monetary autonomy by imposing restrictions on the freedom of their banks to engage in international transactions has itself encouraged efforts by those banks to circumvent national restrictions in the search for the profits of financial business on a Europe-wide scale through the development of the Euro-dollar and Euro-bond markets. In any case, it has been obvious that the main obstacle to European monetary independence in relation to the dollar has been the unwillingness or inability of individual European countries to take independent action, owing to the interdependence among them. The obvious answer, at least to those who think in political terms, would be to establish a single European currency that could rival the dollar as an instrument of private international trade and payments, and whose exchange value in relation to the dollar could be changed by central decisions which would not raise the issues of individual national costs and benefits, especially in relation to other European countries, that now inhibit European resistance to inflationary pressures emanating from the United States.

These two motivations towards the establishment of a common European currency, however, are in sharp inconsistency with one another. The strategy of inducing acceptance of the symbolic goal of a common currency as a means of forcing policy harmonization and eventually the pre-conditions of political union assumes that the necessary preconditions for unified political decisions have not yet been established, but need to be secured by a species of political chicanery. The desire to confront the dollar with a rival currency of comparable power assumes that political agreement on both this objective and the means of achieving it already exist, and need only to be suitably organized through supranational institutions.

The danger in this conflict of assumptions – which will be discussed further below – is that Europe will stall somewhere on the way to monetary union, immobilize itself in an effort to unify the European currencies that will preclude any action to free the European participants in the international monetary system from subservience to the monetary policies of the United States, and so pave the way for the international dominance of the U.S. dollar. This would be a result ironic in the extreme, for since the pound, franc, and mark crises of 1967–9 the United States and other leading countries have come to recognize the problems resulting from rigidity of exchange rates in the present international monetary system, and have been discussing greater flexibility of exchange rates as a means of avoiding these problems. This has involved a willingness of the United States to abnegate the power in the system which the unwillingness of other countries to change their exchange rates now gives it. And the commitment of the European countries to greater rigidity in the form of the establishment of a common currency threatens to forestall that development without putting anything in its place.

The history of the evolution of the common currency objective may be briefly described as follows. It began with the so-called 'Barre Plan' of February 1969, proposed by the Commission to the member states, and concerned with the coordination of members' economic policies and with monetary cooperation. Its starting-point was the difficulties posed for the Common Agricultural Policy in particular, and trade relations among members in general, by the measures taken by Germany and France in 1968 to avoid exchange rate changes. Its main recommendations were that members should work out possible inconsistencies among their medium-term objectives with respect to growth and inflation, coordinate their current economic and financial policies to forestall short-term external imbalances, consult with one another prior to the final adoption of economic policy measures, and establish facilities for short-term and medium-term monetary assistance within the EEC. As a result of the Hague Summit Conference of December 1969, the meeting of the Council of Ministers of January 1970, and the meeting of EEC Finance Ministers of February 1970, substantial parts of the Barre Plan were approved. The Council of Ministers accepted the need for increased monetary cooperation and policy consultation; and the Community's central banks set up arrangements to provide $2 thousand million of credit facilities for the assistance of members in balance of payments deficit.

In addition, the so-called 'Werner Group' was set up to pursue the subject further. Its interim report of May 1970 led to agreement by members not to widen the exchange margins among their currencies – a decision which in effect blocked further progress towards increased exchange flexibility in the international monetary system as a whole. Its final report, on 8 October 1970, presented a plan for complete monetary union, and with it economic union, to be established by the end of the 1970s. The first stage of the Werner Plan, to be completed in three years, called for the establishment of free convertibility among the six currencies; rigid and irrevocable fixation of the parities of the currencies with one another; establishment if possible of a single Community currency – if national currencies were retained, their existence should have no economic significance; centralization of budgetary and monetary policy at the Community level; the adoption of a common external monetary policy; complete integration of members' capital markets by appropriate fiscal and institutional changes; and the establishment of regional policies determined at the Community level. This programme would require the establishment of two new supra-national institutions: 'a centre of decision for economic policy' – a Community Ministry for Economic Policy, responsible to the European Parliament; and 'a Community system for central banks', involving coordination of exchange-market interventions, the pooling of international reserves, the adoption of a common representative unit, and the narrowing to zero of the margins of market exchange rate variations around the official parities.

This plan was not, however, unanimously accepted. At the Council of Ministers in December 1970, Germany and the Netherlands argued that it was pointless to narrow the bands for exchange rate variation unless at the same time common institutions were established, whereas France refused to surrender the economic sovereignty such common institutions would demand. Nevertheless, the Werner Plan is by now firmly established in the thinking of the Community, most importantly as regards the terms on which new members may join the group.

This paper will discuss three subjects: the basic economics of fixed exchange rates among the members of a free trade arrangement, of which the extreme case is a common currency in an economic union; the implications of such a common currency for the economic policy autonomy of the member countries; and the implications of the effort to establish a common European currency for the evolution of the international monetary system.

FIXED VERSUS FLEXIBLE EXCHANGE RATES

The basic economics involves the long-standing controversy over fixed versus flexible exchange rates, and the more recent formulation of that issue in terms of the economics of optimum currency areas.

Put very briefly, the basic argument for fixed exchange rates is the advantage of the equivalent of a common currency in promoting international competition over distance and other barriers to international trade, and so promoting international economic integration. The basic argument for flexible exchange rates, on the other hand, is to give countries an extra degree of freedom of domestic economic policy relative to other countries, and so reduce the pressures to intervene in international trade and payments that are likely to arise in a fixed-rate system as a consequence of divergent domestic developments or policies. The issue is essentially empirical: will the advantages of fixed rates outweigh the disadvantages of loss of autonomy in economic policy, or not, in any particular case? The theory of optimum currency areas poses this question in terms of the economic characteristics of the regions of a country, or the members of a fixed-exchange-rate area, that will enable a common currency to function smoothly, or alternatively cause it to function badly, given the facts of freedom of trade among the constituents of the currency area and the existence of trade with the outside world. Analysis of the required characteristics has focused on two rather different criteria, according to whether freedom of trade or autonomy of member policies has been the starting-point of the analysis. Freedom of trade focuses attention on structural characteristics that make adjustment to economic change in the face of a commitment to a fixed exchange rate difficult or easy, and suggests that mobility of factors of production among the regions of the currency area or diversity of economic activity within each region or both is conducive to beneficial participation in a common currency area. Autonomy of national economic policies focuses attention on the harmoniousness or otherwise of national economic policy objectives, and suggests that a common currency area requires homogeneity of attitudes in particular towards the trade-off between unemployment and inflation.

In the context of the European Community, the question arising is whether the objective of economic integration is best served by the adoption of a common currency. The advocates of a European currency assume that there is only one possible answer to that question; but their argument rests on analogy with existing national states rather than on economic analysis of the problem. That problem is whether the economic advantages of the free movement of goods and factors of production within an economic union are most likely to be secured by this or by another of the alternative exchange rate arrangements available. There are three main alternatives that might be employed.

193

The first is a system of floating exchange rates among member currencies. This alternative was recommended over a decade ago, in connection with the European Free Trade Area proposal, by James Meade. This is the proper policy if member countries want the advantages of freedom of trade but have divergent policy objectives with respect to inflation, unemployment, and economic growth, because by ensuring automatic balance-of-payments equilibrium it enables the members to pursue those objectives without obliging them to choose between sacrificing one or more of their objectives and imposing restrictions on their international trade and payments. The objections to floating exchange rates are founded either on misunderstanding of the economic logic or on misinterpretation of the facts of experience; but this is not a subject that can be elaborated on here.

The second alternative is the present international monetary system, under which exchange rates are normally fixed but the parities can be changed in cases of 'fundamental disequilibrium'. This system is appropriate if members are in broad harmony on policy objectives, but occasionally domestic or international developments or errors of domestic policy make an existing exchange rate inappropriate. The events of May 1968 in France are an example of the kind of development for which this system is appropriate; the difference between France and Germany in the determination of the political resistance to inflation would be coped with more effectively by a floating rate system.

The chief 'European' objection to this system stems from the Common Agricultural Policy, which seeks to establish conditions of equality of competition among farmers in the Common Market area; the argument is that changes in exchange rates among members confer a competitive advantage or impose a competitive disadvantage on one nation's farmers in competition with the farmers of other nations. This argument, however, is fallacious. If inflation is proceeding more rapidly in one member than in another, its farmers are being put at a steadily increasing competitive disadvantage by rising costs in conjunction with fixed product prices, and exchange rate adjustment simply restores the lost initial equality of competitive conditions. Objection should be made, not to exchange rate adjustment *per se*, but to making exchange rate adjustments by large and infrequent changes, which allows the loss of initial competitive parity to proceed gradually and virtually imperceptibly, and then corrects for it by arbitrary and substantial changes in relative competitive position. A floating exchange rate system would cope with this problem far more readily and satisfactorily.

The third alternative is completely rigid exchange rates among member currencies, or a common currency. This assumes both that members can agree on a common policy with respect to inflation, unemployment, and growth, and that they will live with the consequences of any adverse economic developments or errors in economic policy formation. This the members of the Community, on the evidence of experience in the past few years, have not been willing to do. Instead, they have shown themselves willing to intervene in freedom of trade and payments within the Community in order to protect their domestic policy autonomy – notably in the measures taken by France and Germany to stave off devaluation and revaluation respectively. The Werner Report places its faith in the proposition that, with sufficient 'political determination', a common currency can be established; the evidence is that the political determination is to preserve and not subordinate domestic policy autonomy.

The central point is that an economic union can obtain the benefits of free trade and factor movements under a variety of exchange rate arrangements, and that which one is appropriate depends on the circumstances and objectives of the membership. A common money is an outward symbol of, but not a prerequisite for, effective economic integration. If it could be established, it would undoubtedly promote economic integration by making commercial calculations easier throughout the market area; but the advantage of this would depend on prior effective agreement to harmonize monetary and fiscal policies. The symbol is not the reality. If the prior agreement did not exist, or existed subject to reservations in case of conflict between national and Community interests, the commitment to a common currency will create tensions among the members, and encourage resort to policies employing interventions in the freedom of trade and factor movements among the members designed to reconcile autonomy with balance-of-payments equilibrium and inimical to the overall objective of economic integration.

As already mentioned, the hope of the 'Europeans' is that, by securing prior commitment to the objective of establishing a common currency – which has the twin appeals of symbolizing European unity and permitting resistance to the domination of the American dollar – they will be able to persuade, cajole, or blackmail the members of the Community into the adoption of central coordination of monetary and financial policies and hence bring them to a stage of economic integration at which political union will seem a small further step to take. This, however, is a gamble of very dubious outcome. The difficulty is that at some stage the member countries must definitely and irrevocably give up their domestic policy autonomy in the fiscal and monetary fields. They must make an all-or-nothing choice. But the need for this choice can be disguised by the making of successive gestures towards it that involve little real cost or can be revoked if they come to do so. Thus little real sacrifice is involved in agreements to narrow the bands of exchange rate variation about parity, or to consult and communicate about national fiscal and monetary policy decisions. And commitments can be accepted in fair weather in the knowledge that a government always has the last-resort option of repudiating them in foul weather – as the fate of the Common Agricultural Policy testifies. One can flirt interminably with the idea of marriage, without ever actually sacrificing one's technical virginity.

SURRENDER OF AUTONOMY IN MONETARY POLICY

To turn to the implications of a common European currency for the member countries, the main implication is the surrender of autonomy in monetary policy. There are two aspects of this. The first is that the institutional changes required to create a common monetary area and capital market will require individual countries to give up their present reliance on specific controls over their commercial banking systems to implement their monetary policies; competitive pressures and the need for policy coordination in a Community-wide financial system will force the adoption, gradually, of a homogeneous system of central bank monetary management. This will be a desirable development: there is an eccentric differentiation in European thinking between the production of goods, where competition is deemed to be beneficial, and the production of financial services, where competition is deemed to be anti-social and regulation desirable. The second aspect is the need to align national monetary policies with the requirements of a centralized Community policy. It is questionable how much sacrifice of autonomy this will entail: the present degree of integration of world financial markets imposes severe constraints on the freedom of individual countries to pursue really independent monetary policies, and the different measures of detailed intervention favoured by the different national central banks appear more as means of preserving the symbolism of autonomous choice than as instruments of real independence. Whatever the truth may be, however, the individual national central banks will have to surrender whatever trappings and substances of autonomy they still possess, and become mere delegates to a central policy-making conference. This will be hard for the proud tradition of national central banking, with its ingrained belief in the superior wisdom of central bankers as compared with mere politically-selected and transient Ministers of Finance, to swallow.

A second implication, made much of in European thinking and in the Werner Report, is the need to subordinate fiscal autonomy to central control of national budgets. This emphasis seems overdrawn, and probably counter-productive in terms of achieving the objectives of European monetary and economic union, in the light of the observed roles of state and provincial governments in federal countries. In such countries, the regional governments have autonomy of fiscal policy; but that autonomy is constrained by the fact that the financing of deficits has to be obtained by borrowing in the national or international capital market on competitive terms, and cannot be provided by the creation of money. With a common European currency, the money supply would be centrally controlled and no national government could create money in its own favour; hence there would seem to be no need for central coordination of national fiscal policies. The perceived need for such coordination presumably stems from the assumption that the Community, like existing national governments, will in fact still have the option of resorting to inflationary finance in order to relieve its governments of the need to finance expenditures by either taxation or borrowing on commercial terms. On that assumption, there will obviously be a need to apportion fair shares of the proceeds among the members of the group.

In the longer run, there are more fundamental implications of the adoption of a common European currency for the member countries, implications derivable from the theory of optimum currency areas. The centrally coordinated policies of the Community will have to be devised to serve the average or majority interests of the members; and this will involve conflicts of interest. As is well known from the experience of national states, a policy designed to serve the overall

197

national interest is not necessarily beneficial to, and indeed may bear cruelly on, the residents of the constituent regions of the nation. Similarly, a Community economic policy could bear severely on the welfare of an individual member nation. There is likely to be a national analogue to the existing regional problem within nations, in a Community currency area. Maintenance of overall balance in the Community's balance of payments with the outside world, or (with adequate flexibility of the exchange rate against the outside world) implementation of the monetary and fiscal policies required to achieve the desired Community trade-off between inflation and unemployment, may well mean that some member nations prosper while others suffer from chronic stagnation. If nothing is done in compensation, there will be pressure for emigration of labour and capital from the stagnant to the prospering regions (nations). Within existing nations, compensation is offered in the form of regional development policies involving substantial transfers of resources from the richer to the poorer regions; but these policies have been of very questionable successfulness. It is even more questionable whether Community-level policies would be capable of resisting the competitive pressures for the concentration of resources in the more prosperous nations and regions of nations.

This, incidentally, is the basis for one of the major fears of the opponents of British entry into the EEC, as represented particularly in the recent writings of Nicholas Kaldor. The fear is that, instead of the hoped-for stimulus to British economic growth, the result will be economic stagnation, consequent on the British tendency to inflationary wage increase and the peripheral position Britain will occupy in relation to the major industrial centres of the Continent; and that the result of stagnation will be large-scale emigration of British labour and entrepreneurship to the Continent. This would pose a serious problem for the British politicians who favour entry, though they do not seem to be aware of it. Their aspiration is to take over the political leadership of Europe, on the basis of Britain's assumed technological leadership and their own assumed superior capacity for leading others. But political leadership rests on economic strength; and it would be ironical if British politicians sacrificed their economic power base futilely in their quest for new political fields to conquer. The possibility of loss of industrial strength as a consequence of membership in a European monetary union is, of course, ignored or denied by the financial experts of the City of

London, who see entry into a common currency area probably quite rightly as offering them the prospect of financial leadership in the Community, and also the chance to escape from the heavy burden of present policy restrictions on their freedom to compete in the international financial and capital markets.

THE COMMON EUROPEAN CURRENCY AND THE INTERNATIONAL MONETARY SYSTEM

Finally, let us consider the implications of the adoption of the objective of establishing a common European currency for the international monetary system. As a result of the exchange rate crises of 1967–9, the international monetary authorities came to the view that more flexibility of exchange rates was desirable and should be introduced by institutional changes in the IMF system. This change of view entailed, most notably, recognition by the United States authorities of the special position of the U.S. dollar as the lynch-pin of the system and the burdens that rigidity of rates against the dollar imposed on the other countries, in terms particularly of having to accept the rate of inflation set by domestic American policy. Specifically, it involved the United States becoming willing to allow other countries an escape valve from U.S. dominance of the system. The European movement to establish a common currency has effectively blocked further progress towards implementation of these ideas; the question is what the implications are for the world system.

The idea of the proponents of a common European currency is to establish a currency able to rival the dollar as a private international money, and whose exchange value can be manipulated to counter the dominance of the dollar. This, it should be noted, constitutes a reversal of the previous reluctance of the major European countries (in contrast to British policy with respect to the pound) to allow their currencies to become international monies. There is a grain of sense in this objective inasmuch as the close trading relationships among the European countries have made them individually reluctant to make use of the international monetary autonomy the present system allows them. It would clearly be easier if the exchange values of the European currencies could be changed uniformly in relation to the dollar, by central decision, rather than individual countries having to decide whether or not, and if so by how much, to change their parities, on the basis of informed guesses about how their European partners would react. But this observation presupposes the existence of a central decision-taking process capable of taking such a decision about the exchange value of the European currency in terms of the American, or of deciding to let the European currency float. To establish such a central monetary authority would require the prior establishment of the machinery of policy harmonization discussed above; and, as pointed out, this will involve a once-for-all decision, the approach of which can be indefinitely delayed by agreement on the making of apparently meaningful but substantially empty gestures. The danger is that the European countries will procrastinate indefinitely, in order to avoid actually reaching the chasm that has to be crossed at the end, and that in so doing they will deprive themselves of the possibility of individual exchange rate action that they enjoy under the present system, without arriving at any effective possibility of collective exchange rate action, as envisaged in the plan for a common currency. The result would be that control of the international monetary system would pass to the Board of Governors of the Federal Reserve System, whose domestically-oriented policy decisions would determine the world rate of inflation. Moreover, in the absence of an existential European international money, with a monetary domain extending unrestrictedly over the European economy, the dollar would continue to expand in its present role as the international money used in private international transactions. In short, the difficulties involved in the process of establishing a common European currency may mean that the Europeans will achieve precisely the reverse of what they want – namely, a world economy dominated still more than at present by the United States dollar.

10

THE EXCHANGE-RATE QUESTION
FOR A UNITED EUROPE*

HARRY G. JOHNSON

INTRODUCTION: THE PROBLEM

The title of this paper is intended to describe the major issue involved
in the future monetary arrangements of the European Economic
Communities once the Community has been expanded from six to
ten members. This is whether the European countries should retain
their individual national currencies and the associated freedom of
exchange-rate adjustment as an instrument of national economic
sovereignty, or adopt a common currency – either *de facto* through
absolute fixity of the exchange rates prevailing among themselves,
or *de jure* as well by formal adoption of a European unit of account,
reserve money, and possibly an eventual common circulating
medium – harmonize their domestic economic policies to the extent
that such a change would require, and establish a collective authority
to effect exchange-rate adjustments between the common currency
and the currencies of the outside world. The title implicitly assumes
that the third alternative – complete rigidity of exchange rates all
round – is ruled out of consideration by the facts of nature, that is,
that in the relevant future the collectivity of major countries will not
be able to achieve via conscious harmonization of their domestic
economic policies the same degree of automatic coordination of
policies via the pressures of international monetary flows that
prevailed – at least in theory – under the classical gold standard.

THE BACKGROUND THEORY

In the middle 1950s, long before the monetary arrangements of
European economic integration became a live topic of discussion,
James Meade analysed in a classic paper the balance-of-payments
problems that would be likely to arise in a free trade arrangement,
and after examining the alternative possible methods of adjustment

* *Europe and the Evolution of the International Monetary System*, Geneva
Conference, 1972.

that could be employed, concluded strongly in favour of a system of flexible exchange rates among the member countries, subject to interventions in the exchange market by national monetary authorities (and if possible a supranational monetary authority) provided that such intervention were not used to establish unfair competitive advantages for the intervening country [1]. (Meade did, however, state that the 'integrationist' or in more modern parlance 'common currency' approach offered the best long-run solution to the problem *provided* (a point important for the subsequent argument) that the member countries understood and accepted its political implications in terms of policy harmonization.) Analysing the same problem subsequently in a paper that was translated into French so as to permit decent burial in an obscure Conference volume [2], I raised the question whether the aggravation of balance-of-payments problems by the freeing of trade might not be counterbalanced by the effects of increased international competition in keeping national wages and prices in line with those prevailing generally in the free-trade area.

On this question of whether balance-of-payments problems requiring exchange-rate adjustments would continue to recur under conditions of free trade, experience has shown Meade to be clearly right and my own question naively irrelevant. Yet there is a theoretical problem here that requires some answer, beyond induction from the observed facts of experience [3]. Contemporary 'monetarist' models of balance-of-payments theory, derived from Hume's analysis of the price-specie-flow mechanism [4], typically assume a small country facing fixed prices on the world market, all goods being traded. In such a model, balance-of-payments deficits are a consequence of excessive domestic credit expansion, or in more familiar Keynesian terms of an excess of expenditure over production, and can be remedied by monetary and/or fiscal restraint without the need for exchange-rate changes. One would expect the same proposition to apply to the individual members of a customs union among industrially diversified national economies, especially one providing also for factor mobility internally: excessive expenditure in relation to income might be expected to spill outwards into the rest of the union through reduced exports and increased imports without raising domestic wages and prices sufficiently seriously to require a devaluation as well as a deflation for the restoration of internal and external balance. Indeed, this proposition, if it were correct, would make it a simple matter for the union to adopt a common currency or its equivalent in terms of rigidly fixed exchange rates.

In formal theoretical terms, an answer can be provided along several possible lines. One obvious one, in terms of the theoretical models, is that in spite of industrial diversification members' manufactures are imperfectly or monopolistically competitive with one another, so that excess demand can raise the prices of exportables and importables above the level consistent with balance-of-payments equilibrium, and devaluation is an easier method than deflation and the accompanying unemployment for restoring the competitive price-relationships required for external and internal balance. An alternative explanation consistent with the assumption of perfect competition in the pricing of traded goods, entails the assumption of a significant sector of non-traded goods and services whose prices may move independently (and may be peculiarly responsive to government demand-management policies with inflationary developments of wages and prices in this sector communicating themselves to factor prices and the profitability of exporting and import-competing production, so that excess demand makes wages – but not prices – uncompetitive and requires again a choice between deflation of production and employment, and devaluation as means of restoring the international competitiveness required for external and internal balance). A third explanation would appeal to ignorance, lags, and overshooting in the adjustment of domestic wages and prices to changes in demand pressure at the micro-economic level; this explanation gains plausibility from recent research into the micro-economic foundations of the Phillips curve in the economics of wage-determination under local bargaining, which relies on the costs of information and market research. A fourth and not very intellectually satisfying explanation appeals to 'noise' or stochastic elements in the operation of competition.

Meade's analysis of the problem of balance-of-payments adjustment in a free-trade area (and mine also) was based on theory of exchange-rate flexibility as it stood at that time; and that theory implicitly identified national economies with currency areas. Contemporary analysis of the problem is based on the theory of optimum currency areas as developed by Mundell, McKinnon, and others. Mundell [5] was primarily concerned with the question of whether the optimum currency area might not be smaller than the whole national economy, and made the optimum currency area a question

203

of the mobility of factors of production within the area, though he recognized limits on the possibility of reducing the range of a currency area set by the necessity for money to retain its characteristic of being a form of generalized purchasing power. (Incidentally, I now think that the emphasis placed by Mundell and many other writers on regional differences in unemployment rates as an indication of non-optimality of currency arrangements is mistaken; according to the theory of the micro-economics of labour markets mentioned above, the persistence over long historical periods of regional differences in unemployment rates represents differing equilibrium adjustments to the choice between labour and leisure.) McKinnon [6] made the question one of the 'openness' of the economy, which would determine the 'moneyness' of the money of the area, i.e. the extent to which a change in the exchange rate would not be offset by a compensating automatic increase in the domestic currency prices of tradeable goods and services. Kenen [7] subsequently attempted to make the optimum currency area a matter of the diversity and flexibility of economic activity in the area; while Haberler, in discussions of the problem, and with the exchange rate relationships among the major nations rather than Mundell's original problem in mind, made it a matter of the degree of similarity of the national policy objectives of governments with respect to the trade-off between inflation and unemployment.

All of these analyses contain important clues about or insights into the conditions under which either a national currency can be managed (via monetary or exchange rate policy) to preserve external equilibrium without excessive internal regional or sectoral strains, or a group of countries can maintain fixed exchange rates or a common currency among themselves. Unfortunately, they tend to cancel each other out, so that by the end of the Chicago Conference on International Monetary Problems of 1966 [8] the theoretical problem seems to have reached a dead end of analysis. The problem has since been revived in the context of world inflation and the proposal for a common European currency [9], but more as a concept for debate than as a fruitful theoretical foundation for policy progress [10].

Experience of exchange-rate problems in my judgement strongly supports Haberler's emphasis on harmony or discord of national demand-management policies as the most directly useful idea to emerge from the discussion of optimum currency areas and their crucial economic characteristics. At any rate, I shall focus on policy harmonies and discords. And I offer as a preliminary point the observation that the exchange-rate problems of recent years have been due to the interaction between a shift of United States policies from policies that produced a reasonable degree of price stability in that country to policies that produced an uncomfortable rate of price inflation, and differences among the European countries (including the United Kingdom) in their domestic tolerance for inflation and hence their willingness to accept the infusion of a U.S.-led world inflation that for some meant an undesired importation of both inflation and U.S. dollars and for others a welcome relief from the adverse balance-of-payments effects of domestic inflation necessitated by political pressures. In other words, so long as the United States maintained reasonable price stability, it suited the other major countries to live with the international financial dominance of the dollar and to retain some autonomy of domestic policy on the basis of being able to change their national exchange rates against the dollar if necessary; once the United States became a potent source of world inflation, the question naturally arose of establishing a basis for common action to resist the importation of inflation. I shall later suggest that the key question for the future is whether the prospect of continuing inflation in the United States is sufficiently strong and sufficiently distasteful to the European countries to make them willing to adopt a common currency or internally-rigid-exchange-rate equivalent and introduce the necessary harmonization of domestic economic policies, in order to be able to counter American inflation by harmonized upward exchange-rate flexibility, or whether they will be willing to live with the dominance of the United States in the recently-restored fixed-rate system (sustained of course by the hope of gradually reducing that dominance through the extension of the Special Drawing Rights system and the funding of outstanding dollar balances) as the price of retaining more freedom of domestic policy action than would be allowed by a rigid commitment to fixed exchange rates among the European currencies.

THE PROPOSAL FOR A COMMON EUROPEAN CURRENCY

In my admittedly jaundiced view, the proposal to establish a common European currency represents only the most recent phase of the continued efforts of the Brussels bureaucracy of the European Economic Communities – the powerful institutionalized relic of the entirely understandable and in some respects admirable postwar-two movement for European political and economic integration – to force ever-further integration on countries which are no longer convinced of its political necessity [11]. After the establishment of the Common Agricultural Policy, it was widely asserted and even more widely believed that that policy ruled out any possibility of change in the exchange rates of the Common Market countries' currencies against one another, an assertion that implied that the member governments would willy-nilly have to harmonize their economic policies to the extent required to maintain internal exchange rate rigidity. (With hindsight, it can be said also to have involved the implicit assumption that American prices would remain stable, so that internal rigidity would also mean rigidity against the dollar.)

The assertion was unfounded in theory, as has frequently been shown, because differential rates of inflation among member countries distort competitive conditions among groups of national agricultural producers and the exchange-rate changes necessary to correct for them merely restore the *status quo ante*. But discrete exchange-rate changes as under the International Monetary Fund system are nonetheless disruptive, and theory suggests that flexible exchange rates would provide more continuous conditions of fair competition among farmers in the different member countries confronted with different national trends in their input costs. In fact, different price trends among the member countries, in the face of the American inflation, forced exchange-rate adjustments in the German mark and the French franc, and the temporary suspension of the Common Agricultural Policy. When it came to the test, it was the dam and not the river that gave way. The Common Agricultural Policy did not force harmonization of domestic policies, and the lack of such harmonization finally forced adjustment of exchange rates among the major European countries, while the consequences for the Common Agricultural Policy had to be met by *ad hoc* adjustments.

The Commission reacted to this set-back by tackling the question of permanent fixation of intra-Community exchange rates directly, and won agreement from member governments on acceptance of the objective of establishing a common currency and recognition of the implications of achieving this objective in the way of harmonization of monetary, fiscal and other policies. This agreement, incidentally, from the point of view of the international monetary system as a whole had the extremely unfortunate effect of blocking further progress towards a systematized increase in exchange-rate flexibility generally. Such increased flexibility had come to be regarded as desirable by international monetary officialdom after the various international-monetary crises that preceded the franc devaluation and mark revaluation effected very tardily in 1969. At that time, proposals for a widening of the band of permitted fluctuation of market exchange rates about the official parities, for adoption of some version of the 'crawling peg' plan for automatic slow adjustment of the parities themselves to diverging price trends in national economies, and for allowing the undervalued currencies of surplus countries to be temporarily floated so that these countries could avoid the awkward problem of choosing a new parity immediately, were very much under active discussion. Determination on the objective of a common European currency, which would have to be established before it could be made flexible against the dollar, meant the shelving of discussion of these proposals, pending the establishment of the new common currency. That in turn made the dollar crisis of 1971, in some form, an inevitability: if the Europeans were confined by the common currency objective to doing nothing about the overvaluation of the dollar except complain about it, the initiative in securing a devaluation of the dollar relative to the European and Japanese currencies would necessarily fall to the Americans, and to take it they would have to rupture the established pattern of international monetary relationships.

While it originated in the desire to force real integration by winning political acceptance of the symbols of it in advance of the reality, the notion of a common European currency gained considerable additional appeal on two grounds: politically, in terms of providing a rival world currency to the dollar, an objective strengthened by the unpopularity of the war in Vietnam; and economically, from the potentiality of countering the current American inflation and the presumed advantages to the United States of dollar-financed deficits, by revaluation or upward flotation of the common currency against the dollar. In passing, it may be noted that the economic gains to the United States from foreign holdings of dollars, and from its ability to induce expansion of those holdings by imposing inflation on the rest of the world, can very easily be vastly exaggerated by theoretical analysis based on the classical conception of money as inherently non-interest-bearing and ignoring the gains to the holder of liquid assets from financial intermediation. Most foreign-held dollars are held in forms that yield an interest return as well as a liquidity service, and the interest return tends to be adjusted upwards in face of inflation. Further, the growth of the Eurodollar market has meant that much of any 'seigniorage gain' accrues to banks located in Europe rather than in America. Finally, still in passing, the arguments assume that a viable European alternative to the dollar either exists or could be quickly created – and that is precisely the problem, that its creation would require major institutional or policy changes [12]. Be that as it may, these various additional arguments have brought the concept of the optimal currency area back into the realm of discussion – and a very awkward recruit to the cause of a common European currency it has made, to be sure.

In this connection, it should be mentioned that there is a real problem that a common currency could solve if it could be implemented, namely that any individual European country that revalues to protect itself from inflation emanating from the United States has to cope with the uncertainties involved in the fact that most of its trade is conducted with other European countries rather than with the United States, so that common action would be far less disruptive of intra-European trading relationships than individual action. The problem is reminiscent of the reasons why competing oligopolies frequently find it useful to form mergers, cartels, or information-exchanging arrangements. But the problem for the European countries is to establish the foundations and mechanisms for common action against a common cause of trouble, which are now non-existent – as proven by the inability of the European countries to respond to the American challenge to exercise world monetary leadership issued on 15 August 1971.

The absence of the preconditions necessary for the establishment of a common currency had in fact been demonstrated conclusively earlier in the year, when the Common Market countries were unable to agree on any commonly-instituted alternative to the flotation of the German mark in May 1971. That policy event was in a sense more deeply symptomatic of European disunity than either the inability to agree on a common policy stance in response to the American challenge just mentioned, or the fact that the outcome of the crisis of 1971 has been a realignment of exchange rates among the European currencies as well as between them and the dollar, in place of the general and uniform appreciation against the dollar that the imposition of the uniform 10% surcharge and some policy statements at the beginning of the crisis implied that the Americans were seeking. For a commitment to fixed exchange rates, subject to the safety-valve of infrequent use of revaluation or devaluation in case of necessity, puts pressure on countries to harmonize their policies and could possibly eventually produce sufficient harmonization for a binding commitment to fixed exchange rates or establishment of a common currency to be feasible and acceptable, whereas a floating rate as a non-transient arrangement removes the need for harmonization.

It may be added that both the French insistence on a rise in the dollar price of gold, and the British insistence on not appreciating as much as the Germans and Japanese in spite of their strong balance-of-payments position (with the obvious purpose of entering the Common Market with an undervalued currency so that the balance-of-payments costs involved could be absorbed without an explicit devaluation), reflect a degree of concern for purely national policy interests ominous for the prospects of establishing a common European currency with the policy harmonization and acceptance of the primacy of collective over individual national interests that that entails.

FUTURE PROSPECTS

The fixed exchange rate, Bretton Woods and International Monetary Fund, system of international monetary organization has been restored, with a new set of parities intended to represent an international consensus on equilibrium currency values sustainable for the future, though also with some concession to the earlier recognized need for more automatic flexibility of exchange rates through a widening of the band for fluctuation of market exchange rates around their parities. The fact that the wider band but not the crawling peg or temporary flotation proposal has been adopted means, however, that only a very limited concession has been made to what has been, in my judgement at least, the central problem of the system, divergences of national demand management policies leading to divergences of national cost and price trends requiring continuing adjustments of exchange rates [13]. The wider band is suitable for accommodating transient policy errors that will be corrected fairly speedily, transferring part of the responsibility for exchange rate stabilizing operations to private in place of official speculators, and enabling central banks to impose heavier financial penalties on 'unjustified' destabilizing speculation; but it affords only small and short-run scope for exchange-rate adjustments in response to divergent national price trends.

If such divergent national price trends – resulting from divergent national choices on the trade-off function between inflation and unemployment – re-emerge there will be further international monetary crises. And there is every reason to believe that they will re-emerge. The question of relevance, however, is whether there will be greater divergences between the average of the European countries (or perhaps more accurately the average of the European countries' aspirations and tolerances) and the United States, or among the European countries themselves. If, as in the past five years or so, the United States chooses for itself and under the present fixed-rate system forces on the rest of the world an unreasonably high and disturbing rate of inflation, the argument for establishing a common European currency will remain strong, perhaps sufficiently so to induce the European countries to sacrifice a considerable amount of domestic policy autonomy for .the sake of the policy harmonization that would be required to implement it. If, on the other hand, the United States adopts policies that will result in a return to reasonable stability of American prices, the European countries may well prefer to retain the domestic policy autonomy they have enjoyed over the postwar period on the basis of their ability to change their exchange rates against both the United States and their fellow-European countries together, while of course continuing to pay lip-service to the common currency ideal while contriving in practice to make only glacial progress towards it.

If – contrary to present indications – the policies of the United States restored reasonable price stability there, the motivation for establishing a Common European currency would have to be vanity or political symbolism, or the quantitatively trivial economic gain of seigniorage on privately used international money, most of which Europe is already enjoying as a result of the development of the Eurodollar market. The cost, which on past evidence the members of the European Community (including Britain as a prospective entrant) would be very unwilling to pay, would be the abandonment of domestic policy independence for the sake of currency harmonization. Independence of domestic policy is of course a marginal matter in a fixed rate system (except for the reserve currency country), available only to the extent of the willingness to change the exchange rate as a last resort, and countries may eventually become willing to surrender it. But the time for that does not seem to be near at hand.

The Group has not sought to construct an ideal system in the abstract. It has set out rather to determine the elements that are indispensable to the existence of a complete economic and monetary union. The union as it is described here represents the minimum that must be done, and is a stage in a dynamic evolution which the pressure of events and political will can model in a different way.

Economic and monetary union will make it possible to realize an area within which goods and services, people and capital will circulate freely and without competitive distortions, without thereby giving rise to structural or regional disequilibrium.

A monetary union implies inside its boundaries the total and irreversible convertibility of currencies, the elimination of margins of fluctuation in exchange rates, the irrevocable fixing of parity rates and the complete liberation of movements of capital. It may be accompanied by the maintenance of national monetary symbols or the establishment of a sole Community currency. From the technical point of view the choice between these two solutions may seem immaterial, but considerations of a psychological and political nature militate in favour of the adoption of a sole currency which would confirm the irreversibility of the venture.

For such a union only the global balance of payments of the Community vis-à-vis the outside world is of any importance. Equilibrium within the Community would be realized at this stage in the same way as within a nation's frontiers, thanks to the mobility of the factors of production and financial transfers by the public and private sectors.

To ensure the cohesion of economic and monetary union, transfers of responsibility from the national to the Community plane will be essential. These transfers will be kept within the limits necessary for the effective operation of the Community and will concern essentially the whole body of policies determining the realization of general equilibrium. In addition, it will be necessary for the instruments of economic policy to be harmonized in the various sectors.

Economic and monetary union implies the following principal consequences:

(*a*) The Community currencies will be assured of total and irreversible mutual convertibility free from fluctuations in rates and with immutable parity rates, or preferably they will be replaced by a sole Community currency.

(*b*) The creation of liquidity throughout the area and monetary and credit policy will be centralized.

(*c*) Monetary policy in relation to the outside world will be within the jurisdiction of the Community.

(*d*) The policies of the Member States as regards the capital market will be unified.

(*e*) The essential features of the whole of the public budgets, and in particular variations in their volume, the size of balances and the methods of financing or utilizing them, will be decided at the Community level.

(*f*) Regional and structural policies will no longer be exclusively within the jurisdiction of the member countries.

(*g*) A systematic and continuous consultation between the social partners will be ensured at the Community level.

A result of this is that on the plane of *institutional reforms* the realization of economic and monetary union demands the creation or the transformation of a certain number of Community organs to which powers until then exercised by the national authorities will have to be transferred. These transfers of responsibility represent a process of fundamental political significance which implies the progressive development of political cooperation. Economic and monetary union thus appears as a leaven for the development of political union, which in the long run it cannot do without.

The Group does not consider that it will have to formulate detailed proposals as to the institutional form to be given to the different Community organs; it nevertheless indicates the principal requirements to be observed by two organs that seems to it indispensable to the control of economic and monetary policy inside the union: a centre of decision for economic policy, and a Community system for the central banks.

The *centre of decision for economic policy* will exercise independently, in accordance with the Community interest, a decisive influence over the general economic policy of the Community. In view of the fact that the role of the Community budget as an economic instrument will be insufficient, the Community's centre of decision must be in a position to influence the national budgets, especially as regards the level and the direction of the balances and the methods for financing the deficits or utilizing the surpluses. In addition, changes in the parity of the sole currency or the whole of the national currencies will be within the competence of this centre. Finally, in order to ensure the necessary links with the general economic policy its responsibility will extend to other domains of economic and social policy which will have been transferred to the Community level. It is essential that the centre of decision for economic policy should be in a position to take rapid and effective decisions by methods to be specified, especially as regards the way in which the Member States will participate.

The constitution of the Community system for the central banks could be based on organisms of the type of the Federal Reserve System operating in the United States. This Community institution will be empowered to take decisions, according to the requirements of the economic situation, in the matter of internal monetary policy as regards liquidity, rates of interest, and the granting of loans to public and private sectors. In the field of external monetary policy, it will be empowered to intervene in the foreign exchange market and the management of the monetary reserves of the Community.

The implementation of economic and monetary union demands institutional reforms which presuppose a modification of the Treaties of Rome. Certainly, the present provisions already allow substantial progress to be made towards economic and monetary union, but a modification of the treaties will be necessary eventually to make possible a more advanced development of transfers of responsibility and the progressive establishment of the final institutions.

The Group considers that economic and monetary union is an objective realizable in the course of the present decade, provided the political will of the Member States to realize this objective, solemnly declared at the Conference at The Hague, is present.

NOTES AND REFERENCES

[1] J. E. Meade, The balance-of-payments problems of a European free-trade area, *The Economic Journal*, vol. LXVII, No. 267, September 1957, pp. 379–96.

[2] Harry G. Johnson, Les problèmes monétaires dans un zone de libre échange, in *Marché Commun Institutions Communes*, pp. 78–82. Paris: Pichon et Durand-Auzias, 1960.

[3] For an empirical study of this issue, see R. Triffin and Herbert G. Grubel, The adjustment mechanism to different rates of monetary expansion among the countries of the European Economic Community, *Review of Economics and Statistics*, vol. XLIV, No. 4, November 1962, pp. 486–91.

[4] See Harry G. Johnson, The monetary approach to balance-of-payments theory, forthcoming in Michael B. Connolly and Alexander K. Swoboda, *International Economics: Geneva Essays*, London: George Allen and Unwin, 1973.

[5] R. A. Mundell, A theory of optimum currency areas, *American Economic Review*, vol. LI, No. 4, September 1961, pp. 657–65; reprinted in his *International Economics*, New York: Macmillan, 1968, Chapter 12.

[6] R. I. McKinnon, Optimum currency areas, *American Economic Review*, vol. LIII, No. 4, September 1963, pp. 717–24.

[7] P. B. Kenen, The theory of optimum currency areas: an eclectic view, in R. A. Mundell and A. K. Swoboda (eds.), *Monetary Problems of the International Economy*, Chicago: University of Chicago Press, 1969.

[8] Robert A. Mundell and Alexander K. Swoboda (eds.), *Monetary Problems of the International Economy*, Chicago: University of Chicago Press, 1969.

[9] Harry G. Johnson and Alexander K. Swoboda (eds.), *Economics of Common Currencies*, London: George Allen and Unwin, 1972, forthcoming.

[10] It is interesting to record that Mundell has recently become an ardent exponent of fixed exchange rates.

[11] An exception should be made for the United Kingdom, where membership of the European Community became an internal political necessity, in my judgement, after the disastrous failure of the Suez invasion of 1956 and the associated demonstration that neither the special relationship with the United States nor the sentimental support of the erstwhile empire any longer provided a basis for the continuance of imperial assumptions and habits of behaviour in world politics. British subscription to the objective of establishing a common European currency is to be regarded largely as a matter of acceptance of one of the many prices of membership, though of course, as a major participant in the Eurodollar market, which a common currency might hope to replace, the British financial community has, or at least thinks it has, a commercial interest in the proposal.

[12] Mundell and others have argued for the development of the Eurodollar into a European currency; but this proposal has obvious political drawbacks from a European point of view, though some of the plans put forward for a common currency implicitly involve essentially re-naming the Eurodollar a Europa and taking over the existing financial machinery on its behalf.

[13] An alternative view of the problem that should perhaps be mentioned is that demand-management policies have proved incapable of preventing sporadic outbursts of wage-push inflation, and that 'incomes policy' is no more promising a means to that end, so that exchange rate flexibility is necessary to prevent 'union pushfulness' from causing intractable international disequilibria. My own view is that 'union pushfulness' is not an independent phenomenon but only a facet of the inflationary mechanism.

[14] Unofficial translation! Commission of the European Communities.

11

EUROPEAN MONETARY UNIFICATION AND THE INTERNATIONAL MONETARY SYSTEM*

RICHARD N. COOPER

Yale University

NOTE

This paper was first drafted in the spring of 1971, after the German mark had been floated but before the financial turmoil associated with President Nixon's message of 15 August, which suspended gold convertibility of the dollar and imposed a 10% surcharge on most imports into the United States. The surcharge was removed and the question of exchange-rate parities apparently resolved in December 1971, but the fundamental features of the international monetary system were left untenably in place. Much remains to be done. This paper was and remains addressed to those longer-term issues, not to the resolution of immediate problems. It has therefore been changed little to reflect recent developments. The first stage of the Werner Plan for monetary unification in Europe was derailed by the events of 1971, but monetary unification was probably advanced rather than retarded by those developments, for they brought into prominence both the difficulties of unification, thereby promoting a more realistic approach to it, and the great need for it if continued reliance on the U.S. dollar as centrepiece of the financial system is to be challenged, as many Europeans desire. But, these inducements for unification still must gather much strength to overcome the remaining economic and psychological obstacles to it.

INTRODUCTION

In mid-August 1971, while most Europeans and many Americans were basking in the summer sun, President Nixon dropped an

* Adapted from: *Sterling, European Monetary Unification and the International Monetary System*, London: British-North American Committee, 1972.

economic bombshell whose reverberations will be heard for many years to come. On the domestic side, which does not concern us here, it involved measures to expand the American economy, coupled with wage and price controls for the first time since the Korean War of 1950. On the international side, it involved the imposition of an additional 10% tariff on all dutiable imports (comprising about two-thirds of total imports) and the relatively esoteric but emotive declaration that the U.S. dollar would no longer be freely convertible into gold by foreign monetary authorities.

These two steps affecting international transactions represented a direct assault on the leading principles that had guided international economic intercourse since the Second World War. Those principles conferred on gold a central, although somewhat concealed, role in the international monetary system, required fixity of foreign-exchange rates at 'par values' to be changed only infrequently and under specified circumstances, called for gradual reduction of government-imposed barriers to trade, and, above all, involved a recognition by all major countries of mutual interest in matters affecting international commerce and hence close cooperation in managing the international economic system.

This system, embodied in legal form in the Bretton Woods Agreement and in the General Agreement on Tariffs and Trade (GATT), had become, however, subject to severe tensions arising from developments that had not been fully anticipated when it was laid down, and to which it has been unable fully to adapt. These tensions were bound to cause substantial changes in the system, but few anticipated just how soon and in what dramatic form initiation of the alterations would come.

The purpose of this paper is not to discuss the whole range of issues concerning the international monetary and trading system, but rather to focus on two narrower problems: (1) the prospects for a unified European currency, and (2) the impact of a unified European currency on the international monetary system. It will, nevertheless, be necessary to make an excursion into the broader framework of the existing monetary system, for the tensions found there will help not only in understanding, even if not approving, the American moves of August 1971 but also in interpreting the possibilities and problems of monetary evolution in an enlarged European Community.

By now, it has become conventional for economists to approach analytical discussion of the international monetary system under three separate headings, each representing a complex set of problems and offering a range of possible solutions that are partially – but only partially – separable from one another. The headings *liquidity, adjustment and confidence* offer a fruitful organizing scheme, around which most issues of practical as well as theoretical importance can be discussed, and an understanding of which is essential background for considering the concrete policy questions that face nations. However, for completeness, I would broaden these topics by adding a further heading – *interdependence* – which covers a range of issues related to but fundamentally different from the first three topics. These four analytical topics will be briefly discussed before returning to the more specific problems listed above.

I. FOUR PROBLEMS FOR THE INTERNATIONAL MONETARY SYSTEM

1. *Liquidity*

The liquidity problem arises from the alleged need of a growing international economy for a corresponding growth in international reserves to support it, combined with the fact that adequate additions to monetary gold, the traditional reserve asset, are simply not available from extant gold production after deduction for private uses of gold. A rise in the price of gold might solve this problem, both by increasing the value of existing monetary stocks and by enlarging the quantity of gold available for additions to monetary stocks, but it would do so only with costs in terms of potential inflation, maldistribution of the gains (South Africa and Soviet Russia are the leading producers), and waste of economic resources that are best avoided.

The gap between demand for new reserves and available supply of gold has existed for many years and has been filled by the growing use of the U.S. dollar as a reserve asset, initially 'as good as gold' because of the standing commitment of the U.S. Treasury to convert central bank held dollars into gold at a fixed price. But, the Treasury's ability to honour this commitment has become more tenuous over time as the ratio of reserve dollars to the U.S. gold stock has grown, as it inevitably must do under the postulated circumstances, even with U.S. deficits only large enough to satisfy the growth in world demand for reserves. Thus, a 'gold-exchange standard', under which most countries hold the national currency of some central country that in turn holds gold, must necessarily evolve into an 'exchange standard' as the conversion commitment becomes less plausible and ultimately impossible to honour except for proportionally small amounts. In these limiting circumstances, however, the reserve-providing country is able literally to issue international money, and hence to command resources from the rest of the world at will, a prospect that is politically unacceptable. President Nixon's announcement of 15 August 1971, that the dollar would no longer be freely convertible into gold, simply involved formal acknowledgement of the dilemma of a gold-exchange standard, and the subsequent decision by most other major countries to 'float' their currencies against the dollar, at least temporarily, reflected their unwillingness to accept the full implications of a dollar standard [1].

Sterling and the French franc play the role of reserve currency in areas historically associated with Britain and France, respectively, but, in practice, their ability to 'exploit' the reserve currency status of their currencies in recent years has been sufficiently limited to place them in a fundamentally different category from the United States.

While the reserve currency status of the dollar may be subject to abuse and hence is politically and economically offensive, it has performed a genuine social function; calls to eliminate this status, therefore, require alternative solutions. It is in this connection that the special drawing rights (SDRs) at the International Monetary Fund (IMF) were developed, for they potentially provide an international solution to the need for growing reserves, eliminating the world's dependence for reserve growth both on gold and on the dollar. They have had an auspicious beginning, but they are still too new and untested to hail as the reserve asset of the future. Their early life has been complicated by U.S. deficits of unprecedented size, which leads to the second major heading, adjustment. But, before we turn to adjustment, it should be noted that the analytical foundation for the dependence of a growing world economy on growing international reserves is a tenuous one; private finance and trade credit certainly must grow, but they are different from reserves, which are used only to finance residual imbalances between countries beyond what can be financed (or beyond what countries desire to finance) through private markets [2]. It has not been established that payments imbalances must increase with the growth in trade and private financial transactions, although there is some presumption that they will do so. In any case, the relationship is not independent of the adjustment process, for rapid adjustment will reduce the need for reserves. But, since governments and central banks often use imports as a guide to their needs, there is at least a psychological link between the growth in trade and the growth in demand for reserves.

2. *Adjustment*

The adjustment process concerns the capacity of countries to eliminate imbalances in their international payments. The problem arises because both the 'classical' method of deflating the economy of a country in payments deficit and inflating the economy of a country in surplus and the Bretton Woods method (which, in principle, countries today are bound to use) of eliminating 'fundamental' imbalances by discrete changes in the exchange rate meet great political resistance. Deflation or inflation frequently conflicts with domestic economic objectives, which in democratic societies are politically dominant. Discrete changes in exchange rates in a world of high capital mobility invite market disruption and huge national losses as a result of anticipatory movements of funds; they jolt the economy more than most other changes in economic policy; and they are politically risky for those who make the decision. Moreover, countries in surplus have a disincentive to up-value their currencies and deliberately weaken the competitiveness of their industries, and, unlike countries in deficit, they face no limit corresponding to the exhaustion of international reserves.

The adjustment problem is further complicated by the special role that the dollar has come to play in international finance, since it means that the technical solution (currency devaluation for a country in deficit) offered by the IMF is not available to the United States unilaterally in the sense that a successful devaluation of the U.S. dollar against other currencies would require active decisions by other countries to change the rates at which they intervene *vis-à-vis* the dollar in the exchange markets. Thus, decision-making inertia combines with a fear of becoming less competitive with respect to the world's largest trading nation to favour maintaining existing exchange rates in the case of a U.S. move, which to that extent denies the United States control over its exchange rate, as distinguished from the world price of gold. Hence, the U.S. adoption in August 1971 of a 10% surcharge on imports represented an attempt to influence the price at which all (dutiable) imports enter the United

States. The reluctance of many other countries to allow their currencies to float freely upward, and France's insistence on pegging its commercial transactions to the dollar at the prevailing exchange rate, illustrated just how little control the United States had over the relation between its currency and others even in the face of strong inducements for others to appreciate. Weeks of difficult and even acrimonious bargaining were required to achieve the parity changes of late 1971, and then only after the United States had taken measures that threatened the international monetary system itself.

Solutions to the adjustment problem have been sought along the lines of introducing greater flexibility into exchange rates, with a view to reducing both the attractions of speculating on a change in parity and the degree of national prestige and political commitment now involved in maintaining existing parities. The parity changes of sterling, the French franc, and the German mark in the late 1960s removed the major sources of disequilibrium among European countries and thereby lulled the financial community into a false sense of well-being with regard to the adjustment problem. IMF discussions of the subject, at fever pitch in 1969, became desultory, and a complacent report was issued in 1970. The currency flare-up in May 1971, which led Austria and Switzerland to revalue their currencies and Germany and the Netherlands to 'float' theirs, reminded everyone that all was not well. But the insufficient sense of urgency on the part of most national monetary authorities and the IMF led to the unilateral actions by the United States in August 1971. A recurrence of financial crises can be confidently predicted until the adjustment process is improved.

3. *Confidence*

The confidence problem arises from the coexistence of several widely acceptable reserve assets, and hence the possibility of disturbing shifts among them. The emphasis here is on reserve assets, since shifts between financial instruments by private individuals, however massive, can, in principle, be compensated by counteracting shifts among central banks ('recycling'). So long as central banks cooperate, private shifts can disrupt particular markets but they cannot threaten the system as a whole. The possibility of shifts in central bank portfolios, especially shifts out of dollars or sterling, could, in contrast, induce a basic change in the system by compelling the reserve currency countries to declare foreign-held balances henceforth inconvertible (into gold or SDRs in the case of the United States and into dollars, gold or SDRs in the case of Britain) at a fixed price.

The likelihood of such shifts depends in large part on the balance-of-payments positions of the reserve currency countries and the prospect of a change in the value of these currencies against other reserve assets, i.e. a devaluation of sterling or a rise in the dollar price of gold. Thus, it can be argued that the confidence problem is entirely derivative from the adjustment problem, and that a solution to the latter will reduce the former to a problem of negligible importance. If the solution to the adjustment problem encompasses more frequent and possibly continuous changes in the dollar price of sterling or the dollar price of gold, however, the prospect of major shifts between reserve assets remains, for movements in these prices will create incentives to shift from one asset to another, incentives that cannot wholly and continuously be compensated by interest-rate differentials (even if central banks were fully willing to substitute interest earnings for capital losses) without tying domestic monetary policies to largely this objective.

A variety of solutions have been suggested, most having the same central characteristic of involving a conversion of the several reserve assets of today into a single, composite reserve asset – for example, SDRs – which countries would agree to hold exclusively, except for working balances. Thus, the existing reserve assets would be consolidated into a single, central account, subject to international management, and the possibility of speculative shifts among them would be eliminated.

4. *Interdependence*
The problem here is that markets for capital, business enterprise and even labour increasingly exceed the span of national control at a time when citizens are making ever more exacting demands on their governments for economic performance. Yet, the national instruments of economic policy, to be effective, usually require that markets for labour and capital be no larger than the nation. The most obvious and topical area in which the loss of control can be observed is monetary policy, where high international capital mobility under a regime of fixed exchange rates increasingly limits central bank control over domestic monetary conditions. With the Eurodollar market linking most domestic money markets directly or indirectly,

only the largest countries can influence monetary conditions through their actions, and even they have increasing difficulty in doing so, as the 1970–1 German attempt to maintain monetary conditions tighter than those in the United States testifies – it led to abandonment of the fixed exchange rate. The problem is that as any country attempts to tighten its domestic monetary conditions beyond those prevailing in other major countries, and in particular in the United States, it will find its commercial banks borrowing increasingly from foreigners for conversion into local currency. Under the central banks' obligation to buy foreign currency at a fixed price, this practice will automatically lead to an increase in the money supply no matter how hard the central bank is trying through its other operations to limit such an increase. If domestic banks are prevented from borrowing abroad, firms, local authorities and even individuals will go abroad for funds directly, mainly to the Eurodollar market in London. A world money market under fixed exchange rates requires a world monetary policy, and countries will have to find measures other than monetary action (e.g. tax policy) to stabilize domestic economic activity, to the extent that domestic requirements differ from those in the community of nations at large. The tax and expenditure policies of a government can be used to influence the course of domestic demand, and international capital movements will assure that the money supply will accommodate the change in demand, at least in so far as confidence in existing exchange-rate parities persists, so that for any single country, monetary policy becomes passive – a point to which we will return in discussing monetary integration in Europe.

Alternatively, in order to re-establish domestic monetary control, steps will have to be taken to fragment the international market, returning it to the national level. In this instance, greater exchange-rate flexibility, in addition to contributing to adjustment, will serve the latter function by introducing greater uncertainty into the earnings on short-term funds shifted between currencies; the temporary German switch to rate flexibility in 1970 represented such an attempt, as does the widening of exchange-rate margins to $2\frac{1}{4}\%$ on either side of the dollar that took place in December 1971.

Many countries have also imposed or tightened controls on movements of financial capital in an attempt to reassert national monetary control. These efforts can work for a while, but improvements in communication and enlargement of contacts between residents of different nations (including business enterprises) augurs against long-run success in fragmenting the international capital market in this way.

Of the various possible forms of interdependence, monetary interdependence is perhaps the furthest advanced at the present time, and certainly poses the most visible problems for preservation of national economic control. But, the pressure of increased inter-dependence toward coordination of national policies, or even toward supranational control, also exists in other areas, for example, in maintaining competition in the face of transnational mergers and takeovers of business enterprises or in maintaining national influence over the distribution of income in the face of increased international mobility of skilled individuals. These matters will require solutions different from those appropriate to the monetary arena, but they also are less pressing.

It should be noted that while large-scale movements of funds from one country to another in response to divergent interest rates and other monetary conditions do lead to recorded 'deficits' or 'sur-pluses' in the balance-of-payments accounts, these imbalances must be carefully distinguished conceptually from imbalances arising from divergences in long-term growth trends or in cost-price competitive-ness. The adjustment problem discussed above refers to these longer-term divergencies, not, without stretching the term, to large movements of interest-sensitive capital responding to divergent national monetary actions. A change in exchange-rate parities can correct the former problem, but not the latter. Preservation of national monetary autonomy requires either extensive exchange controls or flexible exchange rates to isolate national markets from international flows.

II. MONETARY UNIFICATION IN EUROPE

The members of the European Community have expressed 'their political will to introduce, in the course of the next ten years, an economic and monetary union' which *inter alia* will involve the formation of 'an individual monetary unit within the international system, characterized by the total and irreversible convertibility of currencies, the elimination of fluctuation margins of rates of ex-change and the irrevocable fixing of parity rates' – in short, a single currency in everything except possibly name [3]. Irrevocably fixed exchange rates combined with total and irreversible convertibility imply that balance-of-payments adjustment *within* the Community will be of the same type that prevailed during the gold standard, viz. any net outflow of funds from a region (country) within the Community will automatically result in monetary deflation in that region sufficient to bring the outflow to a halt.

These two conditions also imply a common monetary policy, even if only a passive one, for the Community as a whole, since any attempt by member countries to pursue divergent monetary policies will automatically result in payments imbalances that will, in turn, force countries back into monetary harmony. Thus, national governments will be sharply limited in their ability to finance budget deficits through domestic credit creation; they will have to rely instead on their capacity to raise funds in private markets. The pursuit of a common monetary policy for the Community as a whole raises questions both about the mechanism for accomplishing this and about the political responsibility of those who are entrusted with determining that policy.

Monetary union in Europe does not, however, imply fixity of exchange rates and reliance on gold-standard type monetary adjustment concerning Community-wide payments imbalances with the outside world; these could be handled with the variety of techniques currently available to national governments, such as exchange controls or changes in exchange rates.

1. *Three approaches to monetary unification*
If monetary union is the objective, what are the means for achieving it? Three ways to begin have been proposed:

(*a*) The official Werner Report on European monetary union at operational level lays heavy emphasis on narrowing the range of permissible fluctuation in exchange rates among the European currencies, which, because the dollar is used as the intervention currency, can now fluctuate more against one another than they can against the dollar.

(*b*) European, and especially German, critics of the Werner Report have argued that monetary union cannot be achieved and exchange rates successfully narrowed without first coordinating economic policies, and especially budgetary policies, among the members of the Community. They therefore urge a concerted effort to coordinate policies, with increasing authority for determining policy guidelines to be centred with the Community in Brussels.

(c) Third, Robert Triffin has proposed that the first steps toward monetary union should consist of a limited pooling of reserves with joint management, followed by extension of conditional credit among members of the Community, to help finance payments deficits [4].

These approaches are not, of course, mutually exclusive, and by being cast as alternatives have generated much needless controversy over their relative merits. Triffin's conditional credits, for example, can be linked to some harmonization of policies, and so can the narrowing of exchange-rate movements. Some conscious parallelism in all three approaches is no doubt desirable. Several observations on these current controversies can be made.

First, the strong emphasis placed on the need to coordinate policies, especially by Germany and the European Commission, reflects the dominant European view that government policies are the principal source of disturbance to the balance of payments, and that if only they can be brought into line everything will be all right. It is true that excessively expansionist policies often have been a source of payments difficulty. There are other sources as well, however, and full harmonization of government policies will by no means assure equilibrium in international payments. Cost movements in different national economies may diverge over time for a variety of reasons, including differential strengths and tactics of labour unions, different rates of adoption of new technology, and the like; and demand for foreign products may grow at differential rates as a consequence of the growth in incomes. For all these reasons, and others, a country's balance-of-payments position may gradually slip out of equilibrium under a regime of fixed exchange rates, even when monetary and fiscal policies have been 'harmonized' in some conventional sense of the term, e.g. common rates of growth of money stocks. Pointing to the fundamentally monetary character of all payments difficulties is not sufficient to establish that inappropriate monetary policy is the source of the difficulty, except in the trivial, and to policy makers totally uninteresting, sense that sufficiently stringent monetary action can always eliminate a payments deficit. For it may generate a major depression in the process. An implication of monetary union, as noted above, is that monetary adjustments will be relied upon to assure balance among its constituent parts; but, monetary adjustment may require substantial deflation or expansion in some regions relative to the union as a whole, and, in particular, may cause serious regional unemployment problems in the absence of Community-financed regional policies to mitigate them.

Second, harmonization of national policies within the Community should not be carried too far prematurely. In particular, precisely because of the regional pressures that may be created by a monetary adjustment mechanism, it would be desirable to allow governments considerable latitude to adjust their budgets to their national requirements. The important point is that governments would cease to be able to finance government deficits, beyond specified limits, through domestic credit creation, i.e. at their central banks. Instead, they would have to issue their securities in a Community-wide capital market when they needed to finance a budget deficit, and this would tend to draw funds into the area in question, thus compensating, at least temporarily, for the deflationary pressures of a regional payments deficit. Hence, governments would retain, through the flexible use of fiscal policy, some influence on the level of total demand within each national market. Such flexible use of fiscal policy can be reconciled with tight Community-wide control on monetary policy by the development of an effective and efficient capital market within the Community, so that each region (national member) could, in effect, achieve monetary expansion by selling securities (in the form of government bonds or bills) to residents of other regions, using the proceeds for expansionary policies. Such a programme for regional stabilization is not, of course, sufficient for offsetting persistent differences in regional costs; it will work only if the regional imbalance is a temporary one, or if it is one that can be corrected through sufficient capital investment. There are limits to which borrowers, even national governments, can raise funds for non-productive expenditures.

Third, therefore, exchange rates between members of the Community cannot be fixed irrevocably until the underlying trends of the national economies, not merely the government policies, come into close harmony, or until the Community develops a mechanism for effecting sufficiently large transfers among the regions of the Community to compensate for the depressive effects on some regions of a gold-standard type adjustment mechanism that relies on monetary movements alone. The transfers that take place under the common agricultural policy represent the beginnings of a large intra-Community transfer mechanism, although that particular one may occasionally be perverse from the point of view of cushioning depressed regions by giving rise to transfers from regions of low income and employment to regions of high income and employment (e.g. from Belgium and Italy to France). Movement toward Community-financed unemployment compensation would represent a much more direct and effective step in this direction.

Fourth, the creation of a European Reserve Fund will not in itself help to solve any of the functional problems that will confront national economies during the process of integration. At best, it would permit the conservation of some international reserves, which members of the Community now use (via multilateral clearing through the exchange market) to settle imbalances among members as well as between members and the rest of the world. But, conservation of reserves has hardly been one of the most pressing needs of the Community in recent years, in contrast to the position of some less-developed countries. Creation of a reserve fund would, however, institutionalize concern for the monetary integration of the Community, encourage and accustom national officials to discussion of monetary policies *before* monetary actions are taken, and provide the institutional basis for joint action when other conditions were ripe for it, e.g. for intervention in exchange markets on behalf of the Community as a whole, *vis-à-vis* the dollar or other outside currencies.

Finally, however, the controversy over transitional tactics really conceals divergent objectives. At least one member of the Community, France, does not accept in principle the desirability of supranational control of monetary policy; but, it is very much interested, for foreign policy reasons, in achieving a concerted position of the Community on alterations in the international monetary system, and, in particular, on the role of the dollar and on the creation of SDRs. After President Nixon's announcement in August 1971, other members of the Community have come increasingly to share this desire, but as much out of concern for the continuing viability of the system as for foreign policy reasons. The Commission, in addition, has an institutional interest in maintaining momentum toward a supranational community and sees the monetary realm as the most promising one for this purpose at present.

2. *Monetary unification without a single currency*

The EC Resolution of February 1971 speaks of 'an individual monetary unit' but is otherwise vague on the question of a European money. As far as their monetary autonomy is concerned, the position in which member countries will find themselves after monetary union is similar with or without a common currency, but important differences remain between a single currency and several currencies with irrevocably fixed exchange rates. In particular, with several currencies, a mechanism is required to preserve fixity of rates between them, while still maintaining some flexibility, or at least the possibility of movement, with respect to non-member currencies. A subsidiary problem involves clearing the accounts among the various currency units within the Community.

Broadly speaking, there are three ways in which fixity of exchange rates among a group of currencies can be maintained while preserving flexibility against other currencies. The first involves a direct commitment by each central bank or its agents (e.g. the commercial banks) to buy and sell the currencies of the other member countries at announced buying and selling rates. Net balances accumulated by these transactions would be settled periodically by transfers of some reserve asset directly between the central banks. Central banks would in effect 'make the market', and the present practice of relying on a relatively free private market for foreign exchange would be abandoned.

If the advantages of a vigorous, competitive market in foreign exchange are judged too great to abandon, even among member currencies, then fixity of exchange rates must be maintained through official intervention in the private market to prevent exchange rates from straying outside the permitted range. Past practice has been to do this through the intermediary of the U.S. dollar, leaving to private arbitrage the task of keeping exchange rates between any two currencies other than the dollar in line. This practice has the well-known disadvantage, from the viewpoint of the Community, of permitting twice the fluctuation in exchange rates between any two Community currencies that can take place between any one currency and the dollar. Yet, the objective is, if anything, to *widen* the possible fluctuations against the dollar, while *narrowing* the fluctuations between member currencies. This practice has the further consequence, increasingly resented, of reinforcing the position of the dollar as a reserve currency, for countries routinely deal in dollars and therefore must hold at least working balances in dollars.

External margins can be widened while internal margins are narrowed in two ways consistent with continued reliance on private markets: (1) close coordination of the points of intervention in dollars by all member countries, with a view to assuring that no two member currencies find themselves at sharply different points in the permissible band of variation with respect to the dollar; and (2) substitution of some member currency for the dollar as the intervention currency for all but one of the member countries, calling on the final member to intervene in its markets with respect to the dollar, and leaving it to private arbitrage to take care of the rest. The Werner Report adopted the first of these possibilities, giving rise to the 'snake in the tunnel' metaphor under which coordinated intervention would hold exchange rates between members' currencies to a narrower band of variation than would be permitted for all member currencies, moving together, with respect to the dollar [5].

The alternative of a European intervention currency would permit greater institutional autonomy but would also require a sharper break in prevailing practices. Because of the technical facilities available, sterling would be a natural choice for the new intervention currency within the enlarged Community, but any member currency would do. All members would, in practice, define permissible ceilings and floors for the rates of exchange between their currencies and sterling, just as they do now in dollars, and would intervene by buying or selling their currency against sterling to assure that those limits were not exceeded. Britain, in contrast, would continue to deal in dollars. This arrangement would break the fixed relationship between exchange margins for the dollar and exchange margins between any pair of member currencies, and would permit wider exchange-rate variation for the former and narrower variation for the latter. The choice of sterling need not involve extension of credit to Britain beyond the minimum working balances which other member countries would have to maintain for daily intervention and which, indeed, several of them maintain already; and even this credit could be avoided if the Bank of England would agree to provide sterling whenever needed for such intervention, or to be the sole intervenor in the market. The choice of sterling would have the disadvantage, from Britain's point of view, of denying sterling the slightly enlarged flexibility against the dollar that the other currencies would enjoy. From this point of view, it would be preferable to choose a currency that is not likely to be either very strong or very weak among currencies of the Community, such as the Dutch guilder, which would also have the attraction of being less controversial politically within Europe than would the choice of sterling or the German mark. But, Dutch financial markets are too small relative to the potential size of the reserve movements required, so special provision would have to be made to insulate the Dutch domestic market from reserve flows of other countries.

3. *Creation of a European currency*

The idea of a genuinely new European currency – call it the Europa – is being increasingly bruited about, and, once in place, the separate identities of existing national currencies would presumably disappear over a period of time, thus eliminating the technical problem of maintaining fixed rates among them. A single currency would be necessary, moreover, to make 'irrevocability' of parities really credible.

It is not technically difficult to design a new currency and its relationship to existing currencies, although it should be noted that the IMF's SDR is not a precedent in this case because it is a claim held by central banks alone, whereas the Europa would circulate with the public. The problem rather would be to gain public acceptance. The efficient financial services of the City of London would be available for the Europa, provided the basis could be established for its use. To make it work, it would be necessary to create both an adequate supply of Europa-denominated claims and a demand for them. Community governments would almost certainly have to issue debt denominated in Europas (to provide the basis for a secondary market in claims) and to accept it in payment for taxes (to create a demand for Europas). Even then, the Europa would face stiff competition from respected national currencies in domestic use, especially under arrangements, such as those described above, that facilitated the easy exchange of one member currency for another at a virtually fixed price. To launch the Europa successfully, it would be necessary not only to solve the problem of basic adjustment within the Community – that would be a political precondition for a common monetary policy – but also to denigrate existing national currencies. Thus, public debt denominated in national currencies would gradually have to be retired and, even then, somewhat higher interest rates might have to be offered on Europa securities to encourage the banks and the public to hold them, although the necessary premium would, of course, diminish as Europas became more widely accepted.

In addition to facing stiff competition in domestic economies from national currencies, the Europa would also face stiff competition on the international plane from the U.S. dollar. Unless it is brought under a persistent cloud by prolonged disequilibrium in the U.S. payments position (which is not the same as a recorded deficit on definitions currently employed by the U.S. government), the dollar is likely to retain and indeed to strengthen its position as an international currency for private transaction and short-term investment. There are substantial economies of scale in any financial market, arising from the greater chance of being able to match supplies of and demands for funds on any given maturity without a sharp change in price – in a phrase, the greater the market, the greater the liquidity of the assets that are traded in the market. It will be difficult for a new and untried currency, even when backed by the world's largest trading area, to overcome the leading advantages of the dollar for many years to come.

A new European currency would have a greater chance of success on the international scene – and even possibly within Europe – if it represented an evolution from some existing currency. If one could abstract from political considerations, and from the balance-of-payments difficulties that are likely to attend Britain's entry into the Community, the logical candidate for this enlarged role is sterling. Important technical facilities already exist for dealing in sterling, not the least of which is the large outstanding public debt, which provides the basis for a sizeable secondary market in interest-bearing claims, and this is essential if a currency is to be widely held outside its country of issue. The transformation of sterling into this European role would, of course, require placing its management in European hands, on the one side, and having other EC members issue their public debt in Euro-sterling, on the other. The Bank of England would become a Bank of Europe, and under European management would determine the amount of issue of Euro-sterling. There would be no special credit to Britain arising from this role. All governments, including the British government, would be limited in their capacity to finance budget deficits by resort to the central bank. Even the outstanding sterling liabilities would remain fully Britain's liabilities, although, of course, the external reserves of the entire Community would be available to 'cover' them against a run.

The only feasible alternative to the pound in this new 'European' role would be the German mark, for which the absence of the technical advantages available to sterling might be more than outweighed by the large external savings (attested by the large German current account surplus) of the German public, making the DM an attractive currency in which to borrow. Even after taking this into account, however, sterling is likely to have the edge.

There is, of course, some relationship between the arrangements under which national currencies are linked at fixed and unchanging parities and the possible evolution of a national currency into a supranational one. A currency that is adopted as an intervention currency for purposes of limiting movements in exchange rates is more likely to evolve naturally into a supranational currency than is another, and this may be a consideration that led the Community to reject the use of one European currency by all member countries in favour of the more cumbersome 'snake in the tunnel' or 'intervention in all currencies' approaches. Indeed, political considerations of national prestige, as well as long-standing suspicion of sterling in European official circles, is likely to militate against what might otherwise be the easiest, the fastest and the most efficient route to the creation of a European currency.

III. IMPLICATIONS FOR THE INTERNATIONAL MONETARY SYSTEM

Suppose now that the practical difficulties have been overcome and a new European currency has been successfully brought into existence, with the corresponding adjustments in European monetary management. What are the possible implications for the monetary system as a whole? Seven can be mentioned briefly, to conclude this survey of the issues.

First, by internalizing much 'foreign' trade into a single monetary area, the demand of the EC members for international reserves would presumably drop substantially because European countries today use international reserves to settle imbalances among themselves, whereas within a monetary union they would not [6]. Unless the European Community willingly held these newly 'excess' reserves, its actions could result in world inflationary pressures or could disrupt the international payments system, depending on the composition of its reserve assets, how it chooses to run them down, and how the rest of the world responds.

Second, sterling balances, if not handled by then in some other way, would become Europa balances by virtue of the conversion of

British public debt from sterling to Europas and, while they would remain British liabilities, they would clearly and automatically be covered against conversion into other currencies by the reserve assets of the enlarged Community.

Third, the Community would have to agree on a common set of exchange controls, or on their removal, since distinctions between national monetary systems would have been eliminated. Thus, either the Germans will have to abandon their predilection for relatively free capital movements or Britain and France will have to relax substantially their present controls and, as a result, might once again become substantial net lenders to the world.

Fourth, the Europa would willy-nilly become a new reserve currency, at least to a modest degree, because of the overwhelming importance of the enlarged European Community as a trading area, the fact that a large fraction of world trade would be denominated in Europas, and the large market in Europa claims that would have developed for internal use. Stringent steps would have to be taken to prevent the emergence of the Europa as an international currency, if that should be desired (as some Europeans claim), requiring the virtual exclusion of non-member governments from Europa financial markets.

Fifth, the emergence of a single European currency would create the possibility for easier movement of exchange rates between the United States and Europe as a whole, movements that are now inhibited by a structural situation involving a number of European countries that cannot revalue or devalue without also considering moves of other European countries, but who find it exceedingly difficult to coordinate effectively among themselves a matter as sensitive as parity changes. During the prolonged transition and breaking-in period, however, the formation of a European currency is likely to involve greater rather than less rigidity in exchange rates *vis-à-vis* the dollar, because interests of the various members of the Community in exchange-rate movements are likely to diverge sharply much of the time; the result will be immobilism.

Sixth, Europe would regain its monetary independence from the United States in the sense that it could more successfully pursue monetary policies at greater variance from those in the United States than is now possible, both because concerted monetary action in Europe would have great influence on world monetary conditions even under a regime of fixed exchange rates, and because greater exchange-rate flexibility would permit somewhat greater monetary autonomy.

Seventh, under a regime of fixed exchange rates, the emergence of a new, major currency with correspondingly strong financial institutions (probably centred in London) will aggravate the problem of large shifts of financial capital between two centres in response to slight interest differentials or slight changes in sentiment regarding exchange rates. These massive shifts of funds will, in turn, complicate greatly the task of monetary management and will occasionally disrupt foreign exchange and money markets. On the other hand, this problem is not unfamiliar even today; and the existence of two strong financial markets both creates the incentive for and holds out the possibility of close and even-sided collaboration between Europe and America in monetary management.

NOTES AND REFERENCES

[1] In the exchange-rate settlement of December 1971, it is true, the European countries and Japan agreed to peg their currencies against the dollar again without the *quid pro quo* of a dollar convertible into gold or other assets – in effect, they agreed to a formal dollar standard. But, this agreement occurred on the short-term expectation that agreement itself (at new exchange parities, with a band of variation around parity widened from 2 to $4\frac{1}{2}\%$) would lead to a large reflow of dollars out of European and Japanese reserves, and on the further expectation that, in the context of longer-range monetary reform to be worked out in 1972, the United States would reestablish some form of official convertibility for the dollar.

[2] There is a confusing ambiguity in the term 'liquidity' that leads some observers to the view that there is no shortage of liquidity *because* the Euro-dollar market and other instruments of private finance have grown so rapidly The 'liquidity problem' discussed here concerns the capacity of monetary authorities to maintain a fixed exchange rate in the face of large swings in private payments and receipts across the foreign exchanges, and, in this sense, the growth of the Eurodollar market, by facilitating movements of short-term funds, may be said to have increased the need for (central bank) liquidity rather than satisfied it.

[3] EC Resolution of 9 February 1971, reprinted as Annex I in *Economic and Monetary Union* (Werner Report), Supplement to *Bulletin of the European Communities* (1970), No. 11.

[4] Robert Triffin, 'On the creation of a European reserve fund, Banca Nazionale del Lavoro, *Quarterly Review*, December 1969, pp. 327–46.

[5] After the currency disruptions of late 1971, the European Commission in Brussels recommended in early 1972 that each member of the community accomplish this objective, not by coordinating their market intervention in dollars as under the Werner Plan, but by intervening in the currencies of *all* other member countries simultaneously. Intervention in dollars would be confined to the vicinity of the borders of the new $4\frac{1}{2}\%$ band of flexibility, whereas exchange variations among member currencies would be held to about half that range by

direct intervention. This proposal greatly underestimates the technical difficulties involved in intervening simultaneously in eight currencies at consistent rates in a changing market, of coordinating that intervention with other member countries who may also be intervening in the market in all member currencies, *and* of coordinating intervention in dollars, all of which would be necessary.

[6] Under certain patterns of intra- and extra-European transactions, the demand for external reserves following unification could conceivably increase; but these are not likely to prevail in practice.

PART THREE

TAX HARMONIZATION

12

BORDER TAXES, BORDER TAX ADJUSTMENTS, COMPARATIVE ADVANTAGE, AND THE BALANCE OF PAYMENTS*

HARRY G. JOHNSON
MELVYN B. KRAUSS

'Border tax adjustments', often referred to briefly and misleadingly as 'border taxes', have been the subject of international discussion recently in two contexts. On the one hand, United States public opinion has been very critical of the decision of certain Common Market and other European countries to move to a system of value added taxes on the destination principle, which change has been seen as harmful to the United States balance-of-payments position [1]. On the other hand, the German decision of November 1968 to compensate for Germany's refusal to revalue the deutchemark by reducing her rates of tax remission on exports and tax imposition on imports was widely regarded as a constructive step towards the restoration of international monetary equilibrium, and official opinion has since occasionally favoured variation of border tax adjustments as a means of promoting international monetary equilibrium.

The purpose of this paper is to demonstrate, by means of a general equilibrium analysis of the border tax adjustment problem, that in both cases cited, the analytical treatment of the effects of changes in border tax adjustments rests on adopting a short-run approach to such adjustments in which domestic prices and exchange rates are assumed to be fixed and no account is taken of the mechanism of international adjustment; and that in a longer-run context in which the international adjustment mechanism is assumed to be functioning, changes in border tax adjustments should make no difference to international trade, provided that the taxes to which the adjustments apply are truly general. In this connection it is remarked that there is

* *Canadian Journal of Economics*, November 1970, 3(4), pp. 595–602.

239

an essential distinction to be drawn between *border tax adjustments*, whose purpose is to equalize the conditions of competition between domestic and foreign producers and so permit comparative cost to govern trade patterns; and *border taxes*, which properly understood are taxes on the crossing by trade of international frontiers (a tariff, for example) and hence restrict trade volumes below what would be indicated as desirable by the principle of comparative advantage. The real problem with border tax adjustments, it is contended, arises when the taxes to which the adjustments relate are not truly general, and/or when the adjustment has to be made by an approximation of the average effect of such taxes on the competitive position of domestic *vis-à-vis* foreign producers.

I

A border tax, properly interpreted, is a tax imposed when goods cross an international border, and as such must be inimical to international trade and therefore to the achievement of the economic benefits of international specialization and division of labour. A border tax *adjustment*, on the other hand, is an adjustment of the taxes imposed on a producer when the goods he produces cross an international border. Such an adjustment may involve an addition to or a subtraction from the taxes he has already paid; and if the adjustment in question implies either equal rates of taxation of imports and subsidization of exports, or equal rates of subsidization of imports and taxation of exports, the effect of the adjustment is to leave the relative competitive positions of exporting and import-competing industries in the domestic market unchanged. This is merely an application of the well-known principle that taxation of imports and subsidization of exports is equivalent to a devaluation of the currency, and that under long-run full-employment and price-flexibility conditions a devaluation will be offset by an equal inflation of domestic prices.

However, only in the long run when the exchange rate or factor prices has adjusted to preserve external balance will it be a matter of indifference which type of border tax adjustment is applied. In the short run, with both domestic factor prices and the exchange rates fixed, taxation of imports and subsidization of exports will give a monetary competitive advantage to domestic goods over foreign goods in both the domestic and the foreign market, tending to improve the country's balance of payments, while the converse will apply when exports are taxed and imports subsidized.

The function of the border tax adjustment, in the long run, and in contrast to the border tax *per se*, is to equalize the conditions of competition between domestic and foreign producers. Border tax adjustments may be based on either of two principles: the origin principle and the destination principle. Under the origin principle, a tax is imposed on the domestic production of goods, whether exported or not, and under the destination principle, the same tax is imposed on imported goods as on domestically-produced goods destined for consumption by domestic consumers, while domestically-produced goods destined for consumption by foreigners enjoy a rebate of the tax. The origin principle involves no visible border tax adjustment, while the destination principle involves a border tax adjustment to the full extent of the tax. But the long-run effect of either principle of border tax adjustment is the same [2].

This point is best understood by considering initially a closed economy. In such an economy, a government imposing a flat rate tax on spending power could choose to impose it either as a proportional tax on factor incomes, or as a proportional tax on total expenditure. In the former case it would appear as a tax on production (the use of factors), in the latter case as a tax on consumption and investment (the expediture of factor incomes). But in either case its real effect would be exactly the same. Its monetary effect, i.e. its effect on either raising domestic commodity prices with factor prices unchanged or lowering factor prices with commodity prices unchanged, would depend on the monetary policy of the government, the latter effect resulting if the money supply were kept constant (or increased at the normal rate) and the former if the money supply were increased (above normal) in proportion to the tax rate.

Now suppose the same country existing in an international economy, and suppose that a general tax is imposed. Whether the form of the tax in a closed economy is initially a consumption tax or a production tax, its form or apparent incidence in the open economy will depend on the border tax adjustment principle employed. Specifically, if the origin principle is employed, with no tax rebate on exports or taxation of imports, domestic factor prices must fall in money terms so as to absorb the burden of the tax, so that domestic products can remain competitive with foreign products in the foreign and domestic markets, and the country's trade remain balanced. Conversely, if the destination principle is employed, domestic factor prices will not be affected, since the tax rebate frees exporters from the burden of the tax, and the compensatory tax imposed on imports equalizes conditions of competition between domestic producers of import substitutes and foreign exporters to the domestic market, and domestic prices must rise to the extent of the tax. Under the origin principle, the tax appears as a tax on production; while under the destination principle it appears as a tax on consumption; but in either case it remains a proportional tax on domestic spending power. Under the origin principle, since domestic commodity prices are unchanged, there is no need for monetary policy to change the domestic money supply; under the destination principle, the rise in the domestic price level requires an increase in the domestic money supply which may be provided either through domestic monetary expansion or through a transitory balance-of-payments surplus.

It follows that it makes no difference to the exploitation of comparative advantage through trade which principle of border tax adjustment is applied, provided again that the tax is a truly general tax. (It should be noted, however, that this is an important proviso, given the importance of trade in invisibles, which generally escape destination-principle adjustment.) Similarly, in the long run a decision by a country or trading group to change from one principle of border tax adjustment to another should make no difference to its international competitive position.

This, however, is not the light in which businessmen and governments see the matter. For this there are two reasons, one fallacious and one valid in content. The first is that practical people tend to look at the form of the border tax adjustment, without appreciating its consequential effects on domestic factor and commodity price levels – that is, to see the tax adjustment or its absence, but not its general equilibrium repercussions. Consequently, the use of the origin principle is typically regarded by the domestic exporter as imposing an unfair competitive disadvantage on him, in so far as he has to pay domestic production taxes higher than those paid by his foreign competitors, while the use of the destination principle also tends to be regarded by domestic exporters as imposing an unfair competitive disadvantage on them, in so far as consumption taxes imposed in foreign countries with destination principle adjustments are at higher rates than domestic consumption taxes, so that the foreign exporter to a country pays a border tax adjustment lower than that paid by the domestic exporter [3]. Both propositions, by ignoring the consequential adjustments of commodity or factor prices to the principle of border tax adjustment, wrongly identify a principle which does not discriminate between foreign and domestic producers with such discrimination. This fallacy is encouraged by the common practice of referring to 'border tax adjustments' as 'border taxes', a practice which implies that explicit adjustments (under the destination principle) or implicit adjustments (under the origin principle) constitute a tax on international as distinct from domestic trade. The fallacy is exemplified by the long-standing belief in the United States that, since the U.S. tax system relies primarily on corporation and personal income tax, to which the origin principle applies, while European tax systems rely more on consumption taxes to which the destination principle applies, United States producers are placed at an unfair disadvantage in international competition, which should be corrected by some policy change; and also the U.S. contention that the decision of the European Common Market countries to move towards a value-added tax with destination principle border adjustments represents increased trade discrimination against the United States [4].

The second and rather more justifiable reason for business and governmental concern about border tax adjustments is that, in the short run in which exchange rates and domestic money factor prices are fixed, a change from one system of border tax adjustment to another can indeed affect a country's international competitive position and balance of payments. Specifically, a change from the origin principle to the destination principle will give a subsidy to exports and impose a tax on imports, and hence tend to improve the balance of payments, so long as factor prices remain unchanged; and conversely for a change in the opposite direction. These changes are in fact equivalent respectively to a devaluation and an appreciation of the currency, with respect to commodity trade. Hence, from the short-run balance-of-payments viewpoint, the United States could snatch some advantage from introducing border tax adjustments for corporation profits taxes, or replacing such taxes by a value added tax with destination principle border adjustments; and it will be placed at a disadvantage by the European move towards such a value-added tax, though only to the extent that that tax does not merely replace previously existing taxes unaccompanied by a border tax adjustment. For the same reason, the reduction in German border tax adjustment rates of 1968 (which amounted to a partial movement from the destination to the origin principle) should have contributed to decreasing the German surplus; the reduction was in fact commonly recognized as equivalent to an appreciation of the mark for the purposes of commodity trade [5]. In either case, however, the change of border tax adjustment principle, through its effects on trade and the balance of payments, will set in motion pressures on factor prices which in the long run will eliminate the short-run balance-of-payments gain or loss. In the long run, the behaviour of countries' balances of payments will depend on other factors than border tax adjustments, specifically, on their over-all demand management policies.

The foregoing analysis has made no explicit reference to tariffs, which interact with the border tax adjustments in determining the commercially profitable trade. Generally speaking, tariffs will simply offset the pattern of comparative advantage, and the resulting effects on trade will generally make the level of domestic factor prices and commodity prices higher than it would be under free trade, as a consequence of the effects of the tariff in drawing factors of production out of exporting into import-competing industries.

The foregoing analysis of the long-run irrelevance of the choice of principle in border tax adjustments has an important application to a recent debate concerned with tax harmonization in common markets, in which it has been contended by several writers that 'mixed systems' of border tax adjustments, i.e. systems that use one type of adjustment for trade with other members and the other type for trade with outsiders, are incompatible with allocative efficiency [6]. This is untrue, as shown by the following argument. Consider first the analogy between a common market and a closed economy consisting of states among which factors of production are immobile but goods are free to move without interference from border taxes. Each state in such an economy can choose whatever system of border tax adjustment it prefers, without affecting the efficiency of the allocation of resources in the economy; all that the choice will affect will be whether its commodity price level is above, or its factor price level below, those of states using the alternative principle. Now consider such an economy to be trading with other countries, again under free trade conditions. Whatever it does in its internal trade, its choice between applying the destination and the origin principles to its external trade should make no real difference, providing that if it uses the destination principle the rates of border tax adjustment are common for all member states. If it applies the origin principle, its internal price level will be equal to the world price level; if it applies the destination principle, its internal price level will be above the world price level to an extent determined by the rate of border tax adjustment. This follows from the equivalence of border tax adjustments with currency devaluation [7]. If now the economy imposes a common tariff against the outside world, internal factor prices and commodity prices must rise to maintain general equilibrium. But any distortions of trade must be the consequence of the tariff, and not of the system of border tax adjustment employed.

II

It has long been recognized that, where consumption or production taxes are not perfectly general (i.e. are non-proportional as between goods), the principle of border tax adjustment does make a difference to allocative efficiency. For example, a country that imposes a specially heavy tax on production of a particular commodity because it wishes to discourage consumption will worsen the efficiency of world resource allocation unless it applies the destination principle; conversely, if the tax is imposed because production of the commodity has social disadvantages, resource allocation will be worsened unless it applies the origin principle. Such cases are well known and require no further discussion, though they are important in practice.

Less well known, however, are the trade effects of indirect taxes that are not truly general. Ordinarily, a consumption tax restricts consumption of the taxed good, the external reflection of which is either a reduction of imports of substitute products manufactured in foreign countries or an expansion of exports of the taxed commodity or both; conversely, a production tax restricts production of the taxed goods, contracts exports, and increases imports of substitute products. The net trade effect of either tax, however, is not clear since the balance of payments adjustments required for external equilibrium induce trade movements opposite to those stemming from the tax's direct trade effect. All that can be said in the way of general principle is that consumption taxes are likely to increase trade should they fall exclusively on exportables and decrease trade should importables bear their essential burden, while production taxes normally will increase trade when levied exclusively on importables and decrease trade in the reverse instance.

Of further interest is the case when taxation is not general and, contrary to what has been assumed previously, the rebates to exporters and compensating taxes imposed on importers under the destination principle are not exactly adjusted to the taxes paid on consumption of domestically produced goods (or on production of goods for the domestic market). In this case the effect will be to tax international trade if the export rebate is too small or the import border tax adjustment too large, and to subsidize international trade if the export rebate is too large or the import adjustment is too small, for the relevant good.

These possibilities are particularly relevant when it is a question of a shift from one type of tax to another, each with destination principle border tax adjustments; for such a shift may have the net result either of subisidizing or of taxing international trade, by comparison with the initial position. A case in point is the decision of the European Economic Community to shift from the gross turnover tax to the value-added tax. Under the former tax the border tax adjustments were necessarily crude, based on rough averages, since the tax burden on industry imposed by the tax depended on the degree of vertical integration in the industry. Under the latter tax, exact adjustments are more feasible, because the tax borne by an individual domestically-produced-and-sold good is more easily identified [8]. Hence the change-over is probably desirable from a global point of view, in so far as it removes distortions of comparative advantage other than those deliberately established by tariff policy. From the point of view of the United States, however, not only might the effect be unfavourable from the short-run balance of payments point of view, but it might be unfavourable from the long-run point of view of increasing United States gains from international trade. Moreover, the short-run and long-run self interests of the United States in the change might conflict. In the short run, with fixed exchange rates and factor prices, the net effect of the change would be to worsen or improve the United States balance of payments, according to whether its net effect was to subsidize European exports and tax European imports or vice versa. In the long run, the United States would gain from European subsidization of international trade, i.e. of both exports and imports, and lose from European taxation of international trade, whether of exports or of imports. Thus a change from one tax to another with destination principle adjustments that would improve the United States balance of payments in the short run might worsen the United States terms of trade in the long run.

The Competence of the Committee can be set forth as follows:

1. Establish if, and should the occasion arise, in what manner and to what point, the disparities existing in public finance of Member States hinder or make completely impossible:

(*a*) The creation of a common market which brings about conditions analogous to those of an internal market and does not contain tax frontiers, as well as

(*b*) The achievement of other objectives of the Community, such as the encouragement of competition and of economic growth.

2. Study to what extent it is possible to eliminate or to compensate the greatest of the disparities referred to, above all without affecting certain local differentiations perfectly compatible with the achievement of the Common Market and with other objectives of the Treaty which have been brought into public expenditure policy and taxation policy as the result of regional dissimilarities conditioned by natural attributes and/or historical evolution and, on the other hand, without applying frequent alterations in the rates of exchange.

3. Show which financial policy it is appropriate to apply if it is not wished to disturb or distort competition between Member Countries; leaving aside all measures disturbing competition or producing distortion of competition other than measures of financial policy.

4. Study under what conditions tax frontiers can be eliminated within the Common Market or at least, reduced to an indispensable minimum.

It is agreed that the common market to be established within the EEC must contain the *same characteristics as an internal market.* Let us assume in principle that among others the characteristics of an internal market are: the free circulation of persons, the free circulation of goods and capital (customs duties and quotas being abolished), a unified currency, relatively uniform transport tariffs, uniform economic and social policy, in general uniform judicial standards and a high degree of security in the supply of durable goods and spare parts. To complement this, let us emphasize that an internal market does not entirely exclude all local (regional) disparities in relation to institutions and to financial measures, but that these disparities must not be of a type and size so as to hinder particularly the free movement of factors of production. Finally, under ideal conditions it would be unnecessary to retain 'tax frontiers' which it might not be possible to abolish in those cases where in the field of indirect taxes major quantitative and qualitative disparities would arise. The question as to whether it is possible to abolish the 'tax frontiers' within the EEC, and if so, how this should be done, will be discussed later on. It is apparent that such an elimination is, in principle, desirable, even though it should be accomplished only in the final stage of the integration, if there is evidence of a genuine wish to achieve conditions analogous to those of an internal market. In dealing with this question, it is necessary to consider as well the possible negative psychological reactions on the part of entrepreneurs, which may be evoked in the event that tax frontiers should be further maintained.

The question of the choice between the principle of the country of destination and the principle of the country of origin is of the utmost importance for all the proposals and measures intended for a harmonization of taxes within a common market. As is well known, discussion of this matter had its origin in turnover taxation within the European Coal and Steel Community. However, it has application currently to a wider framework, without any agreement having yet been reached.

The dispute concerning these two principles has considerable importance from a political–psychological point of view for the future development of the EEC, above all because the decision that will be taken in this respect will also constitute a decision on the question whether it will be possible, and possibly how and when, to remove the so-called tax frontiers existing at the present time.

Except in the case of a tax at the retail trade stage (not including 'use taxes') the principle of destination, assumes the retention of so-called *tax frontiers*. These frontiers exist because of the fact that a good crossing them requires inspection and measures which are necessary because exports are subject to exemptions or refunds, and imports to a compensatory tax.

If the system for exports and imports could function in such a way that each good was completely exempted from the tax of the exporting country that it in fact bears, and be subject precisely to the tax charge of the importing country that a good manufactured in its entirety in that country, must support there, this could clearly not result in any disturbance in trade between the States. However, these conditions do not, or not completely, in reality exist. This is notably the case when one of the Member States applies a turnover tax system which does not allow the *exact* calculation of the tax burden affecting a particular product. Distortions of competition are necessarily the result when tax exemptions or refunds in an exporting country are higher or lower than the amount of the consumption tax effectively borne by a product and, in the same way, when compensatory taxes levied in the importing country are higher or lower than the tax burden borne by a product of the same type entirely manufactured in the country of importation.

The use of the origin principle has the great advantage of *allowing the abolition of the so-called tax frontiers.* Occasionally it is said that for statistical purposes and for reasons of public health, etc. certain frontier inspections would have to be maintained, even if the principle of the country of destination were completely abolished, and that these tax frontiers exist technically and in appearance, but that they are not 'real'. In relation to this, however, it must be emphasized, that the free movement of goods and capital sought and gained through the abolition of *customs* frontiers can only have the result of the establishment of a common market having the character of an internal market if it is complemented by the abolition of *tax* frontiers. Such a measure also seems necessary to the FFC for psychological and political reasons. Thus it is advisable never to lose sight of such an abolition, in the perspective of the ultimate objective of economic integration policy, even if it is only achievable slowly.

Even if, in trade between the Member States, the application of the principle of country of origin and consequently, the removal of tax frontiers is possible if the proposals sketched out above are adopted, the principle of the *country of destination currently practised in a general way* must *naturally* be maintained in trade between the EEC countries and third countries. Two technical difficulties, however, arise in the case of a harmonized net turnover tax in relation to trade with third countries:

1. To the extent that the rates of net turnover taxes at all stages are not strictly identical in all the Member States of the EEC, the question arises as to how the refunds and compensatory taxes

necessary in trade with third countries must be calculated and possibly shared among the interested countries in the case where a good exported from a third country has in part been produced in the exporting country and in part in other Member States of the EEC, or in the cases where a good imported from a third country is made the object of added value as the result of processing, etc. performed in more than one Member State of the EEC. The difficulties resulting from this situation constitute an important argument in favour of *complete* equality of rates relating to net turnover tax. On the other hand, the tax to be levied, according to the present Report, at the retail trade stage at differing rates would, because of its character, hardly raise the problem of sharing as indicated above.

2. Even when the level of turnover tax is the same, it can be asked how refunds to be paid or compensatory taxes to be levied in trade with third countries must be calculated and to which Member State they must be allocated. Clearly this is a problem of supranational financial equalization.

Turnover tax

In relation to turnover tax, there exists a series of more or less differing possibilities which can in part be also combined one with another.

Firstly turnover tax can be levied in the form of a *single phase* tax, a tax on *several stages*, or in the form of a tax *on all stages*. The two latter types may be cumulative cascade taxes or not.

Harmonization of turnover taxation does not seem to be required at first sight, at least as long as differences in the level of taxation are made 'inoffensive' by the application of the principle of the country of destination through the well-known compensatory measures that are already in being (compensatory levies at importation, refunds at exportation). But in reality these compensatory measures cannot prevent there arising from this, less in the average case than in numerous special cases, tax advantages and disadvantages in international trade in certain goods, precisely because there are various types of turnover taxes. Beyond this, certain distortions of competition arise from the fact that the number and nature of goods exempted from turnover tax are different from country to country. Quite apart from differences in the level of effective burden, it is therefore absolutely urgent to go on to a broad harmonization of turnover tax systems, even if the principle of country of destination should be maintained.

The Members of the FFC, with only one exception, are persuaded that in any case it is advisable, in the interests of harmonization which especially in this field is necessary, that *none of the Member States of the EEC maintains a cascade system of gross turnover tax.* This type of tax primarily presents the disadvantage of causing distortions of competition within national economies where it is applied, and of artificially encouraging the concentration of businesses. Moreover this tax distorts international trade through the impossibility of exactly calculating the overall charge of turnover tax for a good and consequently, in the case of the application of the principle of the country of destination, the sum of compensatory duties and refunds corresponding to this charge.

After the abolition of gross all-stage turnover tax, the choice between the other turnover tax systems as well as their form largely depends on the question whether it is wished in relation to this essential tax to retain the current practice of the principle of the country of destination, or that this must be replaced by the principle of the country of origin. If the principle of the country of destination is maintained and at the same time tax frontiers are abolished, there can only be taken into consideration as a turnover tax system, a tax levied at the retail stage which in no case requires tax frontiers with the exception, should the occasion arise, of cases where there is applied what is termed 'use taxes'. If, on the other hand, the principle of the country of origin is supported, any kind of net turnover tax can be employed that may be levied either at the production stage or at the wholesale trade stage. In this case there must not be any, or very small, differences between countries in the different rates if it is wished to abolish tax frontiers.

Some of the Members of the Committee are of the opinion that one could and should give greater or smaller discretion to the various States in the choice of turnover tax systems (leaving aside gross cascade turnover tax). The majority of them are, on the other hand, of the opinion that the application of the same system is desirable, at least over the long term, and more exactly the application of a system allowing achievement of the principle of the country of origin and consequently the abolition of tax frontiers.

For various reasons, notably because of the differing budgetary needs of Member States, it is doubtful that the application of a uniform type of turnover tax, that is to say in fact of a net turnover tax levied on all stages, according to an (approximately) identical rate would be politically achievable and could be considered as a generally satisfactory solution. Therefore the FFC considers the following scheme as the best compromise possible:

A system of net turnover tax of the type indicated is introduced in all the countries of the EEC as a base tax with the same or almost the same rate. In addition, there could be imposed, as a *complementary tax*, a *retail tax* that Member countries can administer – notably in relation to the rate – to a large extent prompted by their particular budgetary needs. It has already been shown that a retail tax is not practicable as the sole form of turnover tax and it has also been shown why this is not so. However, levied as a complementary tax at moderate rates it would not give rise to the same objections and difficulties. Even if there are relatively marked differences of rates between the countries, the character of a retail tax is such that it does not bring about notable distortions in trade between States, given that the goods subject to the tax at the retail trade stage are not exported (with only a few exceptions, relating for example, to certain durable consumer goods for which there could be envisaged the application of use taxes according to the American model).

It is possible to summarize the views of the majority of the FFC as follows: It is desirable to abolish in all the EEC Member States gross turnover tax levied at all stages. In place of gross turnover tax, there should be applied a net turnover tax covering all stages up to that of retail trade, the latter itself being excluded. So as to allow application of the principle of country of origin, it would be advisable that this tax be of the same type and that the rates be nearly the same. Because of differences existing between the budgetary needs of Member States, harmonization of details must take place by stages. But at the end of the process there must be a unanimous agreement with regard to the system, the exemptions from subjective and objective tax liability, the rate of tax, etc.

The aforementioned net turnover tax might eventually be complemented by a tax on retail trade, whose rate can be different according to the country without causing any distortions of competition.

NOTES AND REFERENCES

[1] All the charter members of the European Economic Community employ value-added taxes with the exception of Italy.

[2] This point has been known since the publication of the so-called 'Tinbergen Report' (European Coal and Steel Community, High Authority, *Report on the*

TAX HARMONIZATION

Problems raised by the Different Turnover Tax Systems applied within the Common Market (March 1953)). Actually, as recorded elsewhere by one of the present authors (Johnson), Harry G. Johnson, Paul Wonnacott, and Hirofumi Shibata, *Harmonization of National Economic Policies Under Free Trade* (Toronto, 1968), it was largely the contribution of W. B. Reddaway, a member of the Tinbergen Committee (W. B. Reddaway, The implications of a free-trade area for British taxation, *British Tax Review*, March 1958, 71–9).

[3] Note that in the first case the alleged unfairness consists in the domestic producer having to pay more taxes on production than the foreign producer; in the second case, it consists in the domestic producer having to pay a higher 'price of admission' to foreign markets than the foreigner has to pay for admission to the domestic market.

[4] See, for example, the paper read by Stanley S. Surrey, former Assistant Secretary of the Treasury of the United States, before the 73rd Annual Congress of American Industry of the National Association of Manufacturers, New York City (Washington, D.C., 1968). At present, the U.S. Congress is considering trade legislation containing a proposal (DISC) intended to counter the alleged European tax discrimination against U.S. exporters by granting them a postponement of the corporation income tax due on export profits, so long as such profits are reinvested in export related activities. In effect, this proposal is equivalent to an export subsidy without an import charge of equal rate, and thus, unlike the destination principle border tax adjustments it pretends to counter, is inimical to an efficient allocation of resources. The maximum subsidy per unit of exports is equal to the profits tax rate times the proportion of profits in the export price. This assumes that reinvestment earns the same rate of return as any other dollar the company could obtain; if not, the subidy is less because it is tied to reinvestment.

[5] For an analysis of this equivalency, see Gottfried Haberler, Import taxes and export subsidies, a substitute for the realignment of exchange rates? *Kyklos*, XX (1967).

[6] This view was first put forward in the Tinbergen Report, 25, 37, and later implied by the conclusion of the so-called 'Neumark Report' (*Report of the Fiscal and Financial Committee of the European Economic Community*, unofficial translation by Dr H. Thurston, International Bureau of Fiscal Documentation (Amsterdam, 1963)), which advocated equalization of internal, indirect tax rates to avoid allocative distortions, and has been accepted rather uncritically in the literature. A rationale of it was attempted by one of the present authors (Melvyn Krauss, Tax harmonization and allocative efficiency in economic unions, *Public Finance*, **3**, 1968, 367–71), and accepted by Douglas Dosser, A comment on 'tax harmonization and allocative efficiency in economic unions, by Melvyn Krauss,' *Public Finance*, 3 1968, 376–7); it was also accepted by the other author in a passing reference (Johnson, Wonnacott, and Shibata, *Harmonization of National Economic Policies*, ch. I, 1–41, see p. 19); and also by Paul Wonnacott in this same volume.

[7] Of course, if the rate of rebate on exports is less (greater) than the rate of compensating tax on imports, the effect is to impose a net tax (subsidy) on international trade, with corresponding effects on the relation of the domestic to the foreign price level.

[8] For an analysis of the problems associated with exact border tax adjustments with the value-added tax see M. Krauss and P. O'Brien, Some international implications of value-added taxation, *National Tax Journal*, Dec. 1970.

[9] An unofficial translation by Dr H. Thurston, International Bureau of Fiscal Documentation, 1963.

13

THE VALUE-ADDED TAX: CRITIQUE OF A REVIEW

MELVYN B. KRAUSS
RICHARD M. BIRD

International Monetary Fund

In his recent review of the literature on value-added taxation, Professor Lindholm [1] provided us with an account that demonstrates some confusion presently surrounding this important policy matter as well as the extent of the current interest in it [1]. Unfortunately, after reading Professor Lindholm's review, one is still all too likely to be numbered among those perplexed by the value-added tax (VAT) concept and its probable economic consequences. This comment aims to dispel such lingering confusion by presenting a brief alternative analysis of the nature and significance of value-added taxation. After clarifying the nature of VAT and of certain other key concepts, we show that much of Lindholm's review is vitiated by a failure to consider VAT in a general equilibrium framework. A few comments are also made on other aspects of the Lindholm review.

THE VALUE-ADDED METHOD OF TAXATION

The first point of disagreement is that, properly interpreted, value-added taxation refers to a *method* of taxation and not to some specific new kind of tax on economic activity. VAT is a device for levying taxes on a piecemeal basis, stage by stage, while avoiding double taxation so that the tax collected in relation to final product will be precisely equivalent to that obtained by a single stage tax levied on the same aggregate base with the same *ad valorem* rate.

In a closed economy, with two factors (labour and capital), it can readily be shown that there are three major types of VAT: (1) a 'gross product' VAT, which is equivalent to an equal-rate fully-general

* *Journal of Economic Literature*, December 1971, 9, pp. 1167–73. (Adapted).

sales tax on all final goods and services (i.e. GNP), provided that inventory increases are counted as a positive final good; (2) an 'income type' VAT, equivalent to an equal proportional tax on total factor income, which in turn equals the value of all final goods with a deduction for depreciation of capital goods, provided that inventory decreases are counted as a negative final good [2]; and (3) a 'consumption type' VAT, equivalent to a tax on final consumption goods only [3]. Rather than '. . . somewhat sterile efforts to relate the different to the familiar', as Lindholm claims, these equivalences are fundamental to understanding the essence of VAT – that it is a method of taxation and not a tax in itself.

In its most popular version as a consumption tax, for example, the VAT base may be set equivalent to that of any of the familiar sales taxes (manufacturers', wholesale, retail). In fact, until Denmark led the way in 1967 with a VAT extending through to the retail stage, no VAT extended further than the wholesale (i.e. sale to retailer) level [4]. At the present time, however, all European examples of VAT are consumption taxes of more or less the Danish type; the only current examples of the income and product varieties of VAT are taxes recently proposed in several Latin American countries [5].

Once the assumption of a closed economy is dropped and trade is assumed to take place, a country which imposes a VAT needs to specify not only the tax base but also a principle of *border tax adjustment*. Two principles are possible. The first is the destination principle, under which explicit export tax rebates and import compensatory duties are intended to guarantee that all goods consumed within the taxing jurisdiction are equally taxed regardless of where they are produced. The second is the origin principle, by which exports are taxed and imports exempted to ensure that all goods produced within the taxing jurisdiction are equally burdened regardless of where they are consumed. Most sales taxes in the world today – not just those collected by the VAT method – are on the destination basis, although the EEC member countries propose in the future to move to an origin basis (which requires no explicit border tax adjustment) for intra-Community trade only (taxation outside the community would remain on a destination basis). The introduction of a sales tax or the adoption of a principle of border tax adjustment are, of course, logically quite separate questions from those involved in using the VAT method of taxation as such.

ECONOMIC EFFECTS OF VAT

All existing examples of VAT have either replaced an existing mul-
tiple-stage sales tax (as in Europe) or some other form of general
sales tax. The major reasons for this move to the VAT technique
appear to have been either administrative convenience or in the
interests of efficient resource allocation, as noted below. In the U.S.
and Canada, however, a VAT has often been discussed as a potential
replacement for all or part of the income tax system, especially the
corporate income tax (and similarly in the U.K. – at least until
recently, when, in light of EEC negotiations, the VAT is scheduled to
replace the purchase tax and selective employment tax by 1973).
Usually it appears that a consumption-type VAT imposed on the
destination principle, and with a base equivalent to a general retail
sales tax, is what people have in mind in this connection, although
this is not always made clear. The case for this substitution has
usually been argued on the grounds of its effects on the balance of
payments or economic growth. To understand the likely economic
effects of a given type of VAT in any particular case, however, it is
useful first to analyse the effect of introducing the tax in a closed
economy and then to allow for international trade.

MONETARY EFFECTS

Closed Economy
Suppose a government in a closed economy imposes a general tax of
the VAT variety. As has been pointed out most notably by Harberger
[6] and most recently by Krauss and O'Brien [7], whether this tax
will be reflected in a lower level of production costs or a higher level of
commodity prices depends entirely on the policy followed by the
monetary authority. For the tax to be reflected in a higher level of
absolute commodity prices, the monetary authority has to expand the
money supply by more than the normal amount to accommodate the
increase in commodity prices. However, should the authority simply
provide for the normal secular expansion of the money supply, the
new tax (abstracting from any use of the funds) would exert deflationary pressures on money wages and costs. Should money wages prove
inflexible to the deflationary pressures, this could result in a lower
level of real output and employment in the short run. Given modern
governments' commitment to a high level of employment, however,

presumably the monetary authority would generally be expected to ratify the price increases. In any event, without knowing the precise strategy of monetary policy, it is not possible to predict the absolute price effects of introducing a general tax, whether it is a VAT or not.

Open Economy

If the assumption of a closed economy is dropped and the government wanted the VAT to be reflected in higher prices to consumers, either destination principle border tax adjustments must be employed (the monetary authority has to expand the money supply by more than the normal amount for a closed economy to sustain the increase in commodity prices in this case) or, if under a regime of freely floating exchange rates, origin principle adjustments may be applied. Should the origin principle be utilized under a system of fixed rates, however, and product prices be allowed to rise, adjustment of the consequent balance of payments disequilibrium would in effect convert the consumption tax into one on production (in this case, the increase in the money supply is dissipated *via* the balance-of-payments deficit). Factor costs will then be lower than would otherwise have been the case. Although it should make no real difference either to efficiency in the use of the world's resources or to the distribution of real income which principle of border tax adjustment is applied to a country's foreign trade – since the choice affects neither *relative* commodity nor *relative* factor price ratios – there will be a monetary difference between the two. Choosing the 'wrong' principle of border tax adjustment results in an inappropriate level of absolute money prices and costs and thus, assuming fixed rates of currency exchange, presumably undesired changes in the level of international reserve assets.

The distinction between a tax imposed by the VAT method and the principle by which VAT is applied to international trade is of critical importance to present policy discussions, especially in the United States. Lindholm and others, whom he cites, have mistakenly associated value-added taxation with import taxes and export subsidies (destination principle border tax adjustments) and thus with short-run improvement in the balance of payments. Thus Lindholm quotes Messere [8] as suggesting that 'an increase in VAT rates is equivalent to a devaluation of the currency' and himself claims that 'VAT, by stimulating exports and retarding imports

257

expands domestic investment of savings'. Both claims are incorrect (in our view) in that they mis-specify the cause of any balance of trade improvement, attributing it to VAT instead of the border tax adjustments which could accompany an increase in any sales tax. The latter quotation suffers from the further liability that it is relevant only in the short run when internal money price levels and currency exchange rates are fixed. In a more generalized setting, when the international adjustment mechanism can be assumed to be operating, any balance of payments advantages gained *via* border tax adjustments would tend to be dissipated through either currency appreciation or increases in internal absolute price levels in the improving country, or converse movements elsewhere.

In any event, adoption of value-added taxation for reasons of such short-run balance of payments effects would appear to be unwise policy making. Monetary disturbances are best remedied by monetary measures (exchange rate variation, for example), and questions of tax structure should, in principle, be decided on equity and efficiency grounds, not short-run balance of payments effects, particularly since, in this case, the hoped-for gain could be won simply by changing, either partially or fully, the principle of border tax adjustment independent of changes in tax structure. Of course, the ability of some countries to alter their border tax adjustments is presently constrained by the GATT ruling which limits destination principle border tax adjustments to indirect taxes. The rescission of this regulation would have the positive effect of removing the existing incentive for countries to alter their tax structures for balance of payments gains. However, the allowance of border tax adjustments for direct as well as indirect taxes could very well lead to a variety of other problems, one of which might be, in this neomercantilist age, protectionist overcompensation of export tax rebates and import compensatory duties. In this case, the border tax adjustment, whose purpose is to equalize the conditions of competition between domestic and foreign producers and so permit comparative cost to govern trade patterns, would be used as a *border tax* – a tariff, for example – which taxes international trade and hence restricts trade volumes below what would be indicated as desirable by the principle of comparative advantage [9]. Since most European countries also levy corporate income taxes at rates similar to those in the U.S. they too could, of course, take advantage of any revised GATT ruling in this connection.

Professor Lindholm claims that 'the introduction of VAT as a common tax for the Member States of EEC eliminates ER-IT (destination principle border tax adjustments) on trade among themselves. In doing this it also introduces a new ER-IT hurdle for nations outside of EEC, and a new ER-IT stimulus for nations within EEC to export outside of EEC.' This statement is incorrect for two reasons. First, the substitution of a VAT for a gross turnover tax in the EEC is both logically and politically independent of the decision of the Common Market countries to substitute origin principle for destination principle border tax adjustments with respect to their intra-union trade. Second, as established by Johnson and Krauss [9], the adoption of 'mixed systems' of border tax adjustments, that is, systems that use one type of adjustment principle for trade with other members and the other type for trade with outsiders, neither constitutes increased protection for EEC members against outsiders, nor serves to stimulate exports from the EEC [10].

INCIDENCE

To turn now to the probable effects of VAT on the distribution of real income, Professor Lindholm states that the 'established analyses of incidence of taxes using the transaction as the base conclude a general tax is shifted forward in higher prices'. This statement (as well as the subsequent discussion in Lindholm's review) is both misleading, in that it encourages the reader to believe that there is some vital analytical connection between a tax's incidence and its effects on absolute price levels, and incorrect, in that the 'established analyses' make no such contention. On the contrary, fiscal theorists have consistently pointed out the irrelevance of the absolute price effects of a tax to the question of its incidence – i.e. the manner in which the private real incomes of individuals (households) are altered by the imposition of a tax or, in the more meaningful differential tax approach to the subject, by the substitution of one tax for another [11, 12, and 13, among others]. Since in long-run competitive equilibrium, only households can earn economic rents, regardless of whether a tax is initially imposed on the output of the factors of production (a commodity tax), the use of the productive factors by firms (a production tax), the receipt of factor incomes (an income tax), or the use of factor incomes (an expenditure tax), its ultimate burden must be borne by households either in their role as sellers of productive factors (sources of income side of the household's budget) or buyers of products (uses of income side). As buyers of products (assuming that the average spending propensities of individuals differ), if the imposition of a tax or the substitution of one tax for another cause the *relative* commodity price ratio to change, income is redistributed from those who consume a relatively large proportion of the commodity whose price has increased relative to that of other goods, to those whose average preferences run in terms of the other goods. As sellers of factors (assuming that households possess different relative amounts of labour and capital) if the tax alters the *relative* factor price ratio, income is redistributed from those who own a relatively large share of the factor whose relative return has been lowered, to those who possess a relatively large share of the other factor. The Stolper–Samuelson relation implies that if the fiscal change alters either one of the relative price ratios, it must alter both. The factor-price (sources of income) distributional effect can be isolated only if identical spending propensities for households are assumed; similarly, the commodity-price (uses of income) distributional effect can be isolated only when households possess identical ownership shares of the productive factors.

Whatever the result in the complex world of reality, it is clear that the incidence of any tax, whether imposed by the VAT method or otherwise, or the substitution of a VAT type tax for some other type, bears no necessary relation to whatever effects the accompanying macroeconomic policy may have on the level of absolute prices. The essence of the incidence question is the *differential* effect of fiscal change on individuals resulting from their varied tastes and the different ratios in which they own the factors of production – absolute price changes have no such differential effect. An increase in absolute commodity prices at unchanged absolute factor prices reduces the real income of all individuals in proportion to the price change, regardless of whether they prefer apples to oranges or *vice-versa*. Similarly, a drop in the absolute factor price level at unchanged absolute commodity prices reduces the real income of all individuals in proportion to the price change, regardless of whether they own large amounts of capital relative to labour or *vice-versa*. It is only when relative prices change that individuals are affected differentially.

A final point relates to the question as to whether there exists a meaningful relationship between a method of taxation (VAT) and the distribution of income. It should be clear that the fact that the base of a VAT may be defined so as to be equivalent to GNP, national income at factor cost, or total retail sales, has no necessary bearing on the effects of value-added taxation on the distribution of income. This depends exclusively on the base of the tax and the values of the parameters that link that base with the relative commodity and factor price ratios on the one hand (the price elasticity of demand, the difference between factor intensity ratios between industries at initial factor prices, the elasticities of technical substitution between labour and capital in the relevant industries), and the difference between (1) individual average spending propensities and (2) the ratios in which the productive factors are owned, on the other. The method of taxation would appear to be irrelevant.

EFFICIENCY

Fiscal economists have long been interested in the effects of taxes on efficient resource allocation. Traditionally, these discussions have ignored the method by which the taxes are imposed because on the one hand, application was, after all, only a question of administration, while, on the other, the underlying analytical model considered the factors of production as 'original', thus implying a simplified productive process in which intermediate products were ignored. However, once the productive process is conceived of as a series of steps along which value is added at each level to that supplied by the original productive factors, it becomes apparent that the method of taxation, by discriminating between different forms of business enterprise, can affect the method of doing business – a distortion not generally considered in Paretian welfare analysis. Indeed, once it is realized that the output of one industry may very well be the input of some other industry, and that a tax on the former constitutes one on the latter as well, it becomes necessary to focus analytical attention on the effect of the entire tax structure on *productive processes* rather than on the effect of a tax on *commodities* produced by these processes, a fact well known from the literature on 'effective protection'.

Arguments along these lines have been important in leading the EEC and other European countries to replace their gross turnover taxes by a VAT to improve efficiency. Because the amount of tax a given commodity bears with a VAT, unlike a gross turnover tax, is independent of the number of transactions undergone by that commodity during the process of production and distribution, and independent of the relative amounts of value-added accrued at the several stages of production and distribution, a VAT will be neutral with respect to the structure of business enterprise. In addition, since the tax is levied as a constant proportion of value added at each stage in the production-distribution process, it is a constant proportion of total value added, and thus readily identifiable when, under the destination principle, export rebates and import compensatory duties are effected for goods crossing international borders. This condition will permit precise border adjustments, so that a tax intended to be reflected in higher prices to consumers (with destination principle adjustments) does not affect an industry's international competitive position by altering relative commodity price ratios. Such precision is quite unattainable with a gross turnover tax, although there have been no empirical studies indicating the degree to which vertical integration and imprecise border tax adjustments have in fact been encouraged by the gross turnover tax in Europe. Furthermore, as is well known, neutrality with respect to relative commodity price ratios implies an efficient allocation of resources only in the special case when the adjustment is imposed from an initial position of undistorted competitive equilibrium, which seems unlikely to be the case in practice. Finally, Krauss and O'Brien [7] have shown that, in a world with competitive distortions, it is in fact administratively simple to separate the tax from total value added at the border with destination principle adjustments only with certain forms of a value-added tax.

In short, while it is undeniable that the VAT method of imposing sales taxes possesses substantial advantages in terms of neatness and comprehensibility over the gross turnover tax (if not necessarily over all methods of sales taxation), its comparative advantage in terms of economic efficiency, especially with respect to other methods of general taxation, although significant, is not so overwhelming as commonly argued.

WHY ALL THE INTEREST?

So far we have said that, in fact, VAT constitutes a relatively new method of collecting sales taxes which has found favour in Europe as a replacement for the cumbersome sales taxes previously used there. A number of advantages, primarily administrative, have been claimed for this switch, and there appears to be much merit in some of them [4, 14]. But it is hard to see why such excitement has been aroused by VAT in countries not previously encumbered with clumsy gross turnover taxes.

Two reasons may perhaps be suggested for the current widespread interest in this form of taxation. First, the VAT form of taxation has proved to be a great revenue producer, and second, as Professor Lindholm notes, 'the growth of the use of VAT owes much to the fact it possesses a new name'. The countries which have to date adopted VAT have done so primarily for its alleged administrative and efficiency advantages over existing broad-based sales taxes. Discussions of the 'value-added tax' appear to be the most popular way yet found in which to introduce the idea of replacing income by sales taxes in the English-speaking countries without being immediately accused of the horrendous crime of advocating regressive taxes. As some have argued, sales taxes may indeed be the necessary fiscal oil for the expanding public machine of the future, and the VAT technique the best way of collecting them. But it is hard to avoid the feeling that many have seized upon VAT not so much as a means of increasing the fiscal base of the public sector but rather as a way of reducing income taxes *per se*. This objective too may be quite a valid one, but, if so, it should be discussed on its merits, not obfuscated by presenting the VAT method of collecting taxes as the greatest thing since sliced bread.

The appropriate base for a general tax, the effects of accompanying macroeconomic policy, the effects of the principle of border tax adjustment adopted, and to a large extent the effect on economic efficiency and the distribution of income – all these are logically quite distinct from the use of the VAT technique of tax collection and should be considered separately and explicitly in the interest of analytical clarity.

NOTES AND REFERENCES

[1] R. W. Lindholm, The value added tax: a short review of the literature, *J. Econ. Lit.*, Dec. 1970, **8** (4), 1178–89.

[2] A build-up of inventory in any one taxing period constitutes a positive element in the base of both the gross product and income types of VAT, while a

run-down of inventory constitutes a negative element in the base of the income type but not in the base of the gross product type.

[3] C. S. Shoup, *Public Finance*. Chicago: Aldine Publishing Company, 1969.

[4] C. S. Shoup, Experience with the value-added tax in Denmark, and prospects in Sweden, *Finanzarchiv*, March 1969, **28** (2), 236–52.

[5] J. F. Due, *Indirect taxation in developing economies*. Baltimore: Johns Hopkins Press, 1970; some provinces in Brazil presently employ value-added taxes.

[6] A. C. Harberger, A federal tax on value-added, in *The taxpayer stake in tax reform*. Washington D.C.: Chamber of Commerce of the U.S., 1968.

[7] M. Krauss and P. O'Brien, Some international implications of value added taxation, *National Tax J.*, Dec. 1970, **23** (4), 435–40.

[8] K. Messere, Border tax adjustments, *The OECD Observer*, Oct. 1967, **30**, 5–11.

[9] H. Johnson and M. Krauss, Border taxes, border tax adjustments, comparative advantage, and the balance of payments, *Can. J. Econ.*, Nov. 1970, **3** (4), 595–602.

[10] See the Johnson and Krauss reading in this volume.

[11] C. E. McLure, Jr, Tax incidence, macroeconomic policy, and absolute prices, *Quart. J. Econ.*, May 1970, **84** (2), 254–67.

[12] P. Mieskowski, Tax incidence theory: the effects of taxes on the distribution of income, *J. Econ. Lit.*, Dec. 1969, **74** (4), 1103–24.

[13] R. A. Musgrave, *The theory of public finance*. New York: McGraw-Hill, 1959.

PART FOUR

AGRICULTURAL POLICY

14

THE COMMON AGRICULTURAL
POLICY OF THE EUROPEAN
ECONOMIC COMMUNITY*

TIM JOSLING

London School of Economics and Political Science

The success of the European Community in devising a Common Agricultural Policy (CAP) from the diversity of individual farm policies that existed in Europe has been somewhat overshadowed by the apparent failure of that policy to achieve either a satisfactory balance in the European market for farm goods or a smooth transformation in the structure of rural society within the member countries. Indeed if policies survived on their popularity among economists, the common agricultural policy would be among the first to go. But the policy survives despite continual criticism and the abundant evidence of its own shortcomings.

This paper is in three parts. The first is a discussion of some of the basic objectives of the CAP, in particular those of income maintenance in the farm sector and of competition and specialization within the Community. The problems associated with attaining these goals exist under almost any method of farm support. But much of the criticism of the CAP has in fact centred on the particular type of policies used to support farm prices rather than on the underlying problems of a support policy *per se*. The second part of this paper compares the economic, or real income cost of three support methods using a standard static welfare approach. The third section describes some of the pressures for change which are building up within the Community and outside.

I. THE OBJECTIVES OF THE CAP

As with any other economic policy, the CAP has a number of goals both implicit and explicit. The explicit goals were established follow-

* *Journal of Agricultural Economics*, May 1969, 20, pp. 175–191 (Adapted).

ing the Stresa conference in 1958 convened in accordance with the Rome Treaty. These goals can be grouped into two major objectives: to increase farm incomes not only by a system of transfers from the non-farm population through a price support policy but also by the encouragement of rural industrialization to give alternative opportunities to farm labour; and to contribute to overall economic growth by allowing specialization within the community and eliminating artificial market distortions. There was also a commitment to preserving the family farm and to ensuring that structural and price policies went hand in hand.

It would be churlish to question such a goal of a prosperous agriculture contributing to economic growth in the community. But devising a policy to achieve this uncovers a number of problems. Perhaps the most fundamental has to do with the definition of the farming constituency. Should one's policy be devised to guarantee prosperity to any who might wish at some future date to enter agriculture – and moreover to assure a reasonable rate of return for any amount of capital that they may wish to invest in farming? Or should one's policy be geared to those already in the industry who have made resource allocation decisions based on expectations of the future which governments then feel under an obligation to realize? This is a real political dilemma. Given the competitive structure of the farm sector, returns to resources settle at levels determined by the opportunity cost of the marginal units. Until very recently it was an accepted part of the conventional wisdom of agricultural economics that the low returns commonly noted in agriculture arose from the inability of the labour force to adjust sufficiently fast to the twin pressures of a changing technology and a stagnant market. The new technology was often of the labour-saving type, adding to the pressure for farm labour to be released. This view now seems inadequate. There is ample evidence that the labour market works quite well. The direction of new technology is itself a reflection of a labour shortage in large parts of agriculture – or more correctly of an increase in the price of labour relative to capital often accentuated by government policy. It is much more plausible to assume that low earnings in agriculture are the consequence of low alternative earnings arising from disparities in education levels in rural areas. But in these circumstances any price policy based on some concept of giving to farm resources the ability to achieve parity incomes with the non-farm population is doomed to failure. Higher prices are largely translated into the purchase of more inputs from the non-farm sector (fertilizer and machinery) and into the values of assets the supply of which are fixed (mainly land). Input suppliers and land-holders gain, but the new entrants gets no benefit. This accounts for the seemingly insatiable appetite of farm programmes for public money and the desire to hide the appropriations in the form of higher food costs even if the same transfer could be made more efficiently by direct payments. Agriculture adjusts in size to the level of support it is given; price support policies have never influenced long-run resource returns appreciably. The implication of this is that the only way to raise farm incomes is to control the inflow of resources into agriculture, or to increase the level of education in rural areas.

Equally fundamental are the implications of the objective to promote specialization and encourage competition in European agriculture. The question immediately arises 'competition with whom?' In European policy the emphasis has been mainly on equalizing competition among Community farmers through the establishment of a single market and the harmonization of non-price policies. In an individual country the choice has to be made as to whether to allow agriculture to compete with the rest of the economy or whether to isolate it from secular economic trends. Imagine a country where productivity in agriculture lags behind that in industry, whilst the industrial sector in turn has an increasing competitive edge in world markets. As the exchange rate appreciates, the terms of trade will turn against agriculture if it has a fixed level of protection *vis-à-vis* other agricultural producers. In other words a fixed (or zero) level of market protection implies that farmers are competing with the non-farm sector of the economy. An increasing level of protection in agricultural markets would be needed to isolate the farm sector from the industrial part of the economy. But now imagine this country in a customs union with another where border protection is disallowed. The implication is that however much protected the customs union itself is with respect to the outside world, within its borders it is not possible directly to increase the level of protection to one agricultural sector alone. That sector thus competes directly with its non-farm industry. Even if one allows for differing rates of inflation to substitute for exchange rate changes the implication still holds. To oversimplify: free trade in farm goods between France and Germany forces German agriculture into competition with German

269

industry to an extent that was not true before the CAP was established.

To focus on competition within the farm sectors of a customs union is misleading; it leads to a discussion in terms of absolute cost differences among farms in the member countries, whereas the implications of trade liberalization run in terms of relative cost advantages. Thus the objective should be to allow production to locate where relative costs are less within the Community after account has been taken of monetary adjustments due to differences in industrial productivity and inflation. Of course the agricultural sector of the Community as a whole might still be protected against outside competition. Thus when the dollar was recently devalued relative to European currencies, the levies on American grain increased to offset the extra advantage which these products would otherwise have had on the European market. EEC farmers were being granted an exemption from the full implications of the strong performance of European industrial goods on the world market.

But even having decided on the type of competition that one is willing to allow, one still has to decide whether to bring this about through market prices or by some more *dirigiste* method. The EEC chose free internal markets and a common price system in favour of directed production quotas for various countries. But there appears to have been a serious misconception regarding the operation of a price system. Uniform prices across a market (subject to costs of transportation and quality) are the *result* of free market access; to impose uniform administered prices across countries where trade has previously not been free can deny competition. This may be seen most clearly in the case of the intervention (or floor) price for grains. A common price floor, at which government agencies step in to buy produce off the market, means that low cost countries are unable to undercut less efficient producers. French grain cannot materially supplant German grain in German markets so long as intervention prices in the two countries differ only by transport cost; instead it has to be exported to third countries with the aid of subsidies.

II. SUPPORT SYSTEMS COMPARED

This part of the paper is an attempt to use formal economic analysis to examine the relative efficiency of several alternative methods of price support for agricultural commodities [1]. The policies to be considered are a deficient payment scheme, a variable levy, and a system of direct payments to producers [2]. Traditional analysis of such policies would emphasize the inefficiency or loss in consumer real income of such policies through the misallocation of resources and the distortion of the price mechanism. This analysis departs from tradition by explicitly considering (a) the existence of objectives other than economic efficiency, (b) the effect on markets into which the supported product passes as an input, and (c) the implications of marginal adjustments to policy levels. The analysis begins with a description of the effects of the various policies and a discussion on the quantitative measures of cost and objective variables. The policies are then compared with respect to the relative cost of achieving the objective, both on average and at the margin. The policies are then reconsidered in the light of the impact on markets purchasing the supported products.

(i) *The market*
Consider a product, i, that is both domestically produced and imported. Assume, for simplicity of exposition, that the level of home imports does not significantly alter the import price, and that this price corresponds (with appropriate transport and quality differentials) to the domestic market price. Domestic supply is a function of the relevant producer price, the opportunity cost of the resources used, and a complex of technological factors. Demand for the i-product varies with the market price and, if a consumer good, with the price of related goods and with income and taste changes. If the i-good is an input item, then the demand will be affected by the opportunity cost of cooperating inputs, by factors shifting the demand for the final product(s) such as income and other product prices, and by technical input coefficients, as well as the market price for the i-good.

(ii) *Deficiency payment (DP) scheme*
The results of a guaranteed price imposed by the government above the level of the market price is that this becomes the relevant producer price. The market is illustrated in Fig. 14·1. The effects of the policy can be quickly summarized. Domestic output increases from q_1 to q_2. A deficiency payment of $(G-P)$ is paid on q_2 units – at a budget cost of $R+C$. Saving in foreign exchange out-payments is F. Under the assumption that the supply curve reflects the marginal

(social) opportunity cost of resources used in i-production, it is possible to distribute the extra producer revenue occasioned by the policy. Area $C+F$ approximates the value of extra resources induced into the industry by the policy; area R is the additional producers' surplus, or rent [3]. For the purposes of this paper it will be taken that one objective of agricultural policy is to effect a certain level of income transfer represented by the value of R.

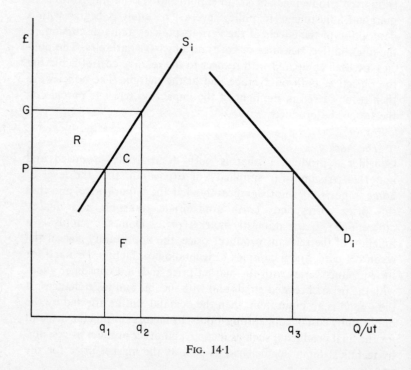

FIG. 14·1

The previous paragraph, together with Fig. 14·1, constitute a description of the effects of the policy; a formal analysis requires that these results are taken a step further. It is possible to derive expressions for the *average* cost (in terms of extra resources or budget payments) of achieving a unit of objective, in this case income transfer. Such calculations are meaningful if comparing the policy with a free market. More relevant in the case of a policy where the level of guaranteed price can be changed from year to year is the *marginal* cost of gaining an additional unit of objective.

(iii) *Variable levy (VL) or quota schemes*

Suppose that, instead of a deficiency payment policy, it was decided to pursue income transfer by means of a threshold price supported by a variable [4]. In this case the relevant producer price would correspond to the established threshold price (adjusted for transport and quality differences). Fig. 14·2 shows a market under such a variable levy scheme. As before, producers' surplus is increased by R, and extra resources worth $C+F$ are encouraged into the industry.

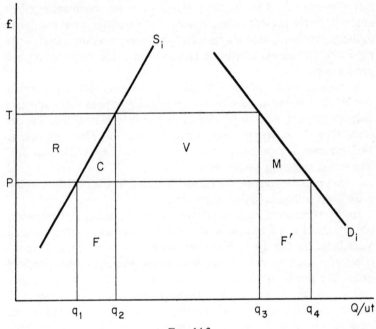

FIG. 14·2

Exchange saving is now $F+F'$ since quantity demanded falls. If all levy revenues are collected (i.e. if there is no discrimination on the part of exporting countries) then these amount to area V; to the extent that exporters discriminate, exchange saving and revenue from the levy will both be less. If the product is purchased by consumers then their expenditure will be less by area F' but greater by $R+C+V$, the net effect depending of course on the demand elasticity. To look at expenditure however is not enough. If one accepts the approximation of consumer well-being given by the area under the demand curve, the consumers are 'worse off' by area $M + F'$. They can how-ever spend the amount F' on other goods to give them at least the same satisfaction. The amount represented by area $R + C + V$ has to be found from elsewhere reducing satisfaction by this amount and the net effect is the familiar loss in consumer surplus of $R + C + V + M$. It is usual in the economic analysis of tariffs to say that area $R + C + V$ is a transfer from consumers to government and producers, and to call the consumer 'cost' of the policy the triangle M. Transfer pay-ments, however much the economist wishes to ignore them, are the diet of politicians. They must be quantified in any meaningful policy analysis. In the present example, area V is a transfer from consumer to the government, area R a transfer from consumers (or users) to the producer, and area C a 'bribe' to factors to enter the sector to increase production.

If instead of establishing a threshold price and enforcing it with a variable levy it was decided to enter into an agreement with exporters that no product were to be offered at less than a minimum import price, then the exchange effects would be different. That area in Fig. 14·2 representing potential levy revenue would be additional out-payments: exchange saving would be $F + F' - V$, and would depend for sign upon the elasticity of import demand. The same effect would arise from collusion among exporters.

In the absence of monopoly practice by importers and exporters the effects of a quota can be illustrated by the same diagram as a VL scheme. In Fig. 14·2, an import quota of $(q_3 - q_2)$ would have the effect of raising the price to the level of the guaranteed or threshold price. The implications for income transfer, user cost, and resource cost are as for the VL scheme. The interpretation of the amount V, the levy revenue under a VL policy, is less straightforward. If the government were to auction off the quotas to importers it could capture that amount in domestic currency. Exchange saving impli-cations and government revenue would be as for the VL scheme. If the government merely set the quotas without such an auction, then exporters could gain by the amount V, and the implications would be as for a minimum import price. The analysis of import quotas under these conditions is therefore subsumed in the previous paragraphs.

(iv) *Intermediate goods*

So far we have assumed that the product is a consumer good. Many agricultural products are in fact inputs into other products (either within the industry or elsewhere). In turn these other products may be imported or produced exclusively at home. Assume, for simplicity, that the input item enters the production of the final good in a fixed proportion (to output, and to other inputs). This enables us to incorporate both product and factor markets (expressed in factor units) on the same graph. Figure 14·3 shows two possibilities. In

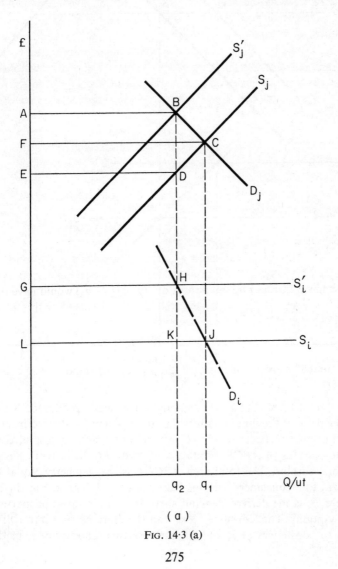

(a)

FIG. 14·3 (a)

275

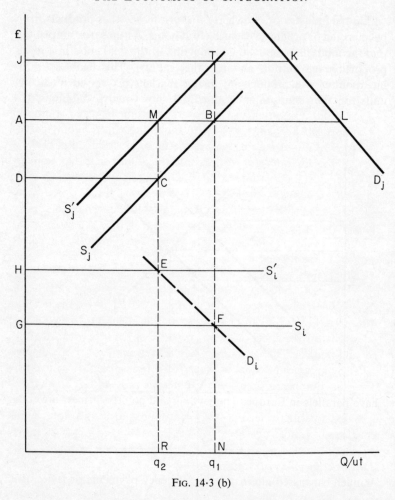

FIG. 14·3 (b)

Fig. 14·3 (a), the final good is wholly domestically produced. A rise in the price of the input (i) shifts the supply curve for the product (j) by the same vertical amount. Consumers of j suffer a loss of consumer surplus of $ABCF$, producers of j lose $FCDE$ in rent or producers' surplus. The total area $ABCDE$ is, by geometry, equal to $GHJL$, the 'consumers' surplus loss' – $R + C + V + M$ in Fig. 14·2 – where D_i is the derived demand curve for i under fixed proportion assumptions. The 'consumer cost' can therefore be split into (i) the loss to consumers of j; and (ii) the loss to producers of j, in the

276

proportion of the elasticities (or more accurately, slopes) of the demand and supply curves for the j-good. The modification is simple to apply to the analysis of a policy for the input i.

If, however, product j is also imported (at a fixed world price, let us assume) then there will also be exchange repercussions. The domestic raising of an input price hurts the competitive position of j-good producers; in effect a tax on their production and a subsidy to competitors abroad. Fig. 14·3 (b) shows this effect. Supply curves S_i and S_j shifts as before. Now domestic production shifts back to q_2 and the quantity $(q_1 - q_2)$ is additional imports. Domestic j-producers lost an amount $ABCD = HEFG$; the full 'consumer cost' (area $R + C + V + M$ in Fig. 14·2) is borne by the j-producers. Foreign exchange is lost to the value of MBNR – which is greater than exchange saving (under a VL system) F' in Fig. 14·2 by the ratio of output to input. Two additional policies can prevent this effect. If product j is supported by a guaranteed price, then that price can be raised to offset the increased input cost. In this case the effect is to compensate j-producers in full at additional exchequer expense of $JTBA$, where guaranteed price is increased by the amount AJ. Alternatively a tariff can be imposed on the j-market. If it compensates fully for the effect of the higher price of the input then there is no additional exchange burden but the consumers of the j-good suffer by an amount equal to area $HEFG$ times the ratio of average domestic disappearance of j to the domestic production. These cases have parallels in European policy; pig and poultry farmers are compensated for higher feed costs by an import levy and flour levies are geared to those of wheat.

(v) *Direct income payments*

A much canvassed alternative to deficiency payments or levies as a means of transferring income to the farm sector is to pay income subsidies. The characteristic of such subsidies of relevance in the present model is that they are not tied to output levels. In a static model such payments involve no economic cost and place no burden on users or on foreign suppliers. To be strictly neutral they should also be paid in such a way as to allow the recipients to leave farming without prejudice to their income from the payments scheme.

(vi) *Comparison of policies*

The three policies can be compared as to the efficiency with which they transfer income to the farm sector. This efficiency can be measured by the economic cost, the budget cost, or the user cost as a proportion of income transferred. It is also interesting to calculate the exchange saving as a proportion of income transfer. If the policy were to be used as a balance of payments instrument then exchange saving would be an objective; in the case of the EEC it is more relevant to consider it as a cost borne by foreign producers who find their sales to the EEC falling as protection is increased. This exchange saving will be called 'foreign cost' in the remainder of this section. As mentioned above, one can discuss either the *average* cost of income transfer, or the *marginal* cost of an additional unit of income transfer. The latter is appropriate when setting the level of policy instruments; the former gives an indication of whether the policy as a whole is efficient. Expressions for the marginal and average budget, user, foreign, and economic cost per unit of income transfer are derived simply from the algebraic specification of the model described above. These costs are dependent upon the level of protection, the elasticities of supply and demand, and the relationship between the quantity produced and consumed [5].

As an indication of the likely magnitudes of these costs the method is applied to the EEC grains sector. The basic assumptions needed are as follows:

EEC grain price	$98/metric ton (tonne)
World grain price	$70/metric ton
EEC 1968 production	70 million t
EEC 1968 consumption	73 million t
Elasticity of supply	1·0
Elasticity of demand	1·0
Therefore, Level of protection	40%
Production at world prices	50 million t
Consumption at world prices	122 million t

With this information, we can estimate the costs of such a policy. The grain policy transfers to producers $1,680 million over and above their net receipts at world prices; the cost to the Community of the present levy policy is $966 million in real income foregone; the budget (FEOGA) gains $85 million in levy revenue, but foreign producer earnings drop by $4,829 million. The cost imposed on users of grain – which, as discussed above, may be offset by policies in other grain using sectors at a further budget and economic cost –

is $2,730 million. With a deficiency payment scheme, giving the same income support, the economic cost would be $280 million, the budget cost $1,960 million, and the foreign cost only $1,399 million. A direct subsidy payment system would transfer the $1,680 million to producers at no economic cost.

TABLE 14.1. *Average and marginal cost of income transfer using alternative policies; grain market, EEC, 1968*

(a) Average cost of $1.00 transferred to grain farmers

Policy	Economic cost	Budget cost	User cost	Foreign cost
Deficiency payment	0·17	1·17	—	0·83
Variable levy	0·57	−0·05	1·63	2·87
Direct income payment	—	1·00	—	—

(b) Marginal cost of additional $1·00 transferred to grain farmers

Policy	Economic cost	Budget cost	User cost	Foreign cost
Deficiency payment	0·29	1·29	—	0·71
Variable levy	0·99	0·94	1·04	2·46
Direct income payment	—	1·00	—	—

Table 14·1 related these costs to the objective of income transfer. Clearly the direct transfer policy out performs the market interference policies. What is striking is the extent to which a deficiency payment policy improves the efficiency of income transfer relative to the variable levy. Each $1·00 transferred costs $0·57 in real income through a levy system but less than a third as much ($0·17) if a deficiency payment system is used. The real income loss to the EEC of raising money through consumers rather than through taxes to pay the transfer is about $0·40 for each $1·00 transferred. Moreover, the depression of the earnings of foreign suppliers is over $2·00 more (per $1·00 transferred) than with a deficiency payment scheme. At the margin, both policies are expensive ways of transferring income, relative to direct payments. But the present system appears to cost almost as much in real income lost ($0·99) as in transfer accomplished ($1·00) at the margin. Moreover, the reduction in levy revenue as imports decline implies a FEOGA loss of $0·94 in addition to the user cost of $1·04 for each extra $1·00 transferred. Foreign costs are slightly lower at the margin, but still very considerable.

These estimates are of course conditioned by the assumptions of the elasticity values. But unitary long-run elasticities for demand and supply are by no means implausible in view of the ease of substitution of grains for other feeds and of the apparent increase in production in those countries where prices rose upon the formation of the CAP. In addition the level of protection of 40% may be somewhat modest. The implication is that however the policy may develop over the next few years, retention of the variable levy as the main protective device for grains is both expensive to the Community and damaging to other grain producers.

III. THE PRESSURES FOR CHANGE

The CAP is under pressure both from within the EEC and from without. The most immediate internal pressure is that arising from exchange rate changes within the Six. It is clear from the discussion above that exchange rate changes are in no way incompatible with the objective of intra-community specialization along comparative cost lines [6]. Competition is distorted only during those periods where countries are moving into positions of increasing surplus or deficit on their balance of payments; whether they use inflation or deflation or whether they allow currency values to change, competition is restored once adjustments have been made. Moreover, if one were devising a scheme which was consistent with exchange rate changes and a unified market one would express administered prices in terms of a common unit of account. The way to make exchange rate changes inconsistent with the Rome Treaty (in agricultural markets) would have been to fix administered prices in the national currencies of each country. But this was not done. The problem that exchange rate changes pose for EEC farmers is that it makes more explicit the fact that they are in competition with their own industrial sectors. It is unfortunate that Germany, the country that had to reduce its prices to harmonize with the common level over the transition period, 1964–7, is the same country whose earnings rate has appreciated most in the last three years. Though transitional measures are no doubt desirable when farmers' expectations have been based on governmental promises of stable exchange rates, any permanent support to offset parity changes will merely lead to a progressive distortion of competition within the Community.

Another internal pressure arises from the accepted principle of 'joint financial responsibility'. This principle when combined with that of a common level of protection against third-country production has some interesting implications for both the Commission and the national governments. For the central decision maker the prospect of retaining the revenue from levies means that there will be an effort to avoid spending on export restitutions that income from levies which could be devoted to other community uses. This implies that in terms of individual agricultural sectors there will be a tendency towards self-sufficiency. If a policy for, say, sugar has zero FEOGA cost then there will be little or no pressure from the Commission to introduce changes. Ideally the Commission's financial aims would be satisfied by imports of some commodities over a protective wall combined with an implicit or explicit export tax on those commodities where the community is more than self-sufficient. But individual countries receive rather different stimuli; for an importing country the 'best' policy is a liberal import stance coupled with high production at home, and for an exporter, the 'ideal' situation would be a sizeable export subsidy paid for largely from community resources on as large a volume of output as possible. Joint financial responsibility removes from the importer the incentive to look outside the area for its supplies, but induces exporters to produce for disposal in third country markets. The incompatibility of the aims of the central authorities and those of the national governments goes some way to explaining the present problems of price fixing and structural reform within the Six.

A more intangible but equally real pressure arises from the feeling that private costs and market prices do not adequately reflect the social costs and benefits of farm production in all areas of the community. This presumed market distortion takes a number of forms. It can be argued that in those regions where there is significant unemployment the social opportunity cost of labour is low relative to the wage rate. A policy which encouraged production in these regions might be consistent with overall objectives even though it appeared to divert competition. Hence the pressure for agriculture to be incorporated in a regional policy. Similarly when other objectives such as that of maintaining a population in the hill areas or in the north of Europe are taken into account it may be reasonable to distort competition in favour of these producers; the social value of their farming activity exceeds the market value of their output. The problem of the elderly farmer has naturally been emphasized in Europe. Here the distortion may lie in the scant availability of pension schemes in rural areas; the solution is more likely to rest with the retirement grants now in operation in some countries rather than any deliberate change in the profitability of farming. The elderly farmer has now been replaced in the centre stage by the small-but-potentially-viable farm. Again the argument for support lies in a market distortion; financial help in the short run will enable these units to 'compete' at some later date. In other words the existence of scale economies implies that private costs exceed the true social costs of expansion. And, to complete the list, there is also the argument that support is necessary to some farmers to enable them to continue to farm in a way which does not exploit the structure and fertility of the land; the cost of conservation should be borne collectively since it does not pay the individual farmer to avoid environmental damage.

Yet another series of pressures on the CAP fall into the category of inappropriate relative prices among goods. It is certainly true that the necessity for large denaturing premia indicate an imbalance in cereal prices. But more fundamentally it can be argued that goods, such as butter, which are close substitutes in consumption with products of the non-farm sector, have been taxed too heavily. Similarly the rapid switch to the use of non-grain feeds by the compounding industry illustrates the consequences of establishing unrealistically high cereal prices. The high price of grain relative to livestock products has meant that the effective level of support has been much higher for cereal farms than for those that use cereals as an input. Thus the only support afforded a large sector of European agriculture is to be compensated for their cost increases arising from the support given to other farmers.

Last, and until recently least among the pressures operating on the CAP, are those arising from outside the Six. These pressures are associated with the current flurry of diplomatic activity by the U.S.A. but they represent the deeper problems of the extent to which industrial countries should take into account the external effects of their own domestic policies on both developing and other developed countries and the degree to which European farm policy as a whole is designed to isolate the market from competition by the low cost suppliers. These problems are not new, but they have found urgency in the context of enlargement and the potential loss of the U.K. market by overseas producers. The U.S., although always disapproving of the CAP, suffered little in trade terms. Exports of first maize and then soybeans were favoured by the price structure of the policy, at the expense of wheat and barley from Canada and other countries. The loss of important Asian markets to subsidized EEC exports and the prospect of enlargement galvanized the U.S. into action. The question of the EEC policy will be at the forefront of international discussion for some time to come. The U.S. has negotiated some short-term changes to accompany the monetary adjustments over the next year or so; in the medium term they anticipate a serious round of negotiations under the GATT charter as tariff bindings have to be released following enlargement of the community under article 24(6). In the longer term they hope that the outcome of the present OECD study group will point to multilateral action on agricultural protection. Further pressure in this direction will come from UNCTAD III which no doubt will repeat its call for trade policies of advanced countries more propitious to primary product exporters.

How the CAP will develop in the light of all these pressures is a question that requires clairvoyance in a number of political and economic areas. All one can do at present is to mention a few alternative paths. A rapid return to the situation that obtained in 1968 – of a relatively free market within the Six under common administered prices – is unlikely. What seems more probable is a tendency to differentiate prices to groups of farmers under various criteria. Thus it is almost certain that there will be a 'hill farming' policy to take account of the special problems of disadvantaged geographical areas. Since Britain has pursued a successful policy of hill subsidies, there would be no opposition from that side of the channel in principle, though there might be disagreement about the distribution of the cost. Secondly the national programme relating to retirement grants for the elderly will be strengthened and may even develop into an EEC-wide policy along the lines of the Mansholt proposals in this field. Again no serious conflicts arise in principle. Thirdly there will be a move to correct some of the relative price ratios among products; but these might take the form of raising the price of the lower-priced goods – oilseeds, beef, and maize – rather than the reverse. There is considerable scope for developing alternative policies, such as direct payments and marketing certificates, to solve the problem of inter-product substitution. Fourthly there will be a growing tendency to support those groups of farmers disadvantaged by exchange rate changes. Political pressures arise when economic forces come into play; the economic cost of the policy will rise over time, and trade distortions increase, if prices are permanently differentiated by monetary blocs. The only hope of a reconciliation here between political and economic forces is if the community develops in such a way that divergent cost trends within the EEC diminish over time. Though forced monetary union will not solve the problem, a *de facto* integration will make the solution easier. Fifth there will be an attempt to generate price levels that will give a satisfactory income to the small but viable farmer. This seems likely to be done on a cost-recoupment basis in much the same way as has been done in the U.K. for many years under the Annual Review system. As indicated in Part I this procedure is unlikely to achieve either the resource allocation or the income parity objectives. Unless the price of goods on the world market takes an unexpected turn upward, the cost of such a policy would increase steadily over time.

One would also predict a trend towards more responsibility in international markets toward the needs of developing countries; in particular the renogation of the Yaoundé Convention and the reformulation of the Commonwealth Sugar Agreement will make explicit the Communities' responsibility toward developing nations. It is in this regard as much as any other that enlargement will change the content in which the policy has to operate.

APPENDIX: MEMORANDUM ON THE REFORM OF
AGRICULTURE IN THE EUROPEAN ECONOMIC
COMMUNITY (MANSHOLT REPORT)
THE 'AGRICULTURE 1980' PROGRAMME

1. *Aims*

The 'Agriculture 1980' programme aims at extricating agriculture from its present position, where it is handicapped both economically and socially. Agriculture has in consequence cut itself off from the rest of the economy, farming has been subjected to special treat-ment, which has meant giving it assistance in connection both with incomes and social conditions and with the conduct of its business affairs. To break out of this situation, farmers will as a start have to free themselves from the constraints imposed on them by the often-outdated structure of production.

Farmers should be able to choose their position in society and their occupation in the light of their own aspirations, gifts and interests. But they will have no effective freedom of choice until they, or their children, can find jobs outside agriculture, to be created as far as possible in their own region.

(a) *A new approach to market policy and price policy.* The productivity of labour in agriculture should be as high as the economic optimum permits. This can be brought about in the main by a reduction of the labour employed, leading to better returns on investment. This higher productivity will raise agricultural incomes, and a larger portion of them can then be used to procure for farmers the sort of living conditions that are the rule outside agriculture.

Once farming is an activity where productivity is high and incomes larger, its economic behaviour will not be the same as today. Investment and production decisions will be economically more rational. In particular, modernized farms will be better able to follow the pointers provided by prices and relative price levels, and will have to take account of them.

Consequently, consumption will guide and limit production via the price mechanism, with the result that agricultural markets can work in a more 'normal' way. The formation of structural surpluses will be avoided and the Guarantee Section of the European Agricultural Guidance and Guarantee Fund (EAGGF) will have to spend less.

With this aim in view, the possibility of revising the common organizations of the various markets should be studied. Responsibility in matters of production and marketing should increasingly be taken over by farmers, who should be encouraged to organize themselves as fully as necessary, especially by forming producers' groupings. The basic principle of the proposed revision should be to give producers an increasingly direct interest in outlets for their produce. It would then be possible to dismantle part of the mechanism of intervention.

The Community's agricultural policy has so far given priority to action on markets and prices.

The introduction of single prices has certainly opened up national markets and made room for a very appreciable increase in intra-Community trade; but in the case of most agricultural products, these prices do not seem to have been fixed primarily with reference to economic criteria and the requirements of the specialization that should exist in the common market. More often than not the price fixed was the result of political compromises acceptable to all Member States.

The Community was thus led to fix the prices for most agricultural products at a level generally well in excess of the prices currently ruling in international transactions or even on the domestic markets of countries with which the Community is in competition.

While this price policy has helped to raise farm incomes, it has not enabled farmers to catch up with the incomes of other comparable social and occupational groups. On the contrary, the income of certain farmers is declining in real terms. The present system of market intervention, with its quantitatively unlimited market support at high prices, encourages marginal farms to stay in business and thus constitutes an obstacle to a Community-wide division of labour in agriculture and to the modernization of farming. It holds up the diminution in the number of farmers, which is one of the essential factors for an increase in farm incomes, and at the same time enables certain more competitive farmers to fatten on the support given.

The system is also extremely costly for the public at large. The policy of high prices, coupled with progress in chemistry, animal health, plant protection and genetics, has greatly raised unit yields. Since demand expansion is limited by the rate of population growth, the Community now finds itself saddled, in the case of many products, with surpluses of which some cannot even be disposed of on the saturated world market. Even when there are outlets, the surpluses bear on the market so heavily that they can be disposed of only at a price which is very costly for the Community. The cost of intervention and refunds in an agriculture producing structural surpluses is a burden which is becoming intolerable for our Member States, and their economies are in consequence being deprived of resources which could be used to better advantage in improving the competitive strength of other economic sectors.

It is therefore essential that a new approach be adopted to agricultural prices.

The suggestion is sometimes heard that producer prices should be lowered, which would reduce consumer prices. Such a policy would have the advantage of stimulating consumption and at the same time cutting down support costs, both in unit and in global terms. It would also facilitate the elimination of marginal producers, who would be hardest hit by such a policy.

But quite apart from the obvious political difficulties involved, such a price reduction would have to be considerable if it were to have the desired effect. If prices were lowered only a little, many farmers might be led to produce more in order to maintain their income unchanged.

The way for the Community to restore more satisfactory conditions to agricultural markets is a combination of long-term strategy and annual adjustments in line with that strategy. Future price policy should be designed gradually to create a new price structure which takes account of demand, costs and the desired pattern of production. Agricultural prices must again assume their real economic significance, which is to guide production with a view to better market balance. Savings on support costs to competitive farms would make room for concurrent help to those farms which are capable of becoming competitive and steps to reduce the number of marginal producers.

The principles by which price policy could be guided in the years ahead are as follows:

Those products of which there are structural surpluses are subject to steady pressure on prices; it would seem that their prices cannot be raised in the immediate future, but only when, after due allowance has been made for foreign trade, demand exceeds supply under the impact of a rising population and growing incomes. The prices of other products can be raised to the extent allowed by the expansion of demand.

Implementation of the 'Agriculture 1980' programme should steadily reduce the net expenditure of the Guarantee Section of the EAGGF, so that by 1980 the figure should not exceed 750 million u.a., of which 250 million for dairy products.

(b) *Measures concerning the structure of production and marketing.* A certain number of measures will be necessary to achieve the aims of the 'Agriculture 1980' programme.

(1) A first set of measures concerns the structure of agricultural production, and contains two main elements:

(i) One group of measures, varying widely in character, must be taken to bring about an appreciable reduction in the number of persons employed in agriculture. Older people will have to be offered a supplementary annual income allowance if they agree to retire and thereby release land; younger farmers should be enabled to change over to non-farming activities; the children of farmers, finally, should be given an education which enables them to choose an occupation other than farming, if they so desire. For the two latter categories, new jobs will have to be created in many regions. These efforts at reducing agricultural manpower should be brought to bear with particular force on one group of persons within agriculture, namely, those who own their farm businesses, inasmuch as the structural reforms of farms themselves, as described below, largely depends upon the withdrawal of a large number of these people from agriculture.

(ii) Secondly, far-reaching and coordinated measures should be taken with a view to the creation of agricultural enterprises of adequate economic dimensions. If such enterprises are to be set up and kept running, the land they need will have to be made available to them on acceptable terms; this will require an active and appropriate agrarian policy.

(2) A second group of measures concerns markets, with the double purpose of improving the way they work and of adjusting supply more closely to demand.

(i) Here the major factor will be a cautious price policy, and this will be all the more effective as the enterprises react more sensitively to the pointers offered by the market.

(ii) A considerable reduction of the area of cultivated land will work in the same direction.

(iii) Better information will have to be made available to all market parties (producers, manufacturers and dealers), producers will have to accept stricter discipline and there will have to be some concentration of supply. Product councils and groupings of product councils will have to be set up at European level and to take over certain responsibilities in this field.

In the case of farmers who are unable to benefit from the measures described, it may prove necessary to provide personal assistance not tied either to the volume of output or to the employment of factors of production. This assistance should be payable within specified limits defined in the light of regional factors and the age of the persons concerned.

2. *Principles of implementation*

The general principles on which the 'Agriculture 1980' programme is to be implemented must be clearly defined, not least because of its scale and its political, economic and social implications.

(1) In accordance with the political philosophy of our society, implementation of the programme must be based on its acceptance by the farmers and must be subject to the decisions they make of their own free choice;

(2) The present diversity of regional conditions calls for a corresponding variation in the measures adopted;

(3) While the programme must be conceived in Community-wide terms, its implementation must be largely decentralized and be the responsibility of Member States;

(4) The Community will have to contribute to financing the programme.

REFORM OF THE STRUCTURE OF PRODUCTION

Reform of the structure of production is the keystone of the proposed agricultural reform. It is indispensable if farmers are to enjoy incomes and living conditions comparable to those of other workers in the industrial society of today.

The new structure envisaged rests, essentially, on enterprises of adequate size. The necessary changes concern, on the one hand, the size of the agricultural population and, on the other, the farms themselves and area available for agriculture. The new agricultural enterprises will employ less manpower than today's farms. Their establishment will be made possible by a certain number of farmers making their land available either beforehand or at the time the enterprise is established. To facilitate such a development, help will have to be extended to two classes of persons:

(i) Those who wish to take up another occupation or to retire.

(ii) Those who will be staying on in modernized farming.

1. *Measures to help persons wishing to take up another occupation or to retire*

Agriculture cannot be finally integrated into the economy as a whole without drastic change, and this change requires a speedy adjustment of the agricultural population to its new tasks, as regards numbers, composition and skills.

To this end, effective steps will have to be taken to accelerate the outflow of manpower from agriculture and to ensure that most of it comes from certain categories and age groups where there are at present surpluses.

The measures concerned are in principle of two kinds, namely those that can be applied to all members of the labour force irrespective of their age, and those that are specific to age groups with particular problems in connection with occupational mobility.

(a) *Measures to help persons wishing to withdraw from farming regardless of their age.* All owner-farmers who give up farming and place their land at the disposal of the 'Agriculture 1980' programme, are to be given a structural reform grant amounting to, say, eight times the rental value of their land. Under the programme, this land is either to be farmed by production units or modern agricultural enterprises, or to be withdrawn from farming altogether. There will have to be appropriate provisions to keep the reform grants within reasonable limits.

It is part of the plan that the beneficiaries of the structural reform grants may retain ownership of their land. They will be free to choose between selling their land, leasing it to a production unit or modern agricultural enterprise, or making it available under the programme for other purposes (afforestation for instance). The use made of land for which grants are paid should be subject to approval by some official body, to be specified by each Member State.

To ensure that farmers in urgent need of capital are not forced to sell, the following provision is recommended. Any farmer who leases his land to a production unit or a modern agricultural enterprise for a period of eighteen years may, on conclusion of the contract, obtain a lump sum representing capitalization of the first nine years' rent, calculated on the basis of a 3% yield on the value of the land.

Equivalent benefits will be made available to owner-farmers who turn their land over to woodland. They are to get afforestation subsidies, and in addition a sum representing capitalization of the returns on the land concerned, so that they get the same income they could have obtained had they leased their land to a production union or a modern agricultural enterprise.

With a view to removing one of the major obstacles to the occupational mobility of the agricultural population, farmers, paid hands and relatives who help should be eligible for grants enabling their children to continue their training beyond school-leaving age.

The annual Community contribution to these grants might be around 600 u.a.

Like all other provisions of the programme, those relating to assistance for agricultural workers who wish to leave the land rest on the principle of free choice on the part of the persons concerned. They must be informed of the occupational opportunities open to them and to their children, they must be enabled to compare these opportunities with their existing situation and, once they have made up their mind to take up another occupation, must be referred to specialized official bureaux which will help them to find a new place for themselves. To this end, a network of socio-economic information offices will have to be set up in rural areas and financial aid will have to be provided for training the specialist advisers needed.

(*b*) *Measures to help persons over 55 who wish to leave farming.* Given the high average age of the agricultural labour force, and especially of heads of farms, who at present constitute the largest single group, special efforts need to be made to promote the withdrawal from agriculture of elderly farmers, whose occupational mobility is of course very limited.

Heads of farms aged 55 or over will therefore be able to draw a supplementary annual allowance to make up their income, on condition that they withdraw from farming and make their land available for the programme.

(*c*) *Measures to help persons wishing to take up another occupation.* The situation which faces people who want to give up farming, or are thinking of doing so, varies so much with the region they live in, the economic situation and their personal circumstances, that it is hard to arrive at any judgement applicable to all. Very many facts must be taken into account and a large number of measures will have to be introduced in order to facilitate the process of adjustment and, in many cases, even to create the conditions in which adjustment can occur. In all cases the principle should be to leave the individual to make his choice; new jobs must be created, to give him a chance of a reasonably comfortable and dignified life and enable him to make his work as productive as possible. We cannot close our eyes to the fact that the present situation not only imposes heavy sacrifices on the individual, but is extremely harmful for the economy as a whole. For these people to shift to better paid jobs associated with more satisfactory social conditions is, therefore, not only a matter of social justice, but a dictate of the present economic situation.

(*d*) *Schooling and vocational training in rural areas.* One of the most important moves in this connection is to improve educational policy in rural areas.

Vocational training should be so recast that the trainee can, in mid-course, change over to other types of training; this, together with the development of a network of efficient occupational advisory services in rural areas, should help to diminish the number of young people who take up farming simply because they are not trained for anything else. In addition, the general improvement of basic schooling and the raising of the school-leaving age already occurring in several Member States can be expected to prove particularly useful in rural areas in connection with the present programme.

Agriculture itself should benefit from anything that is done to give the reserve of gifted children in rural areas easier access to higher education, for it is from amongst them that agriculture will have to draw the cadres which it needs as much as any other branch of our industrial economy.

(*e*) *Readaptation.* People who want to give up farming and to take up another occupation must be able to do so in propitious conditions. It is deplorable that in the past only a very small proportion of the people who changed to another occupation were prepared for the latter.

Assistance to cover the changeover must therefore be made available to anyone working in agriculture who wishes to take up employment outside it.

But the essential point is that people must not only be well trained for some non-farming job but, more important still, must be offered opportunities of employment in the secondary and tertiary sectors without always having to move.

Should a retrained farmer be unable to find suitable employment within a reasonable time, steps will be taken for him to receive unemployment pay like any wage-earner out of work.

On an overall view, the shift of agricultural manpower to the secondary and the tertiary sectors, as well as job creation on the required scale, should raise no major problem for the economy of the Community generally, provided its real growth rate does not fall below 3%. But in practice this is not a general problem that can be solved by a global policy for growth. The policy of structural change in agriculture must, on the contrary, rest on a regional approach which takes account of the regional implications of such a redeployment of the agricultural labour force in secondary and tertiary activities.

(*f*) *Job creation.* The outflow of agricultural manpower to other, more productive, occupations with higher earnings and a better social position may lead to a harmful depopulation of rural areas or to social tensions, unless there are job opportunities in those areas.

In such cases, regional schemes for the creation of new jobs are an indispensable condition of structural reform in agriculture.

But a choice needs to be made. The economic case for promoting the creation of industrial growth points or of similar growth points for the quaternary sector by establishment of the necessary infrastructure will have to be studied. Another question calling for investigation is whether the outflow of agricultural manpower should not be partially offset by the creation of holiday resorts or natural parks. Finally, there is the question of how to solve the problems involved in resettling a whole farming family.

The Commission considers that, if the measures contained in the 'Agriculture 1980' programme to help persons wishing to change their occupation or to retire have the effect expected, the active agricultural population will fall from 10 million in 1970 to 5 million in 1980.

2. Measures to help persons remaining in modernized agriculture

(*a*) *Increasing the size of farms.* Among the measures to help persons who decide to stay on in agriculture the most important will be those concerned with improving the structure of production.

More and more, agricultural production will have to be concentrated in efficiently managed businesses – those with proper accounting and programming and which are large enough to offer the people working in them incomes and living conditions comparable to those of other workers in equivalent occupations.

These farms will be in a better position to follow the pointers afforded by the market, and for this very reason the market itself will work better and supply will more closely follow demand, so that structural surpluses will no longer accumulate. Each of these enterprises, moreover, should have enough people at work, whether

293

wage-earners or otherwise, to ensure that none of them need work excessively long hours each week and that each in turn can take holidays without disrupting production. The average working week should not be longer than elsewhere in the economy, everyone should have annual leave, and it should be possible to replace a worker in case he falls ill or has an accident. With due allowance for all this, however, the aim on each farm should be to have no more workers than are needed to produce the quantities aimed at.

A set of measures will be needed to help farmers, individually or in groups, to achieve the aims described, as regards both the size of farms and standard of living. Benefits under these measures are to be reserved to those whose farm development plans will demonstrably lead to the target results on completion of the proposed changes. Indiscriminate encouragement of investment in any sort of agricultural business might indeed mislead a certain number of farmers into hopeless ventures.

The establishment of 'production units' or 'modern agricultural enterprises', on the other hand, will enable farmers to tackle structural modernization with a higher degree of security.

(b) *Problems of land tenure.* An unsuitable system of land tenure is a major obstacle to the creation and survival of production units and modern farm enterprises. It is important that these should, at the moment of their establishment and in the course of their subsequent development, be able to acquire without difficulty the land they need, without having to incur undue costs in connection with land purchases.

Once holdings have been combined, it must not be possible for part of the land to be withdrawn in conditions which would compromise the profitability of the investments already made.

Two types of measure, both equally indispensable, may be suggested as appropriate solutions for this problem, which is of major importance in the reform of the structure of production, namely, measures involving adaptation of national legislation on land tenure, and measures based essentially on financial incentives.

(c) *Professional competence of farmers.* Measures in favour of that part of the labour force that decides to stay in agriculture consist mainly in a range of economic aids to facilitate the establishment of production units and modern agricultural enterprises.

However, special attention will have to be paid to the question of the farmer's skill at this job. The Commission will propose Community action in this sphere.

A number of different programmes will be needed if the requisite technical and supervisory staff are to be available and the future managers and skilled workers trained.

A special and concurrent effort will have to be made to teach farmers how to set up and run the new-style farms on profitable lines. In many cases they will have to work in different conditions, or even to change their system of production. There will have to be aids for the retraining and further training of farmers and their staff; these aids will have to allow for the need to be absent from the farm during the training period.

In addition, the methods and possibly also the institutions of the advisory services will have to be adapted to the new conditions of agricultural production. No doubt it will prove necessary to mount an information campaign so as to acquaint farmers with the opportunities open to them in the light of their personal circumstances. It is proposed to make grants towards the training and specialization of the advisers and leaders that will be needed.

Finally, pilot production units will be set up.

REDUCTION OF AGRICULTURAL AREA

The problem of structural farm surpluses is one known in practice to all industrial societies. It involves public expenditure on a scale that taxpayers are less inclined to accept, it swallows up financial resources which are deflected from more productive activities and, finally, it impedes the balanced development of world trade.

These surpluses spring largely from two different sources. First of all, too many people are still having to rely for their main or sole income on the production of certain commodities because they have no alternative. Secondly, under the impact of technological progress and relatively high prices, more and more land is being devoted to certain lines of production, and unit yields have been rising.

This being so, it must be remembered that reform of the structure of production by the creation of larger and more rational production units and of modern agricultural enterprises, with their greater openness to technological progress, is bound to speed up the expansion of agricultural output.

While the establishment of modern units should enable farmers to adjust more closely to the market and the larger farms will in certain regions, at least, doubtless adopt more extensive production methods, measures will none the less have to be taken to ensure that the agricultural area in use is in fact used to the best purpose and that output is limited in accordance with demand.

NOTES AND REFERENCES

[1] The analysis refers only to those goods which compete with imports, and thus are amenable to the policy alternatives considered. Export goods can be handled in a similar way.

[2] A deficiency payment scheme is used here to denote a policy with a guaranteed price which the government realizes by means of a deficiency payment; variable levy scheme is defined here as a policy which imposes a threshold price and charges a levy on imports equal to the shortfall between world price and threshold price; a direct payment scheme transfers income in a way that is not tied to the level of output of the good.

[3] This does not, however, accrue to farmers alone; in fact it represents increased return to fixed factors in both farming and in the purchased input industries.

[4] Since the analysis is static (i.e. for only one time period) it does not matter whether the levy is variable, *ad valorem*, or fixed at a certain level per unit. The term 'variable levy' will be used throughout for any of these support methods.

[5] The algebraic formulation is given in T. Josling, A formal approach to agricultural policy, *Journal of Agricultural Economics*, May 1969.

[6] Also see, H. G. Johnson, 'Problems of European Monetary Union,' this volume, Ch. 9.

INDEX OF SUBJECTS

INDEX OF NAMES

299